A PROMISE OF PRESENCE

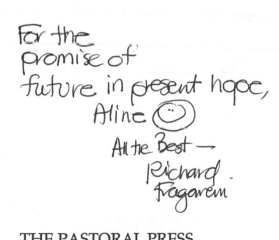

For the
promise of
future in present hope,
Aline ☺

All the Best —
Richard
Fragomeni

THE PASTORAL PRESS
Washington, DC

ISBN: 0-912405-92-9

The Pastoral Press
225 Sheridan Street, N.W.
Washington, D.C. 20011
(202) 723-1254

The Pastoral Press is the publications division of the National Association of Pastoral Musicians, a membership organization of musicians and clergy devoted to fostering the art of musical liturgy.

Printed in the United States of America

Contents

Introduction

THIS COLLECTION OF STUDIES ON LITURGY AND SACRAMENT IS PUBLISHED
in celebration of the sixtieth birthday (14 December 1992) of
David Noel Power, O.M.I., professor of systematic theology
and liturgy at The Catholic University of America in Washington, D.C. Offered in honor of David Power by colleagues and
former students, this *Festschrift* is intended to provide students
and teachers in the field of liturgy and sacrament with studies
that will assist them in their probing and reflection.

Contributors to this collection include David Power's colleagues in sacramental theology and liturgical studies from
The Catholic University of America as well as other colleges
and universities in the United States, former students from the
United States and abroad, and confreres in the Oblates of
Mary Immaculate, the missionary congregation to which David Power has belonged for over forty years. The diversity of
contributors is itself somewhat indicative of the great variety
of students and colleagues with whom Power has worked
over the years in Ireland, Rome, and the United States. The
concerns addressed cover a broad range, from issues pertinent
to a foundational theological anthropology of sacrament to the
grassroots struggle of the churches in Australia and Africa to
create patterns of liturgy that advance true worship and cultural sensitivity.

The authors were not assigned specific topics in view of an
organized plan predetermined by the editors. Rather, they
were invited to bring their own creativity to bear on topics and

issues in line with their own area of research and teaching, or their own pastoral experience and practice. The arrangement and categorization of the studies by heading arises from the content of the contributions themselves, and is intended to provide the reader with a sense of order and cohesion among the various essays.

Many of the contributions give clear indication of the influence of David Power's work. In others, the connections to his investigations are not so apparent. But each one takes up issues of concern to our honoree, and will be all the more useful if read in conjunction with Power's own collection of essays, *Worship: Culture and Theology* (Washington, D.C.: The Pastoral Press, 1990).

We are pleased to include a contribution from our honoree. In "Sacrament: Event Eventing," David Power addresses the crucial issues to be faced in advancing authentic worship at the juncture between modernity and post-modernity. In exploring the frontiers of sacramental and liturgical studies, he has, as on many other occasions, presented challenges that yet await us in our common work.

The appendix includes contributions by two of David Power's Oblate confreres. Ciaran Earley, whose life with the Oblates also took root in Ireland, David Power's native country, salutes his confrere and mentor in a personal testimony. Kenneth Hannon has supplied the biographical note and comprehensive bibliography of Power's works.

The title of the volume, *A Promise of Presence*, expresses salient features of David Power's work. It is intended to evoke the recognition that what is offered in word and sacrament is both realized and anticipated.

This collection represents the work of many. It is likely that each contributor would offer a word of thanks to a colleague or friend for encouragement and support received. But, as co-editors, it is our task to express gratitude to those who have assisted the project as a whole. First, our gratitude is extended to the contributors themselves who have joined with us in this celebration in writing. Each one has done so in a spirit of collaboration and great generosity. Virgil Funk and Larry Johnson of The Pastoral Press welcomed the idea for this collection, and have been of good cheer all along the way. Finally, to David Power, who has been for us and so many others, a mentor, director, guide, friend, and colleague, we are grateful beyond the telling. Ad multos annos!

Michael Downey

Richard N. Fragomeni

For Benefits Received

IN CONCEIVING AND EDITING THIS WORK, RICHARD FRAGOMENI AND Michael Downey have undertaken a work of supererogation. Through the years of teaching and writing theology, my life and thought have been enriched by colleagues and students. If there had been only that, and not the offering of gifts gathered in this book, it would have been enough. If in the book there had been a collection of casual articles, and not this production of high academic and pastoral quality, it would have been enough. I cannot possibly honor the authors in return, so I am content to praise their work and to thank them deeply for the honor which they have done me.

I have enjoyed and benefitted from reading the articles here gathered. It is most pleasing to be celebrated in a way that contributes so much to the field that has been my life work to the present. The book nicely weds academic research, systematic reflection, and pastoral interest. Without the dedication to me, the collection of itself would gain deserved attention and bespeak the merits of editors and publishing house in bringing it together.

I thank Michael Downey and Richard Fragomeni in particular for their generosity of heart and effort. I also thank each and all of the contributors for responding so richly to the invitation extended to them. It is hard to convey my true appreciation. I also thank Larry Johnson and Virgil Funk of The Pastoral Press for undertaking to publish this volume, marked as it is for my honor. The contribution of my essay is but a way of expressing the gratification of being associated with all these people in the service of good liturgy, to the benefit of the church and the glory of God.

David N. Power, O.M.I.

On the Thought of
David N. Power

1

Lex Orandi, Lex Credendi: Taking It Seriously in Systematic Theology

Michael Downey

IT IS NOW MORE COMMONLY RECOGNIZED THAT THE SECOND VATICAN Council encouraged and supported forces of renewal that had been at work in the church for generations. The reforms sanctioned by the council, and the renewal to which it has given rise, have brought about a "sea change" in church life and practice. Perhaps no other area of ecclesial life has been as profoundly affected by the reform and, in turn, furthered the reform and renewal, than has the life of sacramental practice and worship.

The aim of this essay is not to provide a survey of the developments in the sacramental life of the churches brought on by the Second Vatican Council. Nor is it to analyze, assess, or evaluate those developments. It is, rather, to spell out significant characteristics of the work of David Noel Power in such a way as to assist students and teachers of sacramental and liturgical theology in understanding some of the developments in the field during the post-conciliar period. David Power has taken liturgy seriously as a source in doing theology. It is to be hoped that in spelling out significant features in the work of this one theologian, a contribution might be made toward

3

gaining a clearer understanding of the directions taken in the field of sacramental and liturgical theology as a whole, as well as of the challenges that yet await us in our common work.

What many astute students and teachers of sacrament and liturgy have come to see is that the elements of a sacramental theology that one finds in quite disparate fashion in this or that essay or monograph, the insights and snippets unearthed here and there in a given liturgiologist, historian of liturgy, or sacramental theologian, one finds in a more systematic and integrated fashion in the work of David Power. This is not to say that Power simply synthesizes the work of others in such a way that the main lines of post-conciliar developments are more clearly articulated in his writings. If it is true that his work is indicative of significant turns in sacramental theology since the council, it is equally true that he has given methodological form to the study of this subject. This he has done by opening up the discourse about liturgy and sacrament to include other fields, as well as by the nature of his probings, the types of needs he addresses, the kinds of questions he engages, and the way he brings the Christian sacramental tradition to bear on the pressing needs and urgent demands of our age.

David Power is first and foremost a systematic theologian. And there may be a distinct advantage in surveying the writings of this systematic theologian in chronological order. One advantage of such a strategy is that it would provide occasion to take note of the development in his thought from earlier to later stages. Having read all of David Power's work, I have opted for a different course. Rather than providing a tightly-knit survey and synthesis from the "early Power" to the "later Power," I have judged it more useful to draw attention to five *jalons de route*, signposts, or indicators along the way, by which one can navigate part of the course that sacramental theology has taken in the years since the council. These are: (1) Looking to Liturgy as Source for Theology; (2) Text, Context, and the Complexity of Interpretation; (3) The Multivalence of Symbol, Language, and Culture; (4) From Liturgy to Worship: Speaking the Name of God; (5) Prayer as the Praxis of Desire. Careful attention to these indicators may provide further clarity as we navigate the course that yet awaits us at the brink the third millennium of the Christian tradition. Looking to the work of David Power can help us understand where we have traveled, as well as give some indication of the terrain that lies ahead.

Looking to Liturgy as Source for Theology

The work of David Power has been that of a systematic theologian who has taken with utmost seriousness the implications of the aphorism *lex orandi, lex credendi*. This entails the recognition that the prayer of the church is a vital locus for theological reflection. The prayer of the church is brought to fullness of expression in its liturgical life, hence *lex orandi, lex credendi* cannot be properly understood if untethered from a liturgical context. Though liturgy as locus for theological reflection has been a long-standing concern, it is sometimes more readily affirmed in theory than it is validated in practice.[1]

The Second Vatican Council emphasized the importance of the liturgy as "source and summit of Christian life" (Constitution on the Sacred Liturgy 10), and urged the reformation of liturgical rites "as soon as possible" (CSL 25) so as to foster renewal and restoration based on "sound tradition" (CSL 23). Together with this there was a revitalization of interest in liturgical studies and liturgical theology, as well as significant reorientations in sacramental theology.[2] As was the case with the study of Scripture, the patristic sources, church councils, and history, new approaches to the study of liturgy and sacrament emphasized the importance of clearly articulated methods of investigation. The work of David Power may be understood not only as an effort to spell out methods for the study of liturgy and sacrament, but also to open up the discourse about this subject to include the discourse of other fields of investigation.[3]

The existence of several notable learned societies devoted to the ongoing work of liturgical studies and renewal is indication of the recognition that liturgy, prayer, and spirituality are vital sources of rigorous investigation and reflection for Christian life and practice.[4] The singular importance of liturgy as a source for Christian life and reflection that is affirmed in both conciliar documents and theological positions needs to be consistently verified in the doing of systematic theology, influencing thereby its methods, content and conclusions.

Text, Context, and the Complexity of Interpretation

Power's efforts have been given to probing the relationship between liturgy and culture by means of the hermeneutical repertoire of a systematic theologian. Central to this task has been the contextual interpretation and appropriation of liturgical texts and practices, both historical and contemporary. His primary task has been the mediation of worship to culture through theological thought.[5] Consequently, his work has involved different content and methods from those whose primary attention has been given to understanding the history of liturgical rites.

A systematic theological interpretation and appropriation of liturgical texts and tradition requires an awareness of the cultural setting, world-views, ideologies, and philosophies operative in interaction between interpreter and text. Texts must be analyzed with an awareness of the relation of language to meaning. This entails viewing the text within its ritual context which, in turn, must be placed within an ecclesial context of order and ministry, with particular attention to regional differences. In addition, these factors must be interfaced with those theologies operative in the period(s) under consideration, particularly their explicit or implicit understanding of ritual development. Alongside these considerations attention must be given to popular religiosity and the different meanings associated with its ritual enactment vis-à-vis predominant liturgical texts and traditions.

This work of interpretation and appropriation, in contrast to historical or doctrinal analysis pure and simple, is present even in Power's first published work. His dissertation presented for the degree of doctor of theology in the Liturgical Institute of San Anselmo in Rome is an attempt to interpret ordination rites as a source for theology.[6] This he does in view of the shifting perceptions and world-views of the subject, that is, the ordained, the needs of the community, various social factors operative in the formulation of ordination rites, and the relationship between the theologies of priesthood found in the rites to those described in other branches of theology. In his second book, *Christian Priest: Elder and Prophet*, the context for understanding ministry is widened further still so as to include the influence of practical and even political factors in the formulation, interpretation, and appropriation of liturgical texts and practice.[7]

Interpreting the meaning of text in context entails much more than historical or doctrinal hermeneutics of the text itself. Interpretation always entails appropriation. This means that in interpreting a text there is an interaction between where we stand (our world-view) and the standpoint or world-view of the text. In this interaction, effort must be made to examine the presuppositions held by the one interpreting as well as the horizon within which the text is to be properly understood. Thus interpretation and appropriation demand that a wider view be taken so as to render account of thought forms and world-views that influence formulation of texts and practices, and call for a self-critical consciousness of the assumptions and ideologies that underlie any interpretation. Attentive to the further implications of *lex orandi, lex credendi,* Power has been concerned throughout to demonstrate the reciprocal relationship between liturgical practice and ethics, thus attending to needs and concerns well beyond the boundaries of the text itself.[8]

Power's own standpoint or world-view cannot be understood without attention to the "option for praxis" apparent in his own interpretation and appropriation of texts and traditions. The praxis option is already clearly evidenced in *Christian Priest: Elder and Prophet,* underpins the volume of *Concilium* on *Politics and Liturgy* edited together with his mentor Herman Schmidt in 1974, and continues throughout his subsequent publications.[9] No doubt influenced by the Lonerganian schema of conversion in the task of appropriation, and by the crucial role of praxis therein, praxis lies at the heart of Power's dialectic of appropriation. Praxis forges the relationship between what is expressed in liturgy and the doing or activity of the Gospel in human life, history, world, and church. From the vantage point of the praxis option in interpretation and appropriation, liturgy does not precede praxis; one is not followed by the other. Liturgical expression and ethics are co-efficients. Liturgy is "speechifying" in such a way that there can be no truth in a liturgy which preaches a God of love but which is not itself as large as the Gospel.

Integral to this "praxis option" is the critical function opera-tive in reading liturgical texts and traditions.[10] In the interac-tion of appropriation, Power has opted for a critical stance to-ward the ideologies present in liturgical texts and rituals themselves. This critique calls for attention to the "Word be-neath the words." We can speak of the "Word beneath the words" here if we give an analogous meaning to "Word." Power is not looking for some specific idea, metaphor, or con-cept; the "Word" is an address from within, as it were, which is laid bare when texts are dealt with adequately. Cognizant that such a word is not easily discerned, it is nonetheless this which God has spoken, which beckons to ongoing conversion, and which, therefore, is to be gleaned in any interpretation and appropriation of liturgical text and tradition. Critique of ideology allows for attention to this word, along with atten-tion to speech that breaks open common forms of discourse. An ideology critique of prevailing meanings, plus attention to poetic and metaphoric language which "crack" words, makes it possible to hear this inner word that questions assumptions and systems and enlarges desire that reaches beyond the pre-cincts of language and thought. Once freed from obfuscation and untethered from ideological wraps, the "Word beneath the words" can then render critique of ideologies and world-views antipathetic to the freedom of the Gospel.[11]

In this view of interpretation and appropriation, taking *lex orandi, lex credendi* seriously in systematic theology means that any theological understanding of the God-world relation can-not rely purely on doctrinal or scholastic descriptions. Similar-ly, attempts to articulate theological positions primarily in view of a Lonerganian, Rahnerian, Heideggerian, Freudian, Jungian, or Marxian framework prove deficient if account is not taken of the ways in which the perception of the God-world relation is lived out in liturgical practice and in the ethi-cal implications of such practice. Some access to this is given through liturgical texts and practices in context. But such ac-cess is never as easy as it may seem at first. Interpretation of text as well as the appropriation of its meaning is always a complex task which yields results that are necessarily incom-plete and, consequently partial, tentative, and in need of fur-ther revision and refinement.

In the complex task of interpretation of text in context, even and especially when effort is made to include other data beyond the text in service of this aim, it might be thought that arriving at adequate and accurate meanings is indeed always possible.[12] Meanings gained through textual interpretation, however, may be more the result of presuppositions and convictions brought to the text in the process of appropriation than the fruit of rigorous attention to methods and data. Presuppositions and horizons play no small part in adopting this or that hermeneutical repertoire. It is crucial to be clear about what these may be.

Meanings rendered in textual interpretation may in fact conflict with tightly held convictions about precisely what this or that text is supposed to mean. Indeed, caution should be taken if they do not. And when there is conflict of interpretations, a clash between the world-view of the interpreter and the data rendered from the text, or when it becomes clear that meanings rendered do not fit into the horizon of the one appropriating a text's meaning, a challenge is posed. The challenge is not primarily one of deciding which interpretation is correct and which is incorrect. It is rather more a matter of recognizing that in the clash of interpretations new questions arise, broader horizons emerge, and fresh meanings are opened up. Conflict thus plays a positive role in the work of interpretation, which may be likened to a conversation in which both interpreter and text are expressive of a process of coming to greater understanding rather than a tightly-knit world-view.[13]

Tightly-knit world-views are attractive. They provide a sense of unity, coherence, and cohesion. The High Middle Ages, a purported golden age of faith and reason, is often heralded as a high watermark of Christian history, in part because of the magisterial theological synthesis of Thomas Aquinas. But be the synthesis that of Aquinas or another, it must be accepted that such thinkers give evidence of an ongoing struggle to free themselves from ideological blinders, to wrestle with new insight from contrasting, indeed competing worldviews, and to set aside any formal absolute synthesis, including their own, in an effort to come to deeper understanding and insight.[14]

Similarly, the work of interpretation and appropriation of text in context involves the patience and the stamina to resist rushing to incorporate fresh meanings into an already existing, often tacitly held, synthesis. Interpretation of liturgical texts and practice may yield results that do not readily cohere with what is commonly held to be authentic Christian life or doctrine. Indeed sometimes the conclusions to be drawn from the complex task of interpretation, especially when this is done in view of present need and the praxis option, may lead to the formulation of contemporary liturgical texts and practices that find no clear precedent in the Christian tradition.

The Multivalence of Symbol, Language, and Culture

David Power's earliest work is markedly influenced by the "turn to the subject" particularly as expressed in Bernard Lonergan's appropriation of Thomas Aquinas and, to a somewhat lesser degree, Karl Rahner's. Notable influences on his early work also include the writings of Edward Schillebeeckx, Marie-Dominique Chenu, and Yves Congar. These influences must be seen alongside his early interest in post-Kantian interpretation theorist Paul Ricoeur and in the definitions and distinctions of Susanne K. Langer. Attention must also be drawn to the early influence of several historians of religion, most notably Mircea Eliade, and the resultant sensibility to cultural and religious plurality which undergirds the bulk of Power's writings.

Power's early moves within the precincts of Transcendental Thomism put him in touch with approaches to sacrament informed by an appreciation of symbolic causality. Both Karl Rahner and Edward Schillebeeckx treat sacrament from the perspective of symbolic rather than efficient causality, freed from the boundaries of the essentialist or conceptualist mode. With focus on the self, on judgment, action, and being, rather than on essence, Transcendental Thomists developed approaches to sacrament and the causation of grace that eschewed clear definitions and concepts aimed at capturing and communicating the essence of the thing. Karl Rahner moves out of the conceptualist or essentialist understanding of sacrament. This he does by exploring the sacraments in terms of

God's self-communication in Christ with attention to the results of this in the self. In his view of sacrament, Rahner restores to a central position an understanding of grace as God's free and personal self-communication and the human being's response to the divine initiative. The causation of grace is described by him in light of these categories.[15]

The early work of Edward Schillebeeckx is also an approach untethered from an essentialist or conceptualist mode. Within the current of Transcendental Thomism, but more properly understood as an Existential Thomist (at least during the period of his early writings), Schillebeeckx describes the sacraments in terms of shared meaning through personal encounter. His explanation of the causation of grace in sacrament is set in these terms.[16]

In continuity with the insights of both Rahner and Schillebeeckx, David Power's investigations brought him to the question of just how such self-communication and shared meaning come about.[17] No doubt influenced by the methodological investigations of Bernard Lonergan, he attempted to open up the discourse to include insights from other fields. And he turned to the exploration of language as a means of understanding how God's self-communication and shared meaning in personal encounter come about in the reality of sacrament.

In Paul Ricoeur, Power came under the influence of a theorist of interpretation with different orientations and emphases than those of the Transcendental Thomists. Though Ricoeur claims to be a philosopher, not a theologian, his attention is given to revelation, to the word, and to the nature and function of language as the key to all reality. In his work with the language of the Bible, he brings clarity to the different genres of writing in which revelation is expressed. With strong emphasis on the metaphorical as key to understanding language and meaning, and on symbol as it pertains to the bodily in self-communication, Ricoeur's investigations provided Power with a linguistic perspective from which to view sacrament and liturgy. Thus, the abiding question for Power: How do symbol and language, specifically metaphor, constitute the reality of sacramental experience? Because of his focus on language and meaning, Power's concern is not with the "essence" of things that can be pinned down in concepts and clear definitions.

Power's concern with language, specifically with metaphor as the key to understanding the nature of language, as well as his view of culture, symbol, and ritual as dimensions of language, are influenced in no small measure by the investigations of Ricoeur.[18] Language in this view does not refer primarily to the instrument of verbal communication. It may best be described as "expressivity." In this sense language both constitutes and shapes human beings and all other entities. This is to say that everything is what it is by virtue of self-expression. Being is at once given and coming to be through self-expression.

Taking these insights further, it may be useful to note that Power opts for a Gadamerian view of the linguistic character of all reality. In this he differs from the Lonerganian David Tracy and from the Existential Thomist Edward Schillebeeckx, both of whom permit the possibility of pre-linguistic or, perhaps more accurately, sub-linguistic experience. Power, following Gadamer, maintains that there is no thought without language and, consequently, no access to reality which is not linguistic. Language and symbol give rise to thought. There can be no thought aside from the thought expressed which is language, and no access to reality which is what it is by virtue of being expressed or spoken. While it may be said that thoughts and feelings exist in dialectical relation to language and are distinguishable from it, they may not *be* in their fullness without language. The line needs not be drawn too sharply here between Power on the one side, and Tracy and Schillebeeckx on the other. Further investigation would likely yield greater convergence on this point than it may first seem.

Human expression is mediated in and through a multiplicity of forms that together constitute what is referred to as culture. Like time, we know what culture is until we are called upon to describe it. Without prejudice to the complexity of the issue, culture may be described as that constellation of means by which humans express that which is fundamentally constitutive of human being, foremost among them the family, community, society, art, literature, and ritual. Because human beings perceive and pursue the task of human expressivity in various ways, cultures differ, sometimes so much so that they appear to be irreconcilable.

A singularly important instance of language as "expressivity" is symbol and its employment in ritual.[19] In attending to the nature and function of the symbolic, Power avoids naive understandings of both sign and symbol as realities that point beyond themselves. Symbols invite self-expression and facilitate interpersonal communication and communion. Basing his approach on studies in theology, philosophy, anthropology, and perhaps most importantly, sociological theorists Victor Turner and Mary Douglas, Power views symbols as gestures, actions, words, or objects that

> belong within a given cultural context, bear of repetition without being rigid stereotypes, meet affective needs of meaning and belonging, express group identity even though some are more immediately related to the group and others to the individual, and are subject to the changes that come with the evolution of time, moving perspectives and changing values.[20]

In this view the symbolic is related to self-expression as public. It includes the affective as well as the cognitive in the mediation of human expressivity. In addition, the symbolic addresses the personal, unconscious, and the cosmic in expressing human being's relationship to the real.

Two characteristics of the symbolic are important when considering Power's view of symbol and its employment in ritual as part of the task of human self-expression which is language. First, there is a non-identity between the symbol and the reality expressed therein. Words spoken may express the deepest longings of the human heart, but they must be distinguished from those longings in and of themselves. In this view there is a loosening of the connection between symbol or word and its referent, an emphasis on negation, on the distance between image and what is represented, so that any symbolic expression both *is and is not* the reality communicated. If effective "presencing" or communication of such intimate feelings to another is to occur, this distinction must be kept to the fore. Effective "presencing" or communication in and through language demands that one recognize what is not given in self-expression as well as what is.

What is given in symbolic communication is absented in the distance inherent in all communication between the self and the other. This is something which common sense recognizes. When I speak to another there is space or distance between us. This is accepted as part and parcel of effective communication. Legacies of a bygone era are communicated through the distance of time and space in speech. There is, of necessity, distance and absence between narrative and reader or hearer, and this too must be accepted if communication is to occur. At an even more fundamental level, I can only know what I look like through a mirror image of myself, no matter how identical a likeness is projected therein. Further, one cannot know or understand one's own thoughts and feelings unless they are expressed in writing or speech, which is a manner of putting them at a distance from oneself. And I cannot know the heart and mind of another except through what is offered between myself and the other as the medium of our communication.[21] This is all to say that in the "presencing" rendered in and through language and symbol, absence and distance are inextricably a part of the very modality of presence. Absence is a dimension of presence.

This dimension of non-identity must be kept to the fore in understanding sacrament which, for Power, is symbolic in nature. What is expressed in sacrament is mediated in a form other than itself. For example, in the sacrament of the eucharist, Christ is not present in his own form. The presence of Christ in the eucharist is a sacramental presence in and through symbol, that is, a mediated presence which is by its very nature a presence of non-identity with Christ's own form. But this presence is not any the less real by virtue of non-identity. Such non-identity is intrinsic to any and all symbolic expression. Further, it is the very nature and function of religious language and symbol to bring to expression the relation of human being to that with which it can never claim identity: God. Consequently, this dimension of non-identity needs to be kept to the fore all the more in language and symbols of the holy.

A second characteristic of language and symbol to which Power has given considerable attention is that of polysemy or polyvalence. Specifically, when it comes to language and symbols of the divine, he is critical of efforts to pin down meanings in concise concepts and precise definitions. Though it may be judged necessary to stress a singular meaning in

thought and discourse about sacrament, for example, eucharist as sacrament of the body and blood of Christ, or baptism as
sacrament of incorporation into the Body through forgiveness
of sin, these focal meanings can only be enriched by the rich
array of meanings expressed in other language and symbols of
the God-world relation. No matter how appropriate a word or
symbol may be to express the holy, and no matter how adequate in conveying the human response to the divine initiative, no one symbol or constellation of symbols is capable of
fully expressing the ineffable, the Being beyond being, that
mystery which overspills any and all attempts to speak it. The
presence of the holy both *is and is not* expressed in word and
sacrament, due to the surplus of meaning that is not communicated in any presencing through word and sacrament. Said another way, God both is and is not present in this or that sacrament, the Scripture both is and is not the word of God, and
Jesus both is and is not God.

The key to understanding this view of symbol and its employment in ritual is metaphor. Metaphoric predication juxta-
poses unlikes in order to find fresh meaning. The interplay of
contrasting images and stories in metaphor creates new possibilities. Within the juxtaposition of images, similarities are discovered in the very differences that are yoked in the metaphor. Metaphor's first move is to break open perceptions and
commonly held expectations, surprising us with the whisper
that *this* both is and is not *that*, thereby keeping alive the tensive nature of all language. Similarly, symbol invites beyond
itself to the surplus of meanings in other, often surprising,
words and symbols which are also expressive of the holy.
Hence no matter how adequate it may be as a symbol, *this* sacrament is and is not *that* fullness of God's presence which
overspills any and all symbolic mediation.

The metaphorical may also provide a key to the nature of
liturgy. If liturgy is viewed as language, then it may be understood as the central, world shaping act of self-expression on
the part of the Christian people. Be it in the eucharistic assembly or in the province of private devotion, human beings express and receive their identity by what is said and done in
the language of worship, by speaking in response to what
God has spoken. But this language is always a way of "talk-

ing back" to those established wisdoms that are antipathetic to the grace and freedom of the "Word beneath the words." The metaphorical nature of liturgy, once unleashed, untethers the heart from commonly held perceptions, ideologies, and world-views through the whisper of the promise that the freedom and grace expressed in *this* word and sacrament both *is and is not that* which the established wisdom insists is God's will and way in the world. Even further, *this* liturgy must never be confused with *that* fullness of God's presence it expresses. Consequently, authentic liturgical praxis must attend to God's coming in ways that may indeed interrupt and break open our perceptions of what constitutes good liturgical order and ritual performance.

Hopefully, without pressing the point, I would like to suggest here that Power's entire project of mediating worship to culture through theological thought may itself be understood by a turn of this metaphorical key. Power seems to have listened and taken heed to metaphor's whisper: "*this* is not *that*," "it *is* and *is not*." For him, in our words, concepts, and images there is a greater degree of dissimilarity than similarity, more unlikeness than likeness, to the mystery which they stretch to evoke, to name, to express. There are two poles of a dialectical tension that undergirds all of David Power's work in sacramental and liturgical theology. Though his writings evidence a sustained interest in what may be said of God *in esse*, as well as in what may be known of God through reason illumined by faith, there is also an abiding recognition that whatever claims are made about God, or the divine attributes, or God's intention for the world, these are at best partial and incomplete, and our grasp on grace quite tenuous. But rather than shunning or setting aside ontological considerations, Power invites to the doxology of the heart, the culmination of prayer, beyond words and thoughts, though fostered by both.[22]

The metaphorical as key to understanding Power's work is also obvious in the attention he has given to "contrast experience" as revelatory. Power has consistently sought to include alternative voices and lesser known viewpoints in the field of investigation, with particular attention to the experience of those at the margins of social and religious institutions who are weak, voiceless, and powerless. Whether it be his sustained attention to the emergence of base Christian communities as clear expression of the Spirit's voice in the churches,[23] his continuing commitment to the development and support of lay ministries in the church,[24] his attentiveness to the emergent consciousness of women in church and society,[25] his commitment to the mission of evangelization of and by the poor,[26] or even his efforts to assure that the often facilely villainized Tridentine theology of sacrifice be given a fair hearing,[27] his concern is to give attention to those experiences and to those voices which speak a different word from what the prevailing social and ecclesial orders maintain is the way things are and must be. By looking to contrast experiences as revelatory, Power's work is at once a participation in the tensive movement of metaphor as well as an invitation beyond what *is* and *is not* to what *may* or *might be*.

In considering liturgy as the central world shaping expressive act of the Christian people, the task is to think from what is done and said therein. Rather than bringing tightly-knit philosophical preconceptions and definitions of what sacrament is and must be, the grace of sacramental communion is given in attentiveness to the "Word beneath the words," in the invitation to think from the symbol, to attend to what is known in the simple act of blessing, breaking, and sharing of a crust of bread, and in the passing of a cup hallowed by the speaking of Christ's name. Thinking from the symbol is the condition for the possibility of receiving what is given in the sign of the one who washed the feet of others, and of participating in what may be known through the giving of a cup of cold water in his name. Thinking from what is said in liturgy is an invitation to lean on hope, even and especially when there seems no plausible reason to do so, and to be enlivened by that blood poured out for those whose only strength is found in his self-emptying.

If we are to think from the symbol, then interpretive preconceptions of all sorts are to be set aside: philosophical, theological, religious, political, ethical, aesthetic, economic. Each subjective horizon of appropriation provides some access, but also some barriers, to experiencing the polyvalence of symbol. In overcoming the obstacles that thought and speech may impose, we may come to a knowledge of God through the words and symbols that unite us to God in their plurality, as well as through the multiplicity of expression that they may be given at different times and in diverse cultures.

From Liturgy to Worship: Speaking the Name of God

In mediating worship to culture through theological thought, much of David Power's effort has been given to promoting and advancing liturgical practice. This has necessitated the study of liturgical rites past and present, and ongoing analysis of classical and contemporary theologies of sacrament and the causality of grace, as well as a thoroughgoing appreciation of the nature and function of symbol and language. Such studies, helpful though they may be, especially when undertaken in service of liturgical renewal, do not of themselves bring about the realization of liturgy's purpose. Just as the grace of sacramental communion cannot be measured by dogged adherence to rubric, neither can it be guaranteed by efforts to assure that the prayer of the Christian people is "liturgically correct." Preoccupation with rubric on one hand, or with "good," "moving" liturgical celebration (read performance) on the other, can easily lead to reductionism. The nature and work of grace cannot ultimately be explained or guaranteed by ritual study or correct performance.[28] Grace escapes human comprehension, and the best response to its presence is an attentive and receptive faith. The granting of grace and response to it is in the final analysis ineffable. And it is this gift and response which is the aim of any and all liturgy of the Christian people.

The metaphoric is again helpful in avoiding ritual or rubrical reductionism. Power's attention to the metaphorical, or to the ineffable present in all language, even and especially in the language of the holy, serves to underscore the apophatic, the way of knowing by way of unknowing. We do not hear what God speaks or recognize how God is present unless we are able to recognize what God is not. With attention to the metaphorical key, language has the ability to carry the human being beyond preconceptions, tightly-knit world-views, and firmly held convictions, into the region of personal faith wherein one is invited to communion with the unknown God.

Liturgy is understood by Power as the central world shaping expressive act of the Christian people. In his articulation of the nature of Christ's presence therein, he uses the idea of opening up to mystery rather than efficacy in giving grace. Here again our attention is drawn to the apophatic. Apparent in his attention to the metaphoric, to the non-identity of symbol and symbolized, to the multiplicity and surplus of meaning in all word and symbol, to the need to consult alternative, contrast experience as the locus of God's coming, the apophatic or aniconic again comes into play in Power's conviction that Christ's sacramental presence cannot be reduced to any type of localized imagery. Faith in Christ, even when expressed in the words, narratives, actions, gestures, and objects that together constitute the liturgy of the Christian people, is a response to an invitation into communion with the life of God in Christ, the fullness of which is outside the reach of our imagination, comprehension, and speech.

Even with the limits which symbol and word impose, they are nonetheless our means of access to the real. Liturgy as "speech-act" gives way to true worship as the name of God is falteringly uttered within that space which is the very opening up to the divine presence at the limits of language and symbol. In this view worship cannot be confined within the precincts of liturgy as ritual, however much true worship may be fostered by good liturgical practice. Good liturgical form and adherence to the rubrical canon do not necessarily aid us in the articulation of the name of God, the task of true worship to be taken up again and again in different times, in various places and diverse cultures. The purpose of liturgy is to invite to true worship of the God who is in our midst as the Christ, and who is known in contemplation of the name beyond our ability to name definitively.

Here attention must be drawn to the role of narrative and memory in worship. Narrative is context for metaphoric predication. The purpose of narrative is not simply to render a past event present. Nor is it to render the present to the past. It is to tell of a presence present now in and through remembrance, so that the present presence of Christ may be known.[29] In liturgy it takes on much the character of prophetic telling, of speaking a word of hope in view of much evidence to the contrary. Narrative is the naming of that presence present to Mo-

ses (Exodus 3:13-15) which is brought to self-expression in the
name "I am Who I am" or "I will be Who I will be." It is the invitation to remembrance of the Christ in whose life and cross
God comes, and to attend to God's coming in the interruptive
and disorienting events of history. Narrative holds out the
promise of God's presence even and especially at the limits of
language and symbol. It hearkens to faith and true worship
when trust in established wisdom weakens, when confidence
in creeds crumbles, and when all our efforts at good and
sound liturgical practice fail. The "Word beneath the words"
which is untethered through prophetic telling in narrative is
an invitation to respond to a promise of presence. True worship beyond the precincts of ritual purity and good liturgical
form is an activity of the human heart, in communion with
others and with the "Word beneath the words," which is
brought to self-expression in the naming of God as the One
who comes.

Prayer as the Praxis of Desire

Whether the subject of investigation be a liturgical rite, a
theological explanation of sacramental efficacy, or the formulation of contemporary liturgical texts, Power's concern is
with the movement of the human heart toward God in prayer.
It may be useful to offer clarification about what is meant by
the terms "heart" and "prayer," and in so doing bring some of
my own concerns and perspectives into conversation with David Power's contribution.

In speaking of the human heart, I am not referring to the region of "private," "individual" feelings or emotions in contra-
distinction to other dimensions of the self. The term "heart"
describes the deepest, most fundamental center of the self,
and as such is found in Hebrew and Christian Scriptures, and
in the history of Christian spirituality, to describe the whole
person.[30] Properly understood, the heart is the name for "affectivity," or the affective dimension of the person, the very
openness of the human being to be touched by another, others, and God. As such, it is inclusive of communal and social
realities. To have a heart is to possess the capacity to be in relation. Further, the heart describes human being's openness to

relate to the real. It is the very being within human beings toward the good.[31]

In speaking of prayer I have in mind the deeply personal movement of the heart as I have described it. Thus prayer is not necessarily a private and isolated activity. It finds its fullest expression in interpersonal communion in and through communication with another, others, and God. Thus prayer cannot be properly understood if it is thought to exist in opposition to the liturgy which is the coming together of the Christian people. The public liturgy of a people is intended to foster true worship, to lift the mind and heart of this people to God in prayer. To maintain that the prayer of the heart is deeply personal is not to imply that it is a private matter.

With these clarifications to the fore, prayer may be understood as the praxis of the desire of the human heart. The openness to relation which is a constitutive dimension of human beings is in itself an absence, a longing for completion and fullness. Desire is that in the human being which longs for its own increase. For Paul Ricoeur, desire is the yearning for being. Or, said another way, desire may be understood as the effort to be.[32]

Desire, then, is the basis, the root, of all self-expression. Said another way, desire is that which inheres in all "speechifying," language, or expressivity. Desire seeks to participate in being by speaking itself in culture, symbol, and other elements of language systems. For Ricoeur, human being is both given and that which we desire yet to be.

As human being is brought into fuller being through self-expression, this necessarily entails another and others. It lies at the very heart of human being, then, to be in communion with another and others by virtue of this self-expression. This effort to be, that is desire, takes the form of action which may be understood as the self-articulation of human being. For our purposes it is useful to note the importance of the corporate activity that is worship, by which the church expresses and receives its identity as the Body of Christ in and through his grace. Worship, from this perspective, is the "speechifying" of this people as the Body of Christ. In and through worship, the Christian people are brought into being through self-expression as Christ's Body and thereby invited into communion with Being itself. But because being is both given and achieved, prayer of the heart also finds expression in simple loving attentiveness to Being, as well as in the self-expressive action in word and sacrament. Here the corporate activity of worship and the heart's movement of loving attentiveness to Being beyond being are co-efficients in the praxis of desire.

In this view, the effort to be involves the corporate activity of worship, which is the self-expression and articulation of the Christian people as the Body of Christ. But the yearning for being and fuller self-expression entails the recognition that being is also given, a gift, the very condition for the possibility of human being seeking to participate more fully in Being.

Thus liturgy and sacrament find their purpose in fostering prayer as the praxis of desire. As the basis of all expressivity, desire is brought to articulation in what is said and done in liturgy. But it is also articulated when the human heart attends in silence to the "Word beneath the words," and to the symbols of the holy, recognizing therein God's fidelity to the divine promise. This is the promise of future glory in which faith stakes its claim, but it is also the promise of presence of the One who comes even now as speech stretches to make enough room for silence.

* * * * * *

In pointing to five distinctive factors in the work of David Power, I have aimed to give some indication of significant issues and concerns in the field of sacramental and liturgical studies in the post-conciliar period. These arise when liturgy is taken seriously as a source for theology.

My intention has been to give some attention to significant influences on Power's work and to take up the central concerns that have occupied him. This I have done rather than charting his development from early to later stages. The task has been undertaken in the hope that the methodological form he has brought to the field will be instructive in the raising of fresh questions, tackling thorny issues, and probing the mystery of God's love in word and sacrament.

It may seem a bit ironic that an essay which treats the work of one in whom the critical function plays such a large role should itself not offer critique. A sharper analysis of Power's work would likely take issue with some of his interpretations, or call for further clarification of his positions.[33] I do not shun critique. A thorough, careful, and constructive critical analysis of the contribution of David Power is a task that yet awaits us in our common work.

Notes

1. For a very helpful treatment of the use of the *lex orandi, lex credendi* principle, see Geoffrey Wainwright, *Doxology: The Praise of God in Worship, Doctrine, and Life* (New York: Oxford University Press, 1980) esp. chapters 7 and 8.

2. For example, Raymond Vaillancourt, *Toward a Renewal of Sacramental Theology* (Collegeville: The Liturgical Press, 1979), provides a survey of such reorientations in view of the renewed anthropology, Christology, and ecclesiology articulated in the conciliar documents.

3. In consciously striving to open up the discourse about liturgy and sacrament to include discourse from other fields, Power is influenced by the methodological investigations of Bernard Lonergan.

4. Most notable among these professional societies are the North American Academy of Liturgy and Societas Liturgica.

5. This concern is well expressed in both the title and content of the recent collection of his essays spanning nearly twenty years, *Worship: Culture and Theology* (Washington, D.C.: The Pastoral Press, 1990).

6. The doctoral dissertation has been published as *Ministers of Christ and His Church: The Theology of the Priesthood* (London: Geoffrey Chapman Publishing Co., 1969).

7. *Christian Priest: Elder and Prophet* (London: Sheed & Ward, 1973).

8. See, for example, D.N. Power, "Households of Faith in the Coming Church," *Worship* 57 (1983) 237-254.

9. *Politics and Liturgy*, eds., Herman Schmidt and David Power (New York: Herder and Herder, 1974). See esp. Power, "The Song of the Lord in an Alien Land" 85-106.

10. The critical function of liturgy is treated at greater length in David N. Power, *Unsearchable Riches: The Symbolic Nature of Liturgy* (New York: Pueblo Publishing Co., 1984) esp. chapter seven; see also "Liturgical Praxis: A New Consciousness at the Eye of Worship," *Worship* 61 (1987) 290-305; "Unripe Grapes: The Critical Function of Liturgical Theology," *Worship* 52 (1978) 386-399; "Forum: Worship after the Holocaust," *Worship* 59 (1985) 447-455; "Sacraments: Symbolizing God's Power in the Church," *Proceedings of the Catholic Theological Society of America* 37 (1982) 50-66.

11. For a fuller treatment of this point, see Mary Catherine Hilkert, "The Word Beneath the Words" in the present volume.

12. In the 1991 *Berakah* address, "When Words Fail: The Function of Systematic Theology in Liturgical Studies," Power maintains that it is an illusion to think that it is a relatively simple matter to find the meaning of a text from a past age. See the *Proceedings of the North American Academy of Liturgy*, 1991, 18-26, pp. 19-20.

13. See Power, "When Words Fail" 22.

14. Power writes: "We learn more by attending to the process of thinking in the past than by retrieving ideas that have been thought. The sense of *pensée pensante* is more instructive than *pensée pensée.*" "When Words Fail" 22.

15. See Karl Rahner, *The Church and the Sacraments*, trans. W.J. O'Hara (Freiburg: Herder; London: Burns and Oates, 1963); "The Theology of Symbol," *Theological Investigations*, vol. 4, trans., K. Smyth (Baltimore: Helicon, 1966) 221-252; "What Is a Sacrament?", *Theological Investigations*, vol. 14, trans. D. Bourke 135-148; "Considerations on the Active Role of the Person in the Sacramental Event," ibid. 161-184.

16. For Schillebeeckx's early treatment of these themes, see his *Christ the Sacrament of the Encounter with God* (New York: Sheed and Ward, 1963).

17. Power does have misgivings about some of Rahner's views which he judges to be too abstract. See, for example, David N. Power, "The Holy Spirit: Scripture, Tradition, and Interpretation" in *Keeping the Faith: Essays to Mark the Centenary of Lux Mundi*, ed., Geoffrey Wainwright (Philadelphia: Fortress, 1988) 152-178, p. 156.

18. For an introduction to Ricoeur's work, see C.E. Reagan and D. Stewart, eds., *The Philosophy of Paul Ricoeur: An Anthology of His Work* (Boston: Beacon Press, 1978). For Ricoeur on metaphor, see "Creativity in Language: Word, Polysemy, Metaphor," *Philosophy Today* 17 (1973) 105-112; see also his *La Metaphore vive* (Paris: Seuil, 1975) esp. "Metaphore et discussion philosophique" 325-399.

19. For Power's understanding of symbol, see *Unsearchable Riches*.

20. Ibid. 62.

21. The notions of presence, absence, and distance in self-expression and communication, as well as the examples used to clarify this point, are developed in Power's forthcoming study of eucharistic thought and worship, *Eucharistic Mystery: Revitalizing the Tradition* (New York: Crossroad, 1992).

22. See Power, "When Words Fail" esp. 25-26.

23. See, for example, David N. Power, "Liturgy and Culture," *East Asian Pastoral Review* (1984/4) 348-366.

24. David N. Power, *Gifts That Differ: Lay Ministries Established and Unestablished* (New York: Pueblo Publishing Co., 1980, 2d edition 1985).

25. See, for example, David N. Power, "Liturgical Praxis: A New Consciousness at the Eye of Worship," *Worship* 61 (1987) 290-305. It may also be worthwhile noting the number of contributions by women that have been included in the volumes of *Concilium* edited or co-edited by David Power. Especially noteworthy in this regard is his collaborative work with Mary Collins. For example, see *Can We Always Celebrate the Eucharist?*, eds., Mary Collins and David Power *Concilium* 152 (New York: Seabury, 1982).

26. It is not often taken into account that David Power is a member of the Oblates of Mary Immaculate, an international missionary congregation whose primary purpose is the evangelization of the poor.

27. David N. Power, *The Sacrifice We Offer: The Tridentine Dogma and Its Reinterpretation* (Edinburgh: T. & T. Clark, 1987).

28. Power, "When Words Fail" 20.

29. For Power on memory and narrative, see, for example, *Unsearchable Riches* 39, 114ff.; see also "When Words Fail" 23ff.

30. An extensive analysis of the nature of the heart is provided in my doctoral dissertation, *An Investigation of the Concept of Person in the Spirituality of l'Arche as Developed in the Writings of Jean Vanier* completed in 1982 at The Catholic University of America under the direction of David Power. A brief synthesis is also provided in Downey, *A Blessed Weakness: The Spirit of Jean Vanier and l'Arche* (San Francisco: Harper & Row, 1986), chapter 5, "The Heart Knows."

31. For parallels between this understanding of heart and more classical formulations, see Michael Downey, "A Costly Loss of Heart: The Scholastic Notion of *voluntas ut natura*," *Philosophy and Theology* 1:3 (Spring 1987) 242-254.

32. For Ricoeur on desire, see *Fallible Man: Philosophy of Will*, trans., Charles Kelbley (Chicago: Henry Regnery, 1967) esp. 191-202. It may be instructive to note that in a recent interview Ricoeur speaks of the singular importance of this work: "Le travail auquel je suis finalement le plus attaché, c'est *L'Homme Faillible*, qui était une sorte de petite ontologie . . ."; see "Entretien avec Paul Ricoeur," *Revue des sciences philosophiques et théologiques* 74 (1990) 87-91: 89.

33. For example, see Stephen Happel, "Worship as a Grammar of Social Transformation," *Proceedings of the Catholic Theological Society of America* 42 (1987) 60-87, esp. 76ff.

Foundational Issues

2

Toward a Theological Anthropology of Sacraments

Kevin W. Irwin

THE REVIVAL OF AN INCARNATIONAL EMPHASIS IN THEOLOGY IN GENERAL and in spirituality in particular from the years preceding Vatican II and as validated in many of the conciliar and post-conciliar documents (e.g., The Pastoral Constitution on the Church in the Modern World) has led to an appropriate reemphasis on how one experiences God's presence in all of human life. This incarnational emphasis has also marked much contemporary writing on liturgy and sacraments with the result that the discoverability of God outside sacraments can often cause people to ask about the role of sacraments in the Christian life if God can be discovered outside of what were formerly regarded as the central means of experiencing God and receiving God's grace. The particular point at issue in this essay concerns how one ought to argue for the value of sacraments in this post-Vatican II era in light of an incarnational approach to theology and spirituality. Such an apologetic is particularly important at a time when the argument that sacraments and liturgy are the "church's official prayer" is less compelling when left as a quasi-juridical statement and not

29

accompanied by a rationale that is liturgically and theologically cogent and convincing.[1]

The purpose of this essay is to articulate the Christian's
need for sacraments as privileged experiences of the mystery
of the triune God through the paschal mystery of Christ, manifest in the self-expression of the church as they relate to other
experiences of God in innumerable dimensions of human life,
both communal and personal (e.g., other forms of prayer and
acts of self-transcending love). The chief aim of the essay is to
argue that priority ought to be given to sacraments on the basis of anthropological and theological grounds. The article will
discuss the main lines of the arguments on the necessity of
sacraments in important classical and contemporary treat-
ments of sacraments as these contribute to our purpose. The
last section will offer a way of articulating a "theological anthropology" of sacraments. The focus throughout will be on
the western church's tradition of sacramental teaching and
practice. It is hoped that the argument offered will assist ecumenical conversations across denominational lines about the
role of sacraments in the lives of Christians and, where necessary, to critique approaches to sacraments that do not do justice to their context in one's personal and ecclesial life.

Thomas Aquinas

That Thomas Aquinas' treatment of sacraments has remained uniquely influential on almost all subsequent sacramental theology is clear from the evidence of church teaching
(e.g., at Trent), in post-Tridentine theological manuals,[2] and in
much contemporary sacramental theology. In the *Summa Theologica*, 3a, Question 61, Aquinas asks whether sacraments are
necessary for salvation. In the last section of the answer he
argues that we "are saved through faith in the Christ who has
already been born and suffered . . . [and that] sacraments are
the sort of signs in which the faith by which [we are] justified
is explicitly attested . . ."[3] Thus he appropriately distinguishes
between faith which justifies and sacraments which are particular expressions of justifying faith. With regard to sacraments
specifically, he states that since humans arrive at knowledge
deductively through their experience of physical and sensible

realities, it is appropriate that "in bestowing certain aids to salvation upon [us] the divine wisdom should make use of certain physical and sensible signs called sacraments."[4] He then argues from the nature of the human condition. "For by sinning [humans] incurred an affection for physical things and so made [themselves] subject to them. Now the remedy designed to heal [humanity] has to be applied to that part of [their] nature affected by the sickness. Hence it was appropriate for God to apply spiritual medicine . . . by means of certain physical signs . . ."[5] Since humans are "particularly prone to involve [themselves] with physical things [they are given] certain physical practices to observe in the sacraments."[6] In summary he states:

> Through the sacraments, therefore, sensible things are used to instruct [persons] in a manner appropriate to [their] own nature. [They are] humbled by being brought to recognize [their] own subjection to physical things, seeing that [they have] to rely upon them for the help [they need]. At the same time [they are] preserved by the health-giving practices made available to [them] in the sacraments from various kinds of harm in the physical order.[7]

Thus, one can argue on the basis of Aquinas that sacraments are necessary correctives to the fall, and that the means to communicate this salvation are the means that humans use for all communication—word, symbol, and gesture.

Theological Manuals

The post-Tridentine manual of sacramental theology by Pierre Dens, *De Sacramentis in Genere*[8] typifies this genre and, like most others, draws on Aquinas' *Summa* and the canons of Trent for its argumentation. In addressing the question about the necessity of sacraments in general he states that they are not absolutely necessary since God can save through other means. Dens repeats Aquinas when stating that God's power to save is not restricted to sacraments but that sacraments are necessary through *congruentia*, that is, a harmony or symmetry between sacraments and the human condition. When explaining what this harmony consists in, Dens summarizes the argument from Aquinas, *Summa Theologica*, q. 61 (outlined above).[9]

Dens complements these assertions when discussing the necessity of baptism. He argues that church teaching at Trent affirms that after the preaching of the Gospel, baptism is necessary for salvation.[10] He then argues that baptism is necessary in two ways: by dominical precept (Jn 3:5) and by the human person's need for (such external) means, which argument is in line with his explanation of why sacraments are generally necessary. He fittingly concludes this section by referring to the common teaching on the effects of the baptismal character, namely that one is incorporated into the church and able to receive the other sacraments.[11]

Edward Schillebeeckx

In *Christ the Sacrament of the Encounter With God*, Edward Schillebeeckx draws on both Aquinas and church teaching on sacraments and gives them important phenomenological and personalist interpretations. Thus he states that sacraments are "the face of redemption turned visibly towards us, so that in them we are truly able to encounter the living Christ. The heavenly saving activity, invisible to us, becomes visible in the sacraments."[12] He argues for the usefulness of sacraments in light of the fact that sacraments make possible "a reciprocal human encounter of Christ and [humanity] even after the ascension, though in a special manner."[13] This "special manner" of encounter is based on the wider, foundational, and intrinsic requirement of the Christian religion, namely, "a permanent sacramentality" which "bridges the gap and solves the disproportion between the Christ of heaven and unglorified humanity."[14] Like Aquinas (in *Summa Theologica*, q. 60, art. 3) Schillebeeckx considers sacraments under the category of signs and will emphasize how they are not "indifferent" but "compelling" signs of God's love in Christ.[15] The "sign" element of sacraments is crucial for sacramental encounter because this "is the visible manifestation of the act of redemption, and therefore indicates the particular aspect under which the redemptive act is here present."[16] Schillebeeckx insightfully asserts that neither "the spiritual significance" of sacraments (namely, how God works through them) on the one hand, nor "the outward shape" (namely, the rite engaged in, the "matter and form") on the other, are of the essence of a sacrament. Rather, its essence is in the "manifested signification"[17] of sacraments, which assertion provides a dynamism to sacraments fully in line with the tradition (e.g., "sacraments as signs") and which also emphasizes the necessity of a sacramental encounter with Christ that thus avoids any kind of sacramental "physicalism" or "spiritualism." In this work Schillebeeckx offers fresh insight into the relationship between sacraments and the rest of life (which seminal idea is developed at least indirectly in such works as *Jesus, Christ,* and *The Church with a Human Face*) by stating that:

> sacraments are flashes of light within the whole of Christian life, which has a wider sphere of influence. To seek refuge in the liturgy would be the result of a failure to appreciate the full value of the Church's role in society. To seek a solution outside the liturgy, on the other hand, would also be the result of a failure to understand her eschatological character and the fact that she is involved in the profane life of the world . . .[18]

In his more recent work *Christ,*[19] Schillebeeckx ventures briefly into the sacramental arena once more but from a different starting point. Rather than assume the value of sacraments (as he did in *Christ the Sacrament of the Encounter With God*), here Schillebeeckx argues that liturgy and sacraments are essential for the Christian because of limits in human life. That human history is still marred, that reconciliation is still not yet fully accomplished and that human suffering is still all too real grounds Schillebeeckx's conviction that sacraments and living the gospel life are anticipatory, effective signs of love, healing and perfect union with God. His incarnational emphasis in *Christ the Sacrament* is developed in this work when he states:

> History teaches us that there has never been a perfect redemption, but that in Jesus there is a divine promise for us all, and that this is anticipated in any definitively valid act of doing good to our fellow [humans] in a finite and conditioned world in which love is always doomed to failure and yet nevertheless refuses to choose any other way than that of loving service.[20]

He goes on to argue forcefully that gospel living and sacramental celebration must always cede to the full revelation of their center—Jesus himself.

He argues that Christian liturgy is the place where what is celebrated "symbolically and playfully" is the reality of God in Christ who establishes how "the history of human suffering is not necessary" and that "suffering . . . must be overcome."[21] For him "sacraments are anticipatory, mediating signs of salvation, that is, [the] healed and reconciled life."[22] "As long as there is still a real history of suffering among us, we cannot do without the sacramental liturgy: to abolish it or neglect it would be to stifle the firm hope in universal peace and general reconciliation."[23]

> Because in the last resort the one who is experienced and can be known in this action of reconciliation, the living God, is always greater than our action, this experience, this experience of God as an inner element of liberating and reconciling action, always discloses to us a new and greater future.[24]

Schillebeeckx's theological creativity regarding sacraments is thus evident beginning with *Christ the Sacrament* in the way he is faithful to preceding theological and magisterial teaching, in the way he offers a new slant on such traditional data, and in the way he contextualizes the church's cult within the wider sphere of sacramentality discovered in all of human life. He clearly asserts that sacramental encounter places demands on its participants in light of the church's eschatological nature and obligation to incarnate the kingdom of God in this world. It is also evident in the way he advances his thought, notably in *Christ*, where we detect an apologia for sacraments that remains profoundly Christocentric and eschatological, and yet which locates these realities in the context of human suffering, the lack of harmony in human life and the human person's need for integration. In line with some classical approaches to western sacramental theology, we can characterize Schillebeeckx's approach to sacraments as "anticipatory signs" of the fullness of redemption in Christ.

Karl Rahner

Karl Rahner's contribution to the discussion of our need for sacraments rests, among other things, on his foundational insights on the "cosmology" (for want of a better term) of the Christian life. Characteristically, he asserts that "the grace of

God no longer comes . . . steeply down from on high, from a
God absolutely transcending the world, and in a manner that
is without history, purely episodic; [rather] it is permanently
in the world in tangible historical form, established in the flesh
of Christ as a part of the world, of humanity and of its very
history."[25] He then goes on to offer an approach to the theology of sacraments vis-à-vis the rest of life by asserting: "what is
brought to effective manifestation in the dimension of the
Church in the sacraments is precisely *that* grace which, in virtue of God's universal will to save, is effective everywhere in
the world where [the human person] does not react to it with
absolute denial."[26] Rahner articulates a foundational insight
for his sacramental theology when he asserts that "the Church
is the abiding presence of that primal sacramental word of definitive grace, which Christ is in the world, effecting what is
uttered by uttering it in sign."[27]

Another foundational insight derives from what can be
termed a theology of the exhibitive word. Here sacraments are
understood to be effective because they share in the exhibitive
power of God's own word by recalling the power of the divine
utterance at creation and, most particularly, in the redemption
accomplished by the Word made flesh.[28] He asserts that "it
would do no harm if we were to regard the doctrine of the sacraments in general as one quite specific section of the theology
of the word of God and its exhibitive force."[29] Such a grounding for the theology of sacraments enables Roman Catholics to
establish a commonality among all seven sacraments, including those which do not employ the use of physical elements
(i.e., since penance and marriage lack physical elements, or
"matter," such as oil, bread, wine).[30] This approach to sacramental theology can also help ecumenical understandings of
sacraments and sacramentality[31] because it capitalizes on the
notion of sacraments as "visible words."[32] More foundational-
ly, one could argue that such a theology of the word can help
establish the anthropological basis of sacraments in the sense
that human beings communicate on the basis of a theology of
the exhibitive word, whether this means that words used in
human communication are always oriented toward being effective or performing an act (as performance theorists argue)[33]
or words understood as intrinsically symbolic or (as in liturgy)

as necessarily leading to enactment which at times includes the use of symbolic elements.

Another foundation for Rahner's sacramental theology, his theology of symbol,[34] is evident in the way he articulates the relationship between Christ and the church. He explains: to say that the church is the "fundamental sacrament means [that it is] the one abiding symbolic presence, similar in structure to the incarnation, of the eschatological redemptive grace of Christ . . ."[35] Like Schillebeeckx before him, Rahner carefully contextualizes sacraments within the total faith life of the church by stating that "supernatural activity where grace is conferred and promised to us by God, infallibly on his part, and sacramental activity, are not identical. The second is only one of the possible kinds of the first."[36] He notes the importance of sacraments by stating that they are essential self-expressions of the church[37] through which the church "attains the highest degree of actualization of what she always is: the presence of redemptive grace . . . historically visible and manifest as the sign of the eschatologically victorious grace of God in the world."[38] Rahner relies on Aquinas[39] when he states that "God has not attached his power to the sacraments in such a way that he could not also impart the effects of sacramental grace without the sacraments themselves.[40] Such an approach offers real possibilities for the anthropological foundation of the sacraments in that it capitalizes on both the social nature of the human person in emphasizing the role of the church as well as the importance attached to events which solidify one's identity in human life which are part of human life itself.[41] He thus restores to contemporary sacramental theology one of the key retrievals of the postconciliar liturgical reform of the sacraments—the essentially communal, ecclesial event character of sacraments.[42]

Rahner links the important insights about church, sacraments, the word, and grace when he states that the church is "the visible outward expression of grace, not in the sense that she subsequently announces as it were the presence of something already there without the announcement, but in the sense that in the Church God's grace is given expression and embodiment and symbolized, and by being so embodied, is present."[43] Thus, on the one hand, sacraments typify and are the chief embodiments of the church's essential nature; yet, on the other, they are by no means the exclusive locus of Christ as "the actual historical presence in the world of the eschatologically triumphant mercy of God."[44]

Donald Baillie

An important contributor to the contemporary Protestant discussion, Donald Baillie, Professor of Systematic Theology at the University of St. Andrew's, sought to answer the question "why should we have sacraments at all?"[45] in a series of lectures delivered at Presbyterian Theological Seminary (California) in 1952. He began by citing Paul Tillich who had spoken of the "death of the sacraments" over thirty years earlier.[46] He sets out his project by asking:

> What is there in human nature and human needs and our human situation, what is there in the Christian faith, the Christian Gospel, the Christian salvation, what is there in the nature of the divine grace and its ways of working, to demand this strange visible, tangible expression, in material things and in perceptible actions, which we call sacramental?[47]

Baillie begins by asserting that sacramentality is a notion that is much wider than the church's sacred rites. He asserts that the church uses certain elements (e.g., bread and wine) for sacraments "because this universe is [a] sacramental kind of place in which that can fitly happen; because these elements, these creatures of God, do lend themselves to such a use; and because we men and women, who are another sort of God's creatures, do require in our religion such a use of material things and symbolic actions."[48] Natural objects can become sacramental only because we live in "a sacramental universe"[49] created and redeemed by God. Part of that created world is created human beings who can only express themselves "through the material—words uttered by the tongue [or] written with ink on paper . . . Persons also communicate with each other by symbolic movements, smiles and gestures, handshakes, linking of arms, and embraces."[50] Baillie then asserts that human beings engage in social relationships based on our living together; hence a meal is a social occasion, a means of fellowship.[51] Thus Baillie can assert that:

we cannot worship God without words, and we shall impoverish our worship if we try to dispense with all other symbols in the realm of sense—music and gesture and ritual action, standing and kneeling, clasping our hands, closing our eyes. So we need not only the Word but also the sacraments . . .[52]

Baillie then argues that Christianity is of the aorist indicative in that "it tells of something that once happened" and that sacraments have an inseparable connection with that historical fact.[53] Here Baillie notes and debates the usefulness of the common phrase that "the sacraments are the extension of the incarnation."[54] What is most useful here is the way the author will assert, especially from the perspective of sacraments, that the issue "was not that spirit entered into matter, but that the Creator entered into humanity, that the Word became flesh, that God lived a human life and died a human death."[55] This leads him to assert an important factor that theologizing about the relationship between sacraments and the incarnation is also wholly bound up with the idea that the incarnation did not go on for ever, but came to an end, and that since then the divine presence is with us in a new way through the Holy Spirit working in the church through word and sacraments.[56] His important nuances about Christ and sacraments and their relationship with Spirit, word, and grace are worth citing in full.

We ought to think of the living Christ who is with His people in every age through the Holy Spirit,and who establishes with us through His Church, His Word and His sacraments, that personal relationship which is the very meaning of grace . . . Christ is present with us, not incarnate in the Church, but through the Holy Spirit working in the Church by Word and Sacrament. And it all happens that way because Christianity is the religion of the incarnation.[57]

The final aspect of Baillie's argument rests on the eschatological nature of the sacraments because of the eschatological nature of the church. In the interim period of the church, a period of looking back and looking forward, Christ is present with us through the Spirit. "We are *viatores*, present in the body and absent from the Lord, able to see only 'in a mirror and in a riddle'; and a sacrament is a kind of mirror, the kind of mirror of eternal things required by creatures of flesh and blood in a fallen world which has been redeemed but whose redemption is still not yet complete."[58] Thus, he writes, we need sacraments.[59]

Raymond Didier

Raymond Didier's writings on sacraments (particularly in the mid-1970s) reflect the pastoral experience of a French Catholicism faced with having to argue for the value of sacraments and to enliven sacramental practice for large numbers of "baptized non-believers." These were Catholics who did not practice their faith in sacramental celebration or who were at least quite skeptical about the value of sacraments. They raised such questions as "what need do faith and love have of sacraments" and "is Christianity a sacramental religion."[60] His writings also evidence an initial advance toward an interdisciplinary approach to the study of sacraments as drawn, for example, from anthropology, sociology, and psychology.[61] Before addressing how one should raise the question of how sacraments are rooted in human life, Didier offers two descriptions of Christian "sacrament" that inform his search: that sacraments are enduring signs of the paschal mystery[62] and are actual memorials of the dying and rising of Jesus through the medium of the Word of God.[63] Sacraments share in the common appreciation of other public rites in the rest of human life. Like them they are specific social acts that are programmed, repeated and symbolic through which an individual is identified with a social group and with society at large.[64] From this he argues repeatedly that sacraments are necessary because they offer the Christian an important opportunity to experience the church as the body of those who share the same beliefs and hopes.[65]

Didier argues that as memorial rites of the paschal mystery, sacraments use the word of the scriptures and symbols[66] to ensure ecclesial belonging and continued identification with the church. Here he notes the performative value of liturgical language,[67] and how the elements used as symbols are not sources of grace in themselves but rather the means needed for grace to pass to participants.[68] In this way he avoids any "sacralization" of Christian liturgy which could lead to an exclusively other-worldly appreciation of sacraments.

This basic understanding of sacraments is underscored in Didier's discussion of sacraments and hope. Here Didier emphasizes the relationship between sacraments and eschatology and states that sacraments are critical and prophetic moments when participants experience ultimate truth, the reality of God and eschatological hope.[69] This emphasis reminds believers of the "not-yet" character of Christianity and reminds them to view sacraments as important means to challenge the status quo of church and societal life. That such a challenge should derive from sacramental participation is important for Didier. Here he borrows specifically from the Fathers of the church when he argues for the necessity of sacraments to express one's Christian faith because without them (especially baptism and eucharist) the Gospel becomes a moral or theological discourse and faith loses an essential means for a full, complete, and correct identification of life in Christ.[70]

One detects in Didier a pastoral theologian who has reflected on the contemporary needs of the church regarding sacraments and who has brought to his creative treatment important insights from the tradition and contemporary authors such as Schillebeeckx and Rahner.

* * * * * *

This survey of representative works on sacramental theology has disclosed a number of important insights about anthropological and theological value of sacraments. They can be summarized as follows.

Anthropological

At least two points can be made toward arguing for our need for sacraments from an anthropological perspective.

(1) On the basis of what pertains to the nature of a human being, issues undergirding the sacramental act concern how human beings communicate, that is, through word, gestures, and symbols. Together these comprise the ritual action of sacrament. They are appropriate means of communication to fit the human condition. Thus there is an anthropological basis to the church's use of scripture, blessing prayers, and the gestural use of symbols in sacraments.

(2) The common human experience of limitation and estrangement has been interpreted in classical Christian literature in terms of the human's need for redemption because of the fall and original sin. The ritual of sacraments enables one to experience a clear articulation of a balanced and theologically grounded way to deal with both estrangement and redemption. Sacraments employ a balanced theology whereby both sin and forgiveness, the fall and redemption, weakness and strength in God are continually reiterated. Part of this sense of freedom from estrangement and sin is evident in the church's use of paradigmatic myths of the fall and redemption in the scriptures at sacraments, especially in initiation (e.g., the Lenten lectionary readings, especially the temptation account on the First Sunday of Lent preceding the rite of election and the lectionary for penance emphasizing the prodigal son). The use of the word illumines our sense of alienation and estrangement, and at the same time it is a privileged means of renewing our union and communion with God. In addition, the very communal experience of sacraments where the church community together acknowledges its need and together lays claim once more to God's definitive act of reconciliation and redemption in Christ evidences the anthropological experience of humankind yearning for community and relatedness to heal primal estrangement and isolation.

Theological

At least three points can be made toward arguing for the theological importance of sacraments.

(1) Granted the limitation of any particular liturgical rite and realizing that all that one can reasonably hope for is the least inadequate sacramental rite,[71] it is still important to see how the texts used in sacraments reflect a totality of vision concerning God, Christ, grace, salvation, redemption, justification, grace, and the church. One theological justification for sacraments is that they lay bare this totality before believers. Without such specified rites and texts, such communities (or individuals) might have a less than adequate experience and understanding of the multifaceted mystery of God and how the church experiences this mystery in its liturgy, which experience should obviously influence one's spirituality.

(2) Concomitant with this investigation and experience, it is also important to see how the repertoire of a ritual engagement in sacraments sets forth these beliefs in the general instructions to the rituals, in the texts themselves, in ritual gestures, in preaching, and in explanatory comments. This is to suggest that the post-Vatican II model of liturgy allowing for variety, pluriformity, and creativity requires a solid grounding in the theology of the liturgy celebrated derived from the liturgical theology of the sacramental rites themselves,[72] in order that the multifaceted reality of God experienced in sacraments be experienced specifically and directly through sacraments in a given place and time. Particularly helpful means to articulate this experience in sacraments are the homily and intercessions.

(3) That sacraments are the *church's* ritual act of self-expression has been repeatedly stressed in contemporary sacramental theology. One important aspect of this ecclesial expression is that the church sees itself as central to any act of liturgy and that ritual prayer is never private or divorced from the Body of Christ. This establishes a priority in sacraments over other acts of prayer, devotion, or mercy since the biblical doctrine of election and being made part of God's chosen people has a prior claim. Individual needs are placed in relation to the movement of the church toward eschatological fulfillment. Sacraments thus establish a paradigm according to which other experiences of God can be measured, namely, that ultimately such experiences of God should lead one to self-transcendence and to life lived for the sake of the Other and others, not for oneself alone. The ecclesiological underpinning of sacraments by its nature explicitates this required self-criticism and critique.

The priority and paradigmatic quality of Christian sacraments argued here should not be interpreted as eclipsing other ways of coming to experience and know God. This argument does not neglect the reality that the Lord is present where individuals engage in *lectio divina* or other spiritual reading, or when the hungry are fed, the naked are clothed, the homeless are housed, or the poor have the Gospel preached to them. Yet the same Lord is present to the church in liturgy and sacraments in ways that draw on the nature of the human person (word, symbol, gesture, etc.) and which intend to offer a more complete and full picture of divine self-revelation and self-definition (not always found in other ways of experiencing God) in terms of transcendence and intimacy, invitation to communion and enabling us to respond, proclamation of the Gospel and living it in the world, of being converted and of living converted lives, of yearning for Christ who will come again as we luxuriate in the divine presence with us in innumerable ways.

Grace is indeed always available in faith to redeemed humanity through the incarnate Christ. In light of this, sacraments become privileged, but not unique, pivotal, but not exclusive experiences of God through Christ in the power of the Spirit in the church. Sacraments actualize Christ's incarnation and paschal mystery. Sacraments, then, become particularly strong moments[73] of God's self-disclosure. These central saving mysteries become the prism through which we interpret sacraments and the whole Christian life as unfailing signs of God's amazing grace and abiding favor.

Notes

1. Part of the reason why I have selected this topic is that my argument in "Sacramental Theology: A Methodological Proposal," *The Thomist* 54·2 (April 1990) 311-342 (among other recent writing on liturgy and sacraments) lacks attention to this pertinent question. It is hoped that this lack is somewhat adequately addressed here.

2. See, among many others, Pierre Dens, *Tractatus de Sacramentis in Genre* (Mechelen, 1850) *De Sacramentis in Genere*, where he answers the question about the necessity of sacraments (pp. 29-31) by drawing on Thomas *ST, q. 60, n. 1-4* and *De Baptismo* where he answers the question about the necessity of baptism (pp. 38-41) by referring to *ST, q. 66, n. 1-3* (pp. 38-41).

3. Ibid. 49.

4. *Summa Theologica* 3a, q. 61, (*The Necessity of Sacraments*, Blackfriars Edition, vol. 56, ed., David Bourke [New York: McGraw-Hill, 1975]) 39.

5. Ibid.

6. Ibid.

7. Ibid.

8. See note 2 above.

9. Dens, *Tractatus* 29.

10. Ibid. 38; see Trent Sess. 7, can. 5; confer sess. 6, cap. 4. On p. 41 he will repeat this reference and add to it Sess. 5, in the decree on original sin, cans. 4 and 5.

11. Ibid. 41.

12. Edward Schillebeeckx, *Christ the Sacrament of the Encounter with God* (New York: Sheed and Ward, 1963) 43-44. It should be noted that the pre-Vatican II seminal works of Edward Schillebeeckx, *De sacramentele heilseconomie: Theologische bezinning op S. Thomas' sacramenteleer in het licht van de traditie en van de hedendaagse sacramentsproblematic* (Antwerp: H. Neilissen, 1952), and *De Christusontmoeting als sacrament van de Godsmoeting* (Antwerp: H. Neilissen, 1957) are largely based on Aquinas' work on sacraments in the *Summa Theologica*. Hence they are best interpreted in close connection with the *Summa's* questions on sacraments. It should be recalled that the English edition, *Christ the Sacrament*, is a condensed and much impoverished (even, at times, misleading) version of the longer and more detailed original(s).

13. Schillebeeckx, *Christ the Sacrament* 44.

14. Ibid.

15. Ibid. 78.

16. Ibid.

17. Ibid. 96.

18. Ibid. 214.

19. Edward Schillebeeckx, *Christ: The Experience of Jesus as Lord*, trans., John Bowden (New York: Seabury, 1980).

20. Ibid. 836.

21. Ibid. 835-836.

22. Ibid. 836.

23. Ibid.

24. Ibid. 838.

25. Karl Rahner, *The Church and the Sacraments*, trans., W.J. O'Hara (New York: Sheed and Ward, 1963) 15. Like Schillebeeckx before him, Rahner's work *Kirche und Sakramente* (Herder, 1961) is based on Aquinas' work on sacraments in the *Summa Theologica*. Also Rahner himself notes that *The Church and the Sacraments* was intended to be a precise contribution to the *Quaestiones Disputatae* series offering comments on one disputed question, not a full treatise on the sacraments (ibid. 7). Two of Rahner's more significant essays for our purposes are "Considerations on the Active Role of the Person in the Sacramental Event," *Theological Investigations*, vol. 14 (New York: Seabury, 1976) 161-184, and "On the Theology of Worship," *Theological Investigations*, vol. 19 (New York: Seabury, 1983) 141-149 (which essay was written in large part to clarify "Considerations"). In "On the Theology" he states: "salvation history is not made up of succes-

sive spatio-temporal interventions of God in an otherwise secular world, but is the history of freedom (of God and man) which accepts this innermost and enduring deification of the world, gives it historical expression and thus constitutes the history of this deification of the world." "The sacraments accordingly are not really to be understood as successive individual incursions of God into a secular world, but as 'outbursts' (if we can express it in this way) of the innermost, ever present gracious endowment of the world with God himself into history." (143) See especially the second part of the helpful work by Michael Skelley, *The Liturgy of the World: Karl Rahner's Theology of Worship* (Collegeville: The Liturgical Press, A Pueblo Book, 1991) 85-158.

26. Rahner, *The Church* 15.

27. Ibid. 18.

28. This is argued more fully in Rahner's essays "Introductory Observations on Thomas Aquinas' Theology of Sacraments in General," *Theological Investigations*, vol. 14, 149-160, 152, and "What Is a Sacrament?", ibid. 137-141. Edward Kilmartin's critique of Rahner here is instructive; see *Christian Liturgy: Theory and Practice* (Kansas City: Sheed and Ward, 1988) 251-255.

29. Rahner, "Introductory Observations" 152. He goes on to say: "for then we would understand the sacraments as those words in which that which is expressed by them is rendered present by this expression itself when these words are addressed by the Church as basic sacrament to the individual [person] with a radical commitment as the irreversible and historical presence of the grace of God [to that person]."

30. Ibid. 138.

31. Ibid. 148.

32. St. Augustine calls a sacrament a sacred sign, a *signaculum*, a visible word. He states that "one joins the word to the material element and behold the sacrament, that is, a kind of visible word" (*In Johannem* 80, 3; PL 35:1840). This quotation is used by Robert W. Jensen at the introduction to Chapter One of his work *Visible Words: The Interpretation and Practice of Christian Sacraments* (Philadelphia: Fortress Press, 1978) 3.

33. See, among others, J.L. Austin, *How to Do Things with Words*, 2d ed. (Oxford: Oxford University Press, 1962), John Searle, *Speech Acts: An Essay in the Philosophy of Language* (Cambridge: Cambridge University Press, 1969); John Searle, *Intentionality: An Essay in the Philosophy of Mind* (Cambridge: Cambridge University Press, 1983), and J.H. Ware, *Not with Words of Wisdom: Performative Language and Liturgy* (Washington, D.C.: University Press of America, 1981).

34. See Karl Rahner, "The Theology of the Symbol," *Theological Investigations*, vol. 4 (New York: Crossroad, 1982) 221-252.

35. Rahner, *The Church* 23.

36. Ibid. 28.

37. He states: "they can only be so when the signs are posited as signs of the Church as such, when they are ultimately and radically the actual accomplishment of the eternal covenant, operations in which the whole nature of this is actualized, for it alone has this assurance and guarantee." Ibid. 32.

38. Ibid. 22.

39. *Summa Theologica* q. 64, art. 7.

40. Rahner, "Introductory Observations" 158.

41. On the sociological importance of the event of sacraments, see Philip J. Murnion, "A Sacramental Church in the Modern World," *Origins* 14 (21 June, 1984) 81-90.

42. For him sacraments "remain the valid and validly promulgated offer of redemption by God. They are truly *opus operatum*. They can only be so when the signs are posited as signs of the Church as such, when they are ultimately and radically the actual accomplishment of the eternal covenant, operations in which the whole nature of this is actualized, for it alone has this assurance and guarantee." Rahner, *The Church* 32.

43. Ibid. 34.

44. Ibid. 15.

45. Donald Baillie, *The Theology of the Church and Other Papers* (London: Faber and Faber, 1958) 41. Another helpful Protestant approach to sacraments at roughly the same time is Neville Clark, *An Approach to the Theology of the Sacraments* (London: SCM, 1956), esp. 71-85.

46. Ibid. 39, quoted from Paul Tillich, *Essays and Addresses*, First Series (1921) 251.

47. Ibid. 42.

48. Ibid. 44.

49. Ibid. 47.

50. Ibid. 48.

51. Ibid. 49-50.

52. Ibid. 51.

53. Ibid.

54. Ibid. 61. For an example of a classical Protestant exposition of this approach, see Morgan Dix, *The Sacramental System Considered as the Extension of the Incarnation* (New York: Longmans Green, 1902).

55. Ibid. 65.

56. Ibid.

57. Ibid. 65-67.

58. Ibid. 70.

59. Ibid. 71: "We are creatures of flesh and blood in this spoilt and fallen world, and do need the helps which God in His kindness has provided for us in the sacraments of the Gospel."

60. See Raymond Didier, *Les Sacrements de la foi: La Pâque dans ses signes* (Paris: Centurion, 1975) in which his stated aim is to situate Christian ritual within the context of fundamental human experience (5) as he seeks to answer the question "do we need sacraments?" (10) See also his "Des sacrements, pourquoi? Enjeux anthropologiques et théologiques," *La Maison-Dieu* 119 (1974) 51-73.

61. For example, see ibid 146, "Des sacrements, pourquoi?" 36 and P. Beguerie, H. Denis, R. Didier, J.-Y. Hameline, A. Vergote, "Problems sacramentaires dialogue interdisciplinaire," *La Maison-Dieu* 119 (1974) 51-73.

62. Didier, *Les Sacrements* 16.

63. Ibid. 20.

64. Ibid. 22.

65. Ibid., passim, as well as "Des sacrements" 40-41.

66. Ibid. 25.

67. Ibid. 71.

68. Ibid. 69.

69. Ibid. 79-80 and 125-135, as well as "Des sacrements" 48-49.

70. "De sacrements" 41.

71. This statement reflects the present discussion about the importance of the "critical function of liturgical theology" in light of the contemporary reformed liturgy. Among others, see Angelus Haussling, "Die kritische Funktion der Liturgiewissenschaft," *Liturgie und Gesellschaft*, ed., H.B. Meyer (Innsbruck: Tyrolia-Verlag, 1970) 103-130.

72. This distinction between a theology of liturgy as the theological meaning of the act of liturgy, and liturgical theology as systematic theology inspired by the act of liturgy is derived from Alexander Schmemann, "Theology and Liturgical Tradition," in *Worship in Scripture and Tradition*, ed., Massey Shepherd (New York: Oxford University Press, 1963) 175-178. See also Kevin W. Irwin, "Directions for a Method for Liturgical Theology," in *Liturgical Theology: A Primer* (Collegeville: The Liturgical Press, 1990) 64-68.

73. This term is taken from the *Directory for the Celebration of the Work of God: Guidelines for the Monastic Liturgy of the Hours Approved for the Benedictine Confederation* (Riverdale: Exordium Books, 1981) 24-25.

3

The Word Beneath the Words

Mary Catherine Hilkert, O.P.

"BE CAREFUL WITH WORDS; THEY'RE DANGEROUS," WARNED ELIE WIESEL. "Be wary of them. They beget either demons or angels."[1] Preachers, like poets and prophets, spend their lives in the dangerous company of words precisely because they are convinced of their power. Yet preachers claim more than a human craft. From the time of the apostle Paul, Christian preachers, like the Hebrew prophets before them, have insisted that the power of their preaching is the power of God (Rom 1:16; 1 Cor 1:18); the word they speak, God's own. As Karl Barth asserts in his classic *The Preaching of the Gospel*: "Preaching is 'God's own word.' That is to say through the activity of preaching God himself speaks."[2]

That claim presumes, of course, that preaching is rooted in the Bible, the one book that Christians maintain not only witnesses to or transmits the word of God, but in some sense *is* the word of God. As biblical scholar Reginald Fuller relates the two claims:

> There is . . . a superhuman quality to the Bible, and that is why the Christian church has always called it *also* as well as a human product . . . the Word of God. For the Christian church to abandon that affirmation would be for it to lose its very identity . . . [However] the witness of the prophets and apostles to the Christ event, is the Word of God only within the believing

community. Only there does the word *happen* as Word . . .
Preaching is not just an optional activity we do with the Bible.
It is absolutely integral to the Bible as Word.[3]

Whether referring to God's activity in the history of Israel,
in the person, words and deeds of Jesus, in the biblical text, or
in the proclamation event, preaching texts often refer to the
word of God as creative, effective, and prophetic. Preachers
are exhorted to take courage from the biblical promise that
God's word does not return void, but always achieves the purpose for which it was sent (Is 55:11) and challenged by the
claim that "that Word of God is living and effective, sharper
than any two-edged sword" (Heb 4:12). Emphasizing the prophetic dimension of the Scriptures, Leander Keck maintains
that the Bible always remains the church's greatest critic, and
that biblical preaching is the most dangerous form of preaching the church can hear.[4]

Yet some of those who would agree with Keck that biblical
preaching is dangerous have quite a different perspective in
mind. Echoing Wiesel's warning that words can beget demons, feminist biblical scholar Elisabeth Schüssler Fiorenza
suggests that a critical hermeneutics of suspicion would place
the following warning label on all biblical texts: "Caution!
Could be dangerous to your health and survival."[5] The "four
unpreached stories of faith" identified by Phyllis Trible
("Hagar, the slave used, abused and rejected; Tamar, the prin-
cess raped and discarded; an unnamed woman, the concubine
raped, murdered, and dismembered; and the daughter of
Jephthah, a virgin slain and sacrificed") present a far from exhaustive list of what Trible has called "texts of terror" to be
found within the Scriptures believers call sacred.[6] The psalm-
ist's call to dash the heads of the infant children of Israel's enemies against the rocks, the Pauline exhortations of slaves to be
obedient to their masters and wives to be submissive to their
husbands, the passages from John's Gospel used within the
Good Friday liturgy that attribute the death of Jesus to the
Jews, and the insistence of the Epistle to the Romans that "all
authority that exists is established by God . . . civil magistrates
[are] God's ministers" (Rom 13:6) provide some of the most
obvious additional examples of texts that prove problematic

when proclaimed with the liturgical refrain that echoes the prophets: "This is the Word of the Lord."

That preaching has contributed to the use of these texts to reinforce situations of injustice is evident from the recent use of Romans 13 in South Africa (as well as its earlier exercise by Emil Brunner in Nazi Germany) and from the use of biblical texts to legitimate the dominance of men over women and even physical abuse within the home. One of the most chilling testimonies to the power of the word was Hitler's claim made before two German bishops that his policies toward the Jews were "simply completing what Christian preaching and teaching had been saying about Jews for the better part of 1900 years."[7]

Even these few examples highlight a growing conviction that the power of the word is indeed "two-edged," and that only with a critical hermeneutic that is grounded in the vision of the reign of God preached and embodied by Jesus can Christians appropriate and preach the Scriptures as "living and effective." Some scholars have concluded that the problematic texts should be excluded from the lectionary and hence from Christian preaching.[8] On the other hand, it can be argued that precisely because of the history of the ideological use of what have been considered classic Christian texts, they must not be eliminated, but that preaching that is faithful to the Gospel must explicitly address the biases of the historically-culturally conditioned texts and dissociate the Christian community from sinful social structures that have been handed on in name of the Gospel.[9]

While his scholarship has not focused primarily on biblical interpretation or preaching, systematic and liturgical theologian David Power has addressed a number of these questions in foundational terms. He has explicitly critiqued the ideological use of Scripture and religious language as well as of sacraments, liturgy, and ordained ministry, and addressed the need for a critical liturgical praxis and liturgical theology.[10] Throughout his writings can be discovered the threads of a theology of the "Word beneath the words" that evokes both critical response and creative imagination when the preaching of the church fails to be the preaching of the Gospel. Power is well aware that words (and symbols) can beget demons, yet his critical theological appropriation of the power of the word of God (influenced strongly by Paul Ricoeur) allows one to move beyond a first naïveté that emphasizes the power of the word to mediate the divine, through a critical analysis of all human speech about God's word as "flawed," toward a critical reappropriation of "the voice of God between the cracks."

In the Beginning Was the Word

In a 1987 article on liturgical praxis, Power states that "We need an eye for metaphor and an ear for dissonance which dissolves the domineering tendencies of man over man, man over woman, of humanity over cosmos and allows us to hear the voice of God between the cracks."[11] He admits that there is a wager in this use of language—the wager of hope in the service of freedom and the fullness of being for all.

Underlying Power's confidence that the word of God can and must remain at once creative and prophetic is a theology of the word that is profoundly interrelated with an understanding of the human person and human community and rooted in a larger theology of creation. In the beginning the word was spoken to—not by—human beings. The creation myth in the first chapter of Genesis suggests that human beings were called into existence by the word of God, created as the very image of God, and blessed as "very good."

From the beginning, then, everything has been given to humanity in and through the Word, the Word in whose image we are created and for whose reign we are destined. At the core of our being we have been addressed by a word of freedom that grounds both the invitation to transcendence and the possibility of betrayal. Because the Word through whom and in whom we are created is the incarnate Word who will not be "all in all" until the end of history, Power can point to a "transformative dynamic" as "inherent in the human."[12] The final fulfillment of the promise that God's word will not return without accomplishing that for which it was sent (which Christians have understood in terms of Jesus the incarnate Word of God), will not be complete until all of human history and creation have been returned to God in Christ. The word of God remains a promise that always lies ahead of us, summoning us to our deepest truth.

One early influence on Power's approach to the power of the word was Karl Rahner's theology of the word as symbol or sacrament.[13] Rahner offers an incarnational foundation from which to consider that the power of the word derives ultimately from both the trinitarian mystery of God as self-communicating love and the mystery of the human person as body-spirit. In the deepest core of our being human persons remain freedom and mystery, created in the image of God whose freedom is absolute and who remains holy mystery hidden in darkness. God could have chosen to remain the mysterious and distant horizon of our existence. The perspective of faith, however, allows one to perceive that throughout the history of the world (interpreted as a history of salvation by the believer), and ultimately in Jesus, the Word made flesh, and in the community who continue to live in his name through the power of the Spirit, God has been revealed to be God-with-us. The mystery at the heart of reality has been disclosed to be the mystery of relationality and love. From the perspective of Christian faith, all of creation can be viewed as destined for the incarnation—for the total union of divine love and human response in freedom.

But precisely because human persons are constituted as body-spirit, neither the human response to relationship with God nor even perception of the offer is possible apart from the word of faith. Even in human relationships we know the importance and power of words. We have the power to keep our inner self hidden or to reveal (un-veil) ourselves to one another, sharing who we are in vulnerability and truth and hence coming to a deeper identity in and through mutual love.

To an extent, we speak beyond our explicit words—our behavior, our "body language," even our silence—speaks. But only the spoken word can bring the ambiguity of both actions and silence to full clarity. Further, there are words in which we speak our very selves—words which come from the center of our being, words with which we define and create—or lose—our very selves as Thomas More reminded his daughter Margaret:

> What is an oath, but words we say to God? . . . When a man takes an oath, Meg, he's holding his own self in his own hands.

Like water. And if he opens his fingers, *then*—he needn't hope to find himself again.[14]

Words spoken from the center of ourselves, words like "I love you"; "Here I stand; I can do no other"; "I have a dream"—are revelatory—they allow a deeper dimension of reality to emerge. These kind of "depth words" are not merely signs which point to a reality that exists independently of the naming. Rather, the word "embodies" the deeper mystery in a public, conscious, historical way. Here words become sacraments—they function as symbols which make present a deeper mysterious reality.[15]

In a similar way, grace (God's personal self-communication) has been available anonymously throughout creation and history, but the mystery of love at the heart of reality has become explicit, definitive, and irrevocable only in Jesus—the Word made flesh. In other words, as the self-communication of God in love, grace has an intrinsically incarnational or sacramental structure—it is oriented toward the fullness of its expression in embodied word. God has indeed spoken throughout creation and history in "varied and fragmentary ways" as the Letter to the Hebrews states, but "in this the final age, God has spoken to us through the Son who has been made heir of all things and through whom the universe was first created." In Jesus, as Ignatius puts it, God has "broken the silence" (Magnesians 8) and spoken God's own word of self-expression. Jesus, the Word made flesh, becomes the sacrament of God in the midst of human history. As the Body of Christ in the world, the church participates in the abiding sacrament of Christ. Preaching and the sacraments, preeminently the eucharist, function as the church's self-expression, naming, proclaiming, and celebrating the mystery of God's saving self-offering of love in the life, death, and resurrection of Jesus.[16]

Reflection on the unique role of humanity in this sacramental/incarnational view of all of reality discloses a further connection between creation in and through the word and creation in the image of God. To have been created in the image of God is to have been entrusted with "the power of the word." As Michael Scanlon explains:

> Naming is the primordial human *praxis* of "the image and like-
> ness" of God who created the world through the divine Word.
> Just as God's eternal expressibility is the origin of everything
> that exists, so human expressibility is the origin of history. We
> are like God because we can speak . . . our humanity supplied
> the grammar for the divine self-utterance.[17]

It is human beings who make history, who bestow meaning, who constitute the world through words. The human world is always the world as interpreted by human consciousness, that is, mediated by meaning. Meaning is always embodied in word. In reflecting on preaching precisely as "mediating God's meaning," William Hill remarks that "words are events; they happen as do other events and in happening they change, for better or for worse, the course of history. In words, Being itself finds its voice" (Heidegger).[18]

If human beings shape the course of history, however, what contemporary meaning can be found in the complex claim that "God acts in human history"? Power explains that "God speaks" not by making the events of history take place, but through the word of faith that turns the event into a religious one. Challenging the literal or unreflected-upon claims (of preachers among others) that "God speaks in history" as well as the notion that God is the agent-cause of the events of history, Power reminds us that "the power with which the bible accredits God is the power of his word. It is when God is heard that the Spirit renews the face of the earth. God speaks to us in human events when, via the human words of the prophet, these events are made to challenge us to a search for religious meaning."[19]

Faith's recognition and symbolic expression of the religious depth to be discovered in the events of history is necessary for those events to become revelatory. Even the insight that we are called to relationship with God is available to us only in and through the words of a tradition of faith. It is within those frameworks for interpreting (and thus experiencing) human life as rooted in and destined for God that the offer of a relationship with God becomes even a possibility. Religious language opens us to trust in the future based on an awareness of God as at the heart of human history and self-making.

Power would further emphasize, however, the insight of the

political theologians that abstract considerations of human history and self-making are inadequate. Rather, human experience in all its concrete reality—including that of suffering and alienation—must be the starting point for a critical theology of the word needed today. Hence attention to those whose voices are never heard, to those who have been silenced, and to those who speak critically and act in prophetic resistance calling for transformation of the dominant social-symbolic order of both church and society must be attended to in any fully adequate theology of the word.[20]

Finally, the eschatological dimension of the word rooted in the connection between the memory of Christ's passion (which for Christians includes the memory of all human suffering) and the power of the imagination to hope in the possibility of a new and different future is central throughout Power's writings on sacraments and the power of the word. Already in his essays on symbolism written during the 1970s, Power underlined the importance of the future dimension opened up by the word in his critique of some interpretations of Rahner's approach:

> A danger to which this presentation [of Rahner's ontology of symbol] might be subject is that it could be used to give an idea of "God behind us," moving us by his word to action. Hence it needs to be completed by a sense of the word as a word which invites to a future, a word spoken by "God ahead of us," God calling us to himself as object of hope.[21]

In his more recent writings Power has highlighted within his treatment of words as eschatological symbols the nonidentity of symbol and reality. While symbols point us toward the reign of God and draw us into that reign in an anticipatory way, nonetheless, "absence endures until the eschaton."[22] The critical dimension necessary in any understanding of the power of the word of God (that is available only in human words) is rooted not only in the limitations and finitude of the human situation and in the eschatological reservation that recognizes the "absence that endures until the eschaton," but also in the reality of human sin. "Flawed human speech"[23] has the power to mute, if not to silence, God's liberating promise.

Muting the Promise: Flawed Human Speech

Essential to any discussion of the power of the word as foundational to preaching today is critical reflection on the limits of religious language, the role of language in the construction of social reality, and the ideological manipulation of language. As Power has stressed in his writings: "A critical sense is necessary if the gospel is to be truly free in its address to the churches and if people are to be free to listen to it."[24]

Critical reflection begins with the limitations of human words to convey the mystery of God present in human history. As mentioned earlier, Power highlights the dimension of absence and the eschatological reservation that are essential if reverence for the word of God is not to slip into idolatry. Thus he underlines "the nonidentity of the Word with any form in which it is spoken and of the Spirit with any voice in which it speaks."[25] Our words, concepts, and images necessarily are more unlike than like the mystery they try to express, name, or evoke. Only the "odd logic" of religious language can enable human discourse to mediate the disclosure of the divine. As Ian Ramsey's classic work on religious language notes, human language needs to be qualified to the point of infinity in order to express the total commitment and universal significance of the religious claim. Religious language remains always "limit language" that can offer us at best "some intimation of the odd, mysterious, indeed scandalous limit-experience which [the] gospel proclaims as an authentic human possibility."[26] In traditional terms Thomas Aquinas in his doctrine of analogy likewise emphasized that religious language is neither univocal nor equivocal; rather, in the process of naming the unknown God, the human concept is negated, but the directionality of the concept affirmed with an "eminent meaning" beyond human comprehension. Speaking of the revelatory power of sacramental symbols, Power insists in a similar way that "one can never speak of power in a Christian context without being as attentive to what is negated of it in this context as to what is positively affirmed."[27]

Discussions of the power of God's word remain naive at best and ideological at worst if the role of language in constructing social reality is not critically considered. One's

choice of language (in the broad sense of what is given symbolic meaning) is also, even if unconsciously, a choice of what
is to be considered valuable—what is to come to visibility and
speech. As is often pointed out: "the limits of one's language
are the limits of one's world."

In terms of revelation and preaching, this translates into the
insight that while not denying God's gracious presence grounding and summoning humanity toward our future destiny, what
we call "word of God" is also the construct of human words of
faith forged within a concrete historical-cultural context; this in
turn heightens our awareness of the possibility of manipulation, ideology, and cultural bias. The betrayal that always remains a possibility given the human heritage of freedom extends to the power of the word which has been entrusted to us.
Language that was intended to foster human communication,
truth, and love can serve to divide, deceive, and alienate. Ideology takes on its destructive role when the accepted description
of reality that purports to explain how things necessarily are
(often with religious legitimation) is in fact a manipulative way
of preserving the status quo in the interest of those who hold
power in a social system. As South African pastor Allan Boesak
remarked of the religious legitimation of the system of apart-
heid: "There are churches and individual Christians who de-
fend this system as the will of God for South Africa, using arguments from the same gospel that for blacks has become God's
incomparable word of liberation."[28]

Power points to sin at the heart of the abuse of the power of
the word, describing sin with the classic Augustinian term of
hubris or pride. Human beings forget and finally deny our
own source and destiny, which is also the origin and promise
of the word, and begin to distort language in a way that eventually alienates any sense of participation, belonging, or relationship. In attempts to achieve and control the gift that is beyond our grasp and control, we lose our selves and the very
possibility of relationship with one another, with the cosmos,
or with God.

Here it should be noted that while sin has classically been
envisioned as pride, self-assertion, or rebellion against God
and grace as self-sacrificing love that allows one to embrace
the cross, that language can itself serve as ideology in some

contexts. As numerous feminist writers have noted, the language of *hubris* is more appropriate to the dominant members in any social system (white males of a higher economic class in the patriarchal system) who have the possibilities of domination, power, and assertion. The sin of "the other" in that system—women, people of color, the poor—may in fact be better identified as accepting a submissive role, letting someone else define her identity, sacrificing a self she never truly had as an autonomous person, always meeting the demands of others because that is what is expected of her. Grace then takes on a new meaning as claiming responsibility for one's life, as love of self as well as love of others, as ability to say "no" as well as to be self-sacrificing, as the courage to speak the truth of one's own experience, as assumption of power and responsibility. That, of course, has further implications in this discussion of "the power of the word." While the challenge to dominants in the social and ecclesiastical systems may be conversion from a posture of pride, achievement, and control over the word and liturgy, the challenge to the rest of the baptized who have not yet been heard in the Christian community is rather the courage to speak from different experience of life and the Gospel as well as to protest and resist the words, symbols, and ecclesiastical structures that limit the reign of God envisioned and enfleshed by Jesus. Those who are in social positions of subordination also sin by betrayal of our true source and destiny, but more by the failure to assume the power and responsibilities that are rooted in baptism, than by pride and achievement.[29]

In dealing with sin, Power returns frequently to the myth of Adam and Eve in his writings, emphasizing both the transformation of experience when brought to speech and the necessity of symbolic language as the only access to dealing with the experience of evil that, due to its negative nature, eludes philosophical understanding. Underlining that the story of Adam and Eve is a "story of expected redemption" rather than an explanation of the origins of evil, Power criticizes liturgical revisions that limit expressions of evil to scientific or common-sense language, thus losing "the symbolism of evil" that enables the Christian community to express both its encounter with evil and its sense of God's grace and power at work.[30] Only when the experience of sin has come to expression can the community move through lament[31] to the experience of hope in God's ability to recreate and redeem us even beyond the betrayals of our speech and our lives.

The Voice of God between the Cracks

The wager that, in spite of the limitations and even the sinfulness of flawed human speech, the liberating word of God spoken by the Spirit can and will be heard in the Christian community is rooted in the more fundamental conviction that "where sin abounds, grace abounds still more" (Rom 5:15). Although, as his writings indicate, Power is well aware of the ideological abuse of Christian speech and liturgy, he argues nonetheless that "whatever power the patterns of paradigms of speech adopted from dominative cultures have to silence or misrepresent what is experience in God's Spirit, this same Spirit gives the power and freedom to hear an alternative word."[32]

While the power of the Spirit has too often been ignored in recent writings on the power of the word, both the Scriptures and the classical Christian tradition remind us that it is in and through the power of the Spirit that the word of God is spoken and received.[33] The Spirit of God indwells all creation, renews the face of the earth, inspires the prophets, is the source of the power of resurrection and hence of all eschatological hope and freedom, and continues as source of life and witness to truth in the Christian community.

Even the classical theology of Thomas Aquinas reminded us that the revelation of God's word requires both the external manifestation of God's action and the inner anointing of the hearts of believers by the Holy Spirit.[34] The presumption is that when the authentic word of God is preached in the midst of the believing community then the testimony of the proclaimed word will converge with the testimony given by the Spirit in the hearts of believers and in the community's discernment. When preaching is met with conflict or lack of reception, it is possible that the community or the individual may not be fully converted to the difficult word of the Gospel. It is also possible, however, that the Spirit of God is indeed alive and at work in the hearts of the believers, but the liberating word of the Kerygma of Jesus Christ has not been proclaimed. Where the words of the Gospel or the symbols of the church are used to engender submission rather than the liberty of the children of God, to strike fear rather than to stir hopes, to anesthetize rather than empower, the Spirit of God will testify to a deeper truth that is more faithful to the memory of Jesus. As Power suggests: "It is the Spirit who frees the heart from alienation, who inspires right action, and who alerts believers to their fundamental participation in the order of things."[35]

Further, it is precisely in and through the word—through memory of the faith tradition in human consciousness—that the action of the Spirit operates. It is the recreative word that alerts believers to their fundamental participation in creation and the re-creation of the baptismal community; it is the redeeming word that heals all divisions and alienation; it is the generative word that impels the Christian community toward more faithful discipleship (right action or orthopraxis). The recreative, redeeming, regenerative word stirred up in the memory of believers is more specifically the kerygma that Jesus preached in word and deed.[36] The memory of Christ Jesus is both the source of historical ferment as the community expresses eschatological impatience with all that blocks or distorts the reign of God and the promise that the Spirit of God who can raise the dead to life will hold the future open to new possibilities.

Eschatological hope is always a sign of the Spirit's activity. Thus Power describes the role of the Spirit in the protest and lack of reception that emerge as conflict in the Christian community when human biases in either the Scriptures or the proclamation of the church are identified with the word of God:

> We continue to hope in the possibility of being called again, of being surprised by texts that summon us to reckon with realities whose existence we have forgotten, we endeavor to keep the *memoria Christi* as a promise and as a historical ferment, we desire to know once again the voice of the Spirit crying out in our hearts teaching us what we ought to pray.[37]

The difficult question becomes then: "Where is the Spirit to be found speaking the recreative and redeeming Word?" Combining the insights of both the hermeneutical and the political/liberationist theologians, Power locates the presence of the Spirit in the intersection of the poetic speech of the believing community with its agapic praxis. He insists that, like the words and deeds of Jesus, the speech and action of the Christian community are inseparable: "The fundamental power of language, as it comes to speech in the Spirit, is united with emancipatory desire and praxis, each informing the other and testing the other."[38] Precisely because of its eschatological character, the word of God is to be discovered in forms of language that establish space for the freedom of the Spirit by questioning and even subverting the established order thus allowing the imagination to hope in the kind of future possibilities imaged in the parables of Jesus. But hope in the reign of God that is to come remains mere ideology if it is not appropriated by the community in praxis that makes tangible the transformation imagined, thus giving living testimony to "the hope that is within." Unless the community's praxis reveals a visible share in the Spirit's power to "make all things new," the Gospel's poetic redescription of reality is in danger of being heard as mere ideology.

Thus Power calls for a twofold move: (1) an attentiveness to language and in particular, to the emancipatory power of discourse located in the force of metaphor and the intersection of forms of discourse in order to hear the "Word beneath words," and (2) a better understanding of "the transformative dynamic inherent to the human"—the dynamic of the human subject and the human community to which the word makes appeal.[39]

Narrative, the fundamental biblical discourse in which the Christian community and their Jewish ancestors have identified the meaning of the events in their history as an overall story of the redemptive action of God in their lives, has been presumed to establish and to legitimate order and continuity in the community. Paul Ricoeur, who previously described narrative in precisely that fashion, has suggested in his recent writings, however, that narrative functions as "extended metaphor" that subverts traditional expectations of order precisely through "the synthesis of the heterogeneous."[40] Building on that insight, Power suggests that a more creative listening to biblical narrative grasps the subversive twist in the stories that actually subverts the surface meaning and reveals the "Word beneath the words" that is the call of the Spirit to freedom and new possibilities. He detects examples of these subversive twists

> in the locating of victory over death in the death of the inno-
> cent, in the convergence of God's judgment on humankind
> with the judgment of the courts on Jesus, in the sending of a
> woman as apostle to those who, by reason of intimacy with Je-
> sus and by reason of cultural supposition, thought of them-
> selves as apostles, or in the way in which Jesus' judgments of
> people differ so evidently from the judgments made in virtue
> of the law.[41]

Granting that narratives can contain their own twists of meaning, Power nonetheless concedes that, in general, narra-tive as form favors, and is used in the service of, continuity and the established order. Thus he argues for attention to the interaction of multiple forms of discourse as the key to unlock-ing the liberating word of the Spirit within and beneath the ex-plicit words of the biblical texts. In particular he highlights the genres of parables and eschatological sayings and the songs of lamentation as forms of discourse that disrupt and disorient the presumed world of order.[42]

Underlying Power's approach to the liberating power of the poetic word lies his foundational understanding of humanity as rooted in participation with all of reality and grounded ulti-mately in the Trinity—the "recreative word" and the spirit of freedom given at the core of reality. The word is given to us. We neither originate it, nor control it. Poetic language reveals the freedom at the core of the human person—the core which Power and Ricoeur identify as the "mythopoetic core of be-ing" that projects and breaks open the world for which hu-manity is destined and in which we find our truest identities and the deepest call to action. As Power puts it:

> In the midst of various distortions in the use of language, one
> has to be able to hear the word that is not so much spoken by
> the human as spoken to it—even if it is only rarely breathed.
> Recreative Word does not so much break forth from the speak-
> er as break forth in the speaker.[43]

Granting that in our control and achievement-oriented world, that this word is often silenced or at least muted, nonetheless Power maintains that the language of freedom and hope continues to erupt in and through the power of the Spirit of God "who breathes where she wills." If appropriated critically by those engaged in praxis on behalf of the reign of God, the "voice of God between the cracks" can open the community of faith to the possibilities that are offered humanity in the redemptive event and experience of Jesus Christ. The language of freedom and hope has the power to retrieve the originating power of the events of creation and redemption, and thus to reshape reality by disorienting and questioning all patterns of human control and domination and gifting humanity with the imagination of possibility that exceeds and escapes all human achievement.

Rooted in the experience of the mystery of the redemptive word, paradoxical speech emerges most clearly from the experience of those who participate in the mystery of Christ's suffering and hope. Hearing that word will mean listening to the words spoken (and the silence of those unable or not permitted to speak) from the margins and pain of the community. In other words, Power reminds us that we can hear God's word only from within a stance of solidarity with the suffering members of the Body of Christ. Only with consciousness of and commitment to the justice and freedom of the reign of God can we recognize and celebrate the freedom of the children of God, in spite of any misrepresentations of the goodness of creation and humanity or of the power of God's grace.

The power of the subversive symbols of Scripture and liturgy is ultimately the power of God that can never be domesticated or controlled by human structures or misrepresentations. Locating the "power of the word" in the "speech over which in the long run the church can claim no control," Power insists that no matter how distorted or limited the perspective of the biblical writers or preachers, the word of God (and the liturgical symbols) share in the power of the same liberating Spirit of God who remains active in the community to whom these symbols have been entrusted and who are called to appropriate them in freedom and love. Thus he exhorts the hearers of the word: "Similarly, in attending to what is avowed in tradition, the church has to listen keenly for a word that speaks from a deeper experience of redemption than do the paradigmatic patterns of speech adopted from patriarchal, hierarchical, or technological cultures."[44] The power of the word is rooted ultimately in the source of all power in the Christian community—the Spirit of God who animates the entire Body of Christ. The foundational work of David Power reaffirms the "wager of hope" that the Spirit who is to be recognized in the testimony of discipleship and in the bread broken and cup shared, continues to speak the "Word beneath the words" in every age and culture for "those who have ears to hear."

Notes

1. Elie Wiesel, *Legends of Our Time* (New York: Avon, 1968) 31.

2. Karl Barth, *The Preaching of the Gospel*, trans. B.E. Hooke (Philadelphia: Westminster, 1963) 54-55.

3. Reginald H. Fuller, *The Use of the Bible in Preaching* (Philadelphia: Fortress, 1981) 9, 17. See similar statements by Raymond E. Brown, *The Critical Meaning of the Bible* (New York: Paulist Press, 1981) 18 and Avery Dulles, "Scripture: Recent Protestant and Catholic Views," *Theology Today* 37 (1980) 7-26.

4. Leander E. Keck, *The Bible in the Pulpit* (Nashville: Abingdon, 1978) 99.

5. Elisabeth Schüssler Fiorenza, "The Will to Choose or Reject: Continuing Our Critical Work," in *Feminist Interpretation of the Bible*, ed., Letty M. Russell (Philadelphia: Westminster Press, 1985) 130. See *Bread Not Stone* (Boston: Beacon, 1984) x- xiv for political analysis of "the power of the word."

6. Phyllis Trible, *Texts of Terror* (Philadelphia: Fortress, 1984) xiii, 1.

7. Rabbi Marc Tannenbaum quoting from *Hitler's Table-Talk* as found in Walter Burghardt, *Preaching: The Art and The Craft* (New York: Paulist Press, 1987), 153-154. On the relationship between biblical texts and the legitimation of male violence against women, see Susan Brooks Thistlethwaite, "Every Two Minutes: Battered Women and Feminist Interpretation," in *Feminist Interpretation of the Bible*, ed., Letty M. Russell (Philadelphia: Westminster Press, 1985) 96-107. For discussion of recent ideological use of Romans 13 in South Africa, see Allan A. Boesak, "What Belongs to Caesar? Once Again Romans 13," in *When Prayer Makes Sense*, eds., Allan A. Boesak and Charles Villa-Vincencio (Philadelphia: Westminster Press, 1986) 138-156.

8. Elisabeth Schüssler Fiorenza, for example, in calling for a "hermeneutics of proclamation" argues that "Patriarchal texts should not be allowed to remain in the lectionary but should be replaced by texts affirming the discipleship of equals . . . and an inclusive translation is to be made only of those texts that articulate a liberating vision for women." ("The Will to Choose or Reject" 132-133; see *Bread Not Stone* 15-22). See Marjorie Procter-Smith, *In Her Own Rite: Constructing Feminist Liturgical Tradition* (Nashville: Abingdon, 1990) 116-135 for analysis of the androcentric hermeneutic that has controlled the lectionary and for proposals regarding a feminist lectionary and feminist use of typology in preaching.

9. Sandra M. Schneiders, "Feminist Ideology Criticism and Biblical Hermeneutics," *Biblical Theology Bulletin* 19 (1989) 3-10. See Trible, *Texts of Terror* 93-116; Procter-Smith, 124. As a balance to the "hermeneutics of proclamation" (n. 8), Schüssler Fiorenza also calls for a "hermeneutics of remembrance" that recovers *all* biblical traditions and texts through a feminist-historical reconstruction ("The Will to Choose or Reject" 133).

10. See especially "The Holy Spirit: Scripture, Tradition, and Interpretation," in *Keeping the Faith: Essays to Mark the Centenary of Lux Mundi*, ed., Geoffrey Wainwright (Philadelphia: Fortress, 1988) 152-178; "Liturgical Praxis: A New Consciousness at the Eye of Worship 61 (1987) 290-304; "Forum: Worship after the Holocaust," *Worship* 59 (1985) 447-455; *Unsearchable Riches: The Symbolic Nature of Liturgy* (New York: Pueblo Publishing Co., 1984) esp. Chapter Seven; "People at Liturgy," *Twenty Years of Concilium: Retrospect and Prospect*, ed., Paul Brand and Anton Weiler (New York: Seabury, 1983) 8-13; "Sacraments: Symbolizing God's Power in the Church," *Proceedings of the Catholic Theological Society of America* 37 (1982) 50-66; and "Unripe Grapes: The Critical Function of Liturgical Theology," *Worship* 52 (1978) 386-399.

11. "Liturgical Praxis: A New Consciousness at the Eye of Worship" 303.

12. "The Holy Spirit: Scripture, Tradition, and Interpretation" 166.

13. In 1975 Power cited the value of Rahner's ontology of religious symbols as highlighting the fact that the symbol is both a call from God and a corresponding human self-communication that is "the fullest realization of man's nature and being." He noted however, the danger that the eschatological dimension might not be recognized in Rahner's incarnational approach, argued for a phenomenological approach to symbols as a particular mode of language, and supplemented Rahner's ontology of symbol as divine self-communication with Lonergan's explanation of the power of the word to mediate meaning. ("Symbolism in Worship: A Survey III," *The Way* 15 (1975) 56-58). In

his more recent writings, Power endorses the political theologians' critique of Rahner's approach as "too abstract . . . too accepting of an unproblematic originating experience of the question about God." ("The Holy Spirit: Scripture, Tradition, and Interpretation" 156).

14. Robert Bolt, *A Man for All Seasons* (New York: Random House, 1960) 140.

15. See Karl Rahner, "Priest and Poet," *Theological Investigations*, vol. 3, trans., Karl-H. and Boniface Kruger (Baltimore: Helicon Press, 1967) 294-317. See Power's use of Susanne Langer's distinction between discursive symbols and presentational symbols in *Unsearchable Riches* 68-70.

16. For Rahner's own treatment of these themes see especially, "The Theology of the Symbol," *Theological Investigations*, vol. 4, trans., Kevin Smyth (Baltimore: Helicon, 1966) 221-252; "The Word and Eucharist," *Theological Investigations*, vol. 4, 253-285; "What Is a Sacrament?" *Theological Investigations*, vol. 14, 135-148; "Priest and Poet," *Theological Investigations*, vol. 3, 294-317; "Poetry and the Christian," *Theological Investigations*, vol. 4, 357-367; "Considerations on the Active Role of the Person in the Sacramental Event," *Theological Investigations*, vol. 14, trans. David Bourke, 161-184.

17. Michael J. Scanlon, "Language and Praxis: Recent Theological Trends," *Proceedings of the Catholic Theological Society of America* 43 (1988) 83.

18. William J. Hill, "Preaching as a 'Moment' in Theology," *Homiletic and Pastoral Review* 77 (1976-77) 11. Hill explicitly acknowledges that he is building on the foundational work of Bernard Lonergan. For Lonergan's now classic treatment of meaning and the constitutive role of meaning in human living, see *Method in Theology* (New York: Herder and Herder, 1972) 76-81, and "Theology in Its New Context," in *A Second Collection*, ed. William F.J. Ryan and Bernard J. Tyrrell (Philadelphia: Westminster, 1974) 61. See D. Power, "Symbolism in Worship: A Survey III," *The Way* 15 (1975) 57-58.

19. "Symbolism in Worship: A Survey IV" 140.

20. See Rebecca S. Chopp, *The Power to Speak: Feminism, Language, God* (New York: Crossroad, 1989). For Power's discussion of the important role of "contrast experience" (a term borrowed from Edward Schillebeeckx) in this context, see "Receiving What Has Been Handed On," in *Can We Always Celebrate Eucharist?* ed. Mary Collins and David N. Power (New York: Seabury, 1982) 88-90.

21. "Symbolism in Worship: A Survey III" 56-57.

22. *Unsearchable Riches* 72. See also "Response: Liturgy, Memory, and the Absence of God," *Worship* 57 (1983) 326-29. See Louis-Marie Chauvet, *Du Symbolique au Symbole: Essai sur les Sacrements* (Paris:

Cerf, 1979) 37-79, 94-97. Power's stress on the nonidentity between the divine and the human and his emphasis on the power of the word to judge and critique the present situation (influenced strongly by Ricoeur's approach to metaphor) has been criticized by Stephen Happel in "Worship as a Grammar of Social Transformation," *Proceedings of the Catholic Theological Society of America* 42 (1987) esp. 76-82.

23. Power refers to God's voice speaking "in often flawed human speech" in "The Holy Spirit: Scripture, Tradition, and Interpretation" 170.

24. *Unsearchable Riches* 174.

25. Ibid.

26. David Tracy, *Blessed Rage for Order* (New York: Seabury, 1975) 133; see also Ian T. Ramsey, *Religious Language* (New York: Macmillan, 1963).

27. "Sacraments: Symbolizing God's Power in the Church" 55. For Aquinas' classic work on analogy see *Summa Theologiae* I, q. 13 and William J. Hill's treatment of the question in *Knowing the Unknown God* (New York: Philosophical Library, 1971) 111-144. See also Power's discussion of analogy in *Unsearchable Riches* 182-83.

28. Allan Boesak, *The Finger of God*, trans., Peter Randall (Maryknoll: Orbis, 1982) 10. For Power's discussion of ideology in relation to the liturgy see "Liturgical Praxis: A New Consciousness at the Eye of Worship"; "Sacraments: Symbolizing God's Power in the Church"; *Unsearchable Riches* 24-28 and 178ff.; and "Receiving What Has Been Handed On," in *Can We Always Celebrate Eucharist?*, eds., Mary Collins and David Power (New York: Seabury, 1982) 89. See Mark Searle, "The Pedagogical Function of Liturgy," *Worship* 55 (1981) 332-359; and Mary Collins, "The Public Language of Ministry," *The Jurist* 41 (1981) 261-294.

29. For helpful summaries of feminist discussions of sin and grace and further bibliography, see Elizabeth Dreyer, *Manifestations of Grace* (Wilmington: Michael Glazier, 1990) 185-189, and Anne E. Carr, *Transforming Grace: Christian Tradition and Women's Experience* (New York: Harper and Row, 1988) 117-133, 180-214. See Wanda Warren Berry, "Images of Sin and Salvation in Feminist Theology," *Anglican Theological Review* 60 (1978) 25-54; Rosemary Radford Ruether, *Sexism and God-Talk* (Boston: Beacon, 1983) 159-192; and Aruna Gnanadason, "Women's Oppression: A Sinful Situation," in *With Passion and Compassion: Third World Women Doing Theology*, eds., Virginia Fabella and Mercy Amba Oduyoye (Maryknoll: Orbis, 1988) 69-76.

For the connection with preaching, see Chopp, *The Power to Speak: Feminism, Language, God*; Mary Collins, *Worship: Renewal to Practice*

(Washington D.C.: The Pastoral Press, 1987), esp. Section III; Mary Catherine Hilkert, "Women Preaching the Gospel," *Theology Digest* 33 (1986) 423-440; Christine M. Smith, *Weaving the Sermon: Preaching in a Feminist Perspective* (Louisville: Westminster/John Knox, 1989); and Procter-Smith, *In Her Own Rite* Chapter 5.

30. "Sacraments: Symbolizing God's Power in the Church" 50. See *Unsearchable Riches* 110-114, and "Confession as Ongoing Conversion," *Heythrop Journal* 18 (1977) 180-190. See also Paul Ricoeur's classic *The Symbolism of Evil*, trans., Emerson Buchanan (Boston: Beacon, 1967) which Power cites as a definite influence on his own work.

31. "Lamentation expresses the community's perception of its own and of humanity's sin and of the shackles which are placed on human freedom and on God's word and gift. Griefs which have been suppressed and hopes which have been stilled are allowed expression. In this act, the community remembers the question to which the gospel speaks instead of stilling them." *Unsearchable Riches* 165. On the importance of lament, see *Unsearchable Riches* 164-167; Walter Brueggemann, *The Prophetic Imagination* (Philadelphia: Fortress, 1980); Claus Westermann, *Praise and Lament in the Psalms* (Atlanta: John Knox Press, 1981).

32. "The Holy Spirit: Scripture, Tradition, and Interpretation" 167-168.

33. Note Power's use of Spirit Christology in *Unsearchable Riches* 205-206.

34. *Summa Theologiae* II-II, q. 1, a. 4. ad. 4; q. 6, a. 1; q. 2. a. 9, ad. 3.

35. "The Holy Spirit: Scripture, Tradition, and Interpretation" 159.

36. Recognizing plural theological approaches to the relationship between word and action, Power endorses the hermeneutical approach of Paul Ricoeur that places emphasis on Scripture as classic text in preference to the attempts of Edward Schillebeeckx and others to get to the liberating experience behind the text. Power argues: "It is the event come to language and formulated as text that passes into tradition in its most accessible way. This mean that one looks to word for the offer of the possibilities of personal and social transformation and action." ("The Holy Spirit: Scripture, Tradition, and Interpretation" 158).

37. "Sacraments: Symbolizing God's Power in the Church" 50.

38. "The Holy Spirit: Scripture, Tradition, Interpretation" 167. Power explains his understanding of the term praxis as "a conscious doing of whatever we are doing, a doing that is open to reflective critique" ("Liturgical Praxis" 303).

39. Ibid. 168.

40. Paul Ricoeur, *Time and Narrative*, vol. 1, trans., Kathleen

McLaughlin and David Pellauer (Chicago: University of Chicago Press, 1984) ix. See "Toward a Hermeneutic of the Idea of Revelation," in *Essays on Biblical Interpretation*, ed., Lewis S. Mudge (Philadelphia: Fortress, 1980) 77-81. For Power's discussion and use of metaphor, see especially *Unsearchable Riches* Chapter 5, and "Words That Crack: The Uses of 'Sacrifice' in Eucharistic Discourse," *Worship* 53 (1979) 386-404.

41. "The Holy Spirit: Scripture, Tradition, and Interpretation" 169.

42. Ibid. 168-170. See Paul Ricoeur, "Toward a Hermeneutic of the Idea of Revelation," and Walter Brueggemann, "The Message of the Psalms" (Minneapolis: Augsburg, 1984).

43. Ibid. 159.

44. Ibid. 167. Note also Power's approach to the Bible as prototype rather than archetype. "As prototype, it introduces us to the conflicts that emerge with the occurrence of revelatory events and with the proclamation of the gospel, and thus alerts us to the play of language within which value conflicts and meanings come to expression" (Ibid. 170). See Elisabeth Schüssler Fiorenza, *In Memory of Her* (New York: Crossroad, 1983) 33-34.

4

Contributing Credibly
to a Sacramental Theology
of Liberation

Joseph J. Fortuna

THIS ESSAY BEGINS ON THE PATH TO EAST NINTH STREET. THE PATH leads between the parking garage and the cathedral of St. John the Evangelist in Cleveland, Ohio. Halfway along the path, one who fancies himself to be a sacramental theologian recognizes a "street person" sitting on the steps of the church and takes evasive action. He backtracks a few steps, goes into the cathedral, and thus bypasses the poor man. But as he walks through the cathedral, the force of what he is doing inescapably confronts him: he is going *through* the church to avoid the poor.

This story of my journey to East Ninth Street might seem to be more appropriate to homiletic rather than scholarly discourse if it didn't give rise to a disturbing question: Could it be a metaphor for the experience of being a sacramental theologian in the first world in general and in the academy in particular? Is this a metaphor which sheds a penetrating light on my own theological practice? This practice generally takes place in a seminary located in the middle of a ghetto filled with the poor and their many problems. It occurs within a perimeter defined by fortress-like walls, fences, and a guard-shack. The food I eat, the building which shelters me, the security I enjoy—all of which I take for granted as prerequisite for my theological practice— are shared, but only with those within the seminary. The question persists: Is my theologizing about the sacraments in this context any different than going through the church to avoid the poor? Are the usual questions and methods of sacramental theology of any importance in this context? Must walking through the church necessarily imply avoiding the poor?

A possible response to these questions would be to adopt the issues and methods of liberation theology.[1] This would at least permit a theological practice that is self-consciously sympathetic to the cause of the poor. Yet two difficulties immediately surface. First, sacraments seem to be a primarily intraecclesial affair. Effective advocacy for the poor, however, requires addressing the social systems and structures which create and sustain their poverty. Such an address might be made by the ecclesiologist who pursues how the church as social institution can effect transformation of the world, but it normally will not arise in the course of treatment of issues and questions which pertain "properly" to sacramental theology. Thus, the shape of a sacramental theology of liberation is largely unexplored. The second difficulty pertains to the integrity of the theologian and his or her discipline. Even if a first-world theologian or a theologian of the academy should attempt a sacramental theology of liberation, this attempt will inescapably be tied to a crisis of credibility. This is not merely a crisis of consistency raised by the question of whether one can champion the cause of the poor on paper only. It is a foundational crisis, one which questions at two levels the very conditions of possibility of such a theology. First, is there at the basis of liberation theology an epistemological privilege to which the first-world or academic theologian of the sacraments lacks access? Although this theologian might *report* on the work of liberation theologians, can he or she actually *do* liberation theology? Would some kind of active solidarity with the poor provide access to this epistemological privilege, and therefore be a prerequisite to such a theology? If so, this would seem to exclude most theologians from the outset, since scholarship and commitments to their own establishment prevent, or at least make very unlikely, such an active solidarity. Second, would a sacramental theology of liberation be credible to the theologian's peers? Would it meet the demands and criteria of theology as a science and as a serious scholarly discipline?

If the move to a theology of liberation is to offer promise as a way out of my dilemma of going through the church to avoid the poor, it will be necessary to identify and examine some key issues involved in contributing credibly to a sacramental theology of liberation. The way I hope to do this is to bring the work of two different theologians, one writing in the area of liberation theology and the other in the area of sacramental theology, into dialogue with one another.[2] The works I will examine are *Theology and Praxis: Epistemological Foundations* by Clodovis Boff,[3] and *Symbole et sacrement: Une relecture sacramentelle de l'existence chrétienne* by Louis-Marie Chauvet.[4] After identifying the project which each theologian has set for himself, I will examine three issues which represent points of convergence in their work: (1) The priority of praxis; (2) the real and its mediation; and (3) a new way of thinking theologically. Finally, I will consider how these points of convergence bear upon the effort to contribute credibly to a sacramental theology of liberation.

Boff and Chauvet: Their Theological Projects

What motivates Boff's theology is the conviction that liberation theology must become conscious of and articulate its method. Simple assertions that liberation theology is "different" from other theologies may have been sufficient in a first phase in which the urgency of issues shaped theological approaches, but such assertions are no longer so. Nor is it adequate simply to restate one's theological postulates, however compelling they may seem. For Boff, what is required above all else and what he seeks to provide is reflection on the critical basis for the postulates of liberation theologians. This reflection ought to (1) specify the conditions under which these postulates can be elaborated and (2) lead toward the systematization of a method.[5] Therefore, Boff's project is strictly speaking not the creation of a new theology of liberation, but a theory of what is involved in doing liberation theology.

The animating concern of Chauvet's theology is different from Boff's, but no less clearly evident. He is interested in probing the meaning of what appears to be a constitutive characteristic of Christian faith and existence, namely, the sacramental.[6] He attends to the sacramental in order to gain insight into the emergence of Christian identity and the way in which God is involved in this emergence. His project is not a theology of one or more of the sacraments, nor a treatment of the sacraments in general, but rather a sacramental re-reading of Christian existence. As a result, it is as much a theology of grace and a Christian anthropology as it is a theology of sacramentality.

Even such a brief look at the projects of Boff and Chauvet shows why they can be appropriate and stimulating dialogue partners. Each is taking a step back from treatment of specific issues within his respective discipline and attempting a project at the level of fundamental theology, Boff a theory of the theology of liberation and Chauvet a fundamental theology of sacramentality. What is more, there is a sense in which they are both part of a much larger conversation. In their concern to theologize in dialogue with modernity, each cites the work of Lévi-Strauss, Ortigues, Ricoeur, Bachelard, Ladrière, Levinas, and many others. By attending to this larger conversation, however, some differences between the two become apparent. It is obvious, for example, that Boff has a particular affinity for Althusser and Chauvet for Heidegger. Another difference is that each relates this dialogue with modernity to the scholastics, and in particular to Thomas Aquinas, in a different way. As will be seen below, the Thomistic epistemology toward which Boff is so sympathetic is something which Chauvet finds problematic. Identifying the projects of these two theologians thus raises hope that a dialogue between them may yield insight, at the most important and foundational level, into the question of contributing credibly to a sacramental theology of liberation. It is necessary now to examine some specific points of convergence to see if in fact this dialogue can bear fruit.

The Priority of Praxis

Although theology and praxis are simultaneously in a relationship of autonomy and dependence with respect to one another,[7] Boff gives priority to praxis. He is careful to qualify, however, that this priority is practical and not theoretical. Praxis cannot be a principle governing the theological process because theology is governed by its own norms and laws. It speaks a language which exists in a "breach" with respect to the language of ordinary religious discourse.[8]

This practical priority of praxis is rooted in one of Boff's basic theological convictions: it is more important to theorize upon what "the Spirit says in the churches" than to theorize upon what the Spirit said "once upon a time."[9] Thus Boff views the praxis of the Christian community as a place where a Word of revelation comes to the community and is responded to in faith. It is this Word that theologians, with the skills and mediations proper to them, seek to interpret and understand.

To appreciate fully his position it is important to clarify what Boff means by two important and interrelated terms, praxis and the political. Praxis is the *"complexus of practices oriented to the transformation of society, the making of history."*[10] The element of this complexus that is most important to liberation theologians is political practice, since it is through the intermediary of the political that social structures can be influenced.[11] Thus, for Boff, the political is defined with reference to power: it is "the locus of the power of social organization and transformation."[12]

These definitions of praxis and the political give Boff's theological projects a particular direction. To provide a critical basis for liberation theology he must construct *a theory of the theology of the political.* But since the revelation of God to the churches of today is taking place in Christian political praxis, this praxis must be the *medium in quo*[13] of the theology of the political. In other words, if one is going to do a theology which is attentive to where and how the Word of God is being revealed today, one must attend to the political. This is ultimately the basis of Boff's agreement with Gutiérrez: "One does not do the theology one would like; one does the theology one can."[14]

Although he tends to speak of theory and practice rather than praxis, Chauvet is similarly concerned to do a theology which is attentive to where and how the Word of God is being revealed today. Instead of focusing on the political, however,

Chauvet focuses on the sacramental. By sacramental he means not only the seven sacraments officially recognized by the Roman Catholic Church, but any ritual or liturgical activity in which the Trinity is celebrated.[15] For Chauvet, sacramental practice is an instance of the re-inscription of the *logos* of the cross, a manifestation of the *kenosis* of God into the lives of the least among humanity.[16] The participant who in faith assumes an attitude of "disappropriation," i.e., a gracious "letting-be," is one to whom the *logos* speaks. Thus the contours of the re-inscription of the *logos* are diffuse. This re-inscription is a manifestation of God as *unknowable*, as crucified, and as bereft of all traditional attributes of majesty. What is more, this re-inscription is for the individual Christian transformative, a new emergence into his or her Christian identity.

As with Boff, some precisions are necessary in order to fully appreciate why Chauvet gives priority to practice. For Chauvet, sacramental practice is not divorced from sacramental theory. Rather, it shapes theory and is critically informed by it. In one instance he even refers to this relationship as dialectical.[17] To use the language of Boff, one could say that the sacramental and its theory are among practices that collectively constitute that complexus called praxis.

The close and inseparable connection between sacramental theory and practice itself argues for attending to sacramental practice. But Chauvet offers three other reasons as well.[18] First, history has shown practice to be primary in the sense that change in sacramental practice has nearly always preceded change in theory. Second, it sometimes happens that sacraments are idealistically evaluated according to their conformity to a received doctrine. This can contribute to a reinforcement of hierarchical power, because the liturgy may be held in check to a previously announced truth over which the hierarchy reserves to itself the role of guardianship. Third, giving priority to sacramental practice allows it to be a source for many areas of theology. The re-inscription of the *logos* of the cross which occurs in sacramental practice can be a Word of God fruitful for Christology, eccelesiology and other theological disciplines.

Two important points of convergence between Chauvet and Boff are evident from the priority each gives to praxis. First, for each this priority is rooted in a faith conviction that God is indeed in some way involved in Christian existence. Boff attends to this involvement in the political, Chauvet in the sacramental. For each a primary task of theology is the "re-reading" of Christian existence.[19] Second, the praxis to which each attends is in some way transformative. For Boff, the transformation is that which Christian political praxis brings about in society. For Chauvet, the transformation is the ever new emergence of Christian identity in the participants in the sacraments.

These points of convergence give rise to two questions which bear upon the issue of contributing credibly to a sacramental theology of liberation: (1) What is the relationship between Chauvet's sacramental practice and Boff's Christian political praxis? and (2) in what ways are each of these transformative? How are these transformative events related to one another? These are questions to which it will be necessary to return later.

The Real and Its Mediation

There is another very significant point of convergence in the theologies of Boff and Chauvet, but this time the point of convergence is at the same time a point of divergence. In giving priority to praxis, each theologian roots himself in the world not of theological speculation but of Christian living. Each is concerned to theologize on the basis of the real, i.e., the political and the sacramental respectively. Moreover, each maintains that the theologian has no immediate access to the real. The real which gives rise to theological reflection is always in some way mediated. The two differ, however, in the mediation of the real upon which they choose to focus. Boff focuses on what he calls "socio-analytic" mediation, whereas Chauvet's primary concern is the symbolic mediation of the real. This difference is in turn related to different epistemological presuppositions. The most significant point of divergence is over what Boff calls the classic postulate of critical realism, namely, the distinction between cognition and reality, between the logical order and the ontic order, with primacy in the genesis of cognition lying with the second term of each pair.[20] Boff accepts this postulate, but Chauvet, attempting to take seriously the full consequences of the symbolic mediation of reality, cannot. The way each theologian understands the real and its mediation must now be given fuller attention, and the consequences of each of these understandings for a credible sacramental theology of liberation must be explored.

For Boff, there are many different referents to the term, "the real." On the one hand, there is the *cultural* definition. This depends upon the choice made by a society: the real is what society decides "it" should be.[21] The *scientific* definition of the real is chosen by the discipline in question. The sociologist's "real" is not the same as that of the psychologist, biologist, and practitioners of the other scientific disciplines.[22] Boff does not want to admit, however, that the real can be reduced to a simple cultural construction of an era. The term "the real" can also embrace the "transempirical" or the "world of God."[23]

No matter what "real" of which one speaks, however, there is for Boff at the epistemological level an inviolable and central axiom which is at the core of his theory: there is a distinction between the real (the "theologizable" or the "materially theological") and the knowledge of the real (the "theologized" or "formally theological").[24] The structure and logic of knowledge are simply not the same as the structure and logic of the real, on which knowledge depends. To illustrate this point he puts forth a simple dictum: "A rock is material; the concept of rock is immaterial."[25]

Boff maintains that this distinction between the real and knowledge of the real holds for the two areas with which a theology of liberation is concerned, the political real and the theological real. His main interest here seems to be to delimit theological discourse to a regional discourse. He is apparently wary of what he considers to be the totalizing pretensions of some theologians who confuse their knowledge of their real with other knowledge, especially with knowledge of the political real.[26] The theologian's knowledge of the real is regional, circumscribed by the methods and practices of the science of theology. Faith alone and not theology can appropriately make absolute claims concerning the theological real.[27] On the other hand, Boff is wary of allowing the recognition of theology as regional knowledge to serve as justification for a "dialogue" or "pluralism" which is nothing other than an excuse for acceptance of the status quo and political inactivity. He admonishes the theologian to what he calls a constant "ideo-political vigilance."[28]

To ensure that this distinction between the real and knowledge of it is respected in the theology of the political, Boff posits the need for a twofold mediation of the real. The first he calls socio-analytic mediation, which brings to theology the political real as its material object.[29] This mediation occurs through the positive analyses of the social sciences: the political sciences, economics, anthropology, social psychology, history, and especially sociology. Although recognizing their possible legitimate use, he chooses not to engage such mediations as the philosophical, psychological, linguistic, or literary.[30] The fruit of socio-analytic mediation, the political as theologizable, is then subject to a second mediation, the hermeneutic. In this mediation the principles of the Christian faith are brought to bear as the formal object of theology to yield the theologian's apprehension of the theological real. It is this mediation which gives to theology its pertinency, which makes theology theology.[31] The fruit of this mediation is a critical and faith-filled articulation of what God seems to be doing in the churches, an articulation which ultimately seeks further expression in the Christian praxis of *agapic* love. Thus, for Boff theological practice is not the same thing as political practice, but is intrinsically related to it.[32]

In his re-reading of Christian existence, Chauvet focuses on a mediation of the real which Boff recognized but to which he did not give central attention, namely, the symbolic. This difference in focus ought not simply to be interpreted as an arbitrary choice of one mediation over the other, both of which occur at the same level. It is a difference related to a different epistemology and which challenges the postulate of critical realism so central to Boff's theory. The difference might be stated as follows. For Boff, the socio-analytic and hermeneutic mediations are *methodological* requirements of his theory resting on a prior epistemology. For Chauvet, the symbolic mediation of the real is *pre*-methodological and is itself at the level of the epistemological differently understood.

This difference between Boff and Chauvet cannot be pressed without care, for Boff is clearly aware of the key role of symbol and word in both religious and theological discourse. Yet it appears that he accepts a theory of language which Chauvet believes ultimately results in missing the mediation of the real at its most fundamental level, that is, in language itself. That this is so seems to be indicated by the following. Almost as an aside, Boff indicates that words refer univocally to concepts and these concepts in turn refer to their empirical referents.[33] This seems briefly to state the very theory of the word which Chauvet identifies in Thomas Aquinas[34] and which he rejects. Given Boff's affinity for Thomistic epistemology, this would not be surprising. It would fit quite well with his fundamental epistemological axiom regarding the difference between the known and the real: the real is the empirical referent and the known is the concept of that referent. What is key to Thomas' theory is that the empirical referent is known *in se*. To be sure, the concept is the product of a process of cognition, but language is extraneous to the knowing itself.[35] The precondition of the difference between the known and the real is the immediacy of the knower to the known.

For Boff, before that which is known in the immediacy of faith comes to the language of religious or theological discourse, there seems to be an intermediate step, namely, the symbol.[36] Here his notion of symbol is Tillichian. It is a reality which evokes another with which it maintains an internal relation. Boff finds the Platonic notion of "image" helpful, since it implies a participation in an intended reality that becomes partially present in the image itself.[37] On this basis he can then assert that symbol is to be thought of in the line of sacrament, efficacious, an expression-and-realization. The symbolizing thing is more than itself, unfolding within it an energy, a presence, a signification. Between symbol and symbolized there obtains a co-pertinency of content.[38]

The result of all this is that for Boff the symbol mediates between the theological real and that which is known in the immediacy of faith. But if Boff's affinity for Aquinas is operative here as well,[39] what is very important is that what is symbolized is the already-known-in-faith, the result of an immediate already-knowing made possible by the fact that the symbol and the knower somehow participate in the same reality toward which the symbol unfolds and with which it bears this co-pertinency of content. For Chauvet, such an immediate already-knowing is untenable because it neglects the role of the symbolic and language in the knowing itself.[40] For Chauvet, here is the most fundamental mediation of the real. Whereas Boff seems to hold the following relation to obtain, object of faith >>>> concept (the known) >>>> the symbol >>>> language, Chauvet sees things to be ordered this way, symbolic/language >>>> the real/the human/God as manifested. For Chauvet, it is not a question of the symbolic and language mediating between the known and reality, but rather of the symbolic and language mediating at one and the same time the real and the subject to himself or herself. In other words, where Boff posits an immediacy between knower and what is known and so holds to a distinction between the known and the real, Chauvet posits a symbolic mediation between the real and the knower which results in the blurring of the distinction between the real and the known.

Heavily influenced by Heidegger's phenomenology and philosophy of language, Chauvet holds that as a consequence of the symbolic mediation of the real and the subject to himself or herself, it is more proper to say that language speaks the subject rather than the subject speaks a language. Language and the symbolic are prior to the subject and not of the subject's making or control.[41] The best "speaker" is not the one who can attain mastery of a language, but rather the one who can let go of the desire to master the manifestation of being in language and instead let oneself be spoken by language. In this way the most real, the most human, being of the subject can emerge.[42]

The implications of this understanding of the real and its mediation for the sacraments are enormous. The sacraments are not instrumental signs which believers perform as an expression of Christian faith, they are rather expressions of the Christian faith which speak believers.[43] As symbolic acts of the church, the sacraments are instances of Christians being spoken by language in events which are a re-inscribing of the *logos* of the cross.[44] The manifesting of God and the manifesting of the human occur in one and the same event. What is required on the part of the participant is an attitude of "disappropriation" or of "letting-be" which is faith.[45] The sacramental event is judged not according to its validity, but according to its veracity: in what way does the subject who is spoken in the sacrament give expression to this new "most real self" by taking to his or her ethical practice in the community the same gracious attitude of "letting-be" which will permit the reinscribing of the *logos* of the cross to occur there as well?

How does this concern for the real and its mediation, a concern which is a point of both divergence and convergence, bear upon the overriding concern of this discussion, namely, contributing credibly to a sacramental theology of liberation? A first answer is that concern for the real and its mediation is a check against allowing any theology of liberation, whether a theology of the political or a sacramental theology, to be illusory, naive, or the expression of an unconscious and perhaps oppressive ideology. A second is that by attending to the real and its mediation, one can begin to address the issue of epistemological privilege. By knowing *what* real is at issue and *how* this real is mediated, one can determine who has access to it and in what way. For Boff, access to the political as theologizable seems to be attainable to any who respect its socio-analytic mediation. On the other hand, access to "what God is saying in the churches," is open only to those who in faith engage in hermeneutic mediation. For Chauvet, access to "the most real" of genuine Christian subjectivity is gained in the attitude of "letting-be" which allows one to be spoken in the symbolic operating expressions of the church, the sacraments.

New Ways of Thinking

For both Boff and Chauvet, to accept the priority of praxis and to attend to the real and its mediations ultimately involve new ways of thinking. Boff urges dialectical thinking. This is not a particular method or precise technique of investigation or research, but rather a particular manner in which reason operates. It is a fundamental attitude of the human mind, a dynamism which rejects all static and rigid mental constructs and renounces all definitive conclusions and eternal truths. It is the perpetual motion of reason seeking to transgress its previous limits in an ever new beginning.[46] Chauvet, on the other hand, urges what he calls symbolic thinking. Symbolic thinking is a way of thinking *from within* the space between discourse and the real. This involves the "overcoming" of metaphysics, which according to Chauvet seeks to think of all being as reasonable. Metaphysics can occasionally acknowledge the space between discourse and the real, but it is not able to think *from within* this space.[47] It is necessary now to take a closer look at each of these new ways of thinking.

Boff identifies a dialectic between theology and praxis which "plays" in two "keys," one minor and the other major.[48] The play of the minor key is exclusively within theoretical practice, on the level of cognition. It has to do with the reciprocal play between subject and object, between the moment of logical construction and empirical verification. Its movement is not between the abstract and the concrete, but rather from the "thought abstract" to the "thought concrete," from unknown to the known, from the less known to the more known.[49] The play of the major key has to do with the relationship between consciousness and the world, between all manner of thought (reflection, discussion, science, poetry, and so on) and all expression of the real (work, experience, practice, and so on).[50] What is of major import is that for Boff the dialectic between theory and praxis can only be spoken of *theoretically*, in other words, from and within the element of one of the poles under discussion.[51]

Boff subdivides the play of the major key into two fundamental modalities, mutual inclusion (*perichoresis*) and difference (*chorismos*).[52] Attending first to *perichoresis*, he notes that from the polarity of theory three instances of mutual inclusion can be seen. First, theoretical practice is similar in structure to other practices. As the hands work to transform that upon which they work, so does the brain work to transform the concepts upon which it works. Second, the concern of theoretical activity must be the world as sensibility, history, and practice. Third, every mental activity is situated *in concreto* in a whole series of external factors that accompany it and make it possible. From the polarity of praxis two aspects of mutual inclusion can be seen. First, every human activity which is calculated to transform the world has its reasons, motivations, finalities, and so forth. In other words, praxis always includes theory. Second, word—the voice of meaning— often accompanies praxis. Word mediates between the regions of theory and praxis. What is more, through its illocutionary force word often achieves the realization of the meaning it expresses.

Despite these aspects of mutual inclusion Boff underscores that it is not possible simply to reduce theory and praxis to one another. Theoretical practice, though one of the many practices that constitute praxis, is not to be viewed as on an equivalent social plane. There is a "breach" that exists between theory and praxis which requires a "leap" to move from one to the other. There is therefore an irresolvable difference, or *chorismos*, which distinguishes but does not separate them.

As terms of a dialectic, praxis and theory are in a dynamic relation to one another. There is a movement between them which Boff describes in very concrete terms as "ricocheting" or "blow and counterblow." The dialectic is a current receiving its first thrust from the side of praxis. It ricochets off theory, which by means of its symbolic intervention confers upon praxis its specifically human character, and returns to praxis and delivers a counterblow, dislocating it and starting the whole process over again.[53] Given his description of the elements of the dialectic and its movement, one can infer that for Boff to think dialectically is to self-consciously allow oneself into this movement, respecting the distinctiveness of each polarity and yet allowing one's theorizing to be continually moved and challenged to ever new syntheses.

Chauvet's new way of thinking is not dialectical but symbolic. It is not a matter of *recognizing* the space between discourse and the real (or the "breach" between theory and praxis), but rather of thinking *from within* this space. In order to understand what Chauvet means, it is necessary to look briefly at another aspect of symbolic mediation. Symbols mediate not only presence, but also absence. The co-emergence of the real and the human subject in the symbolic is at one and the same time a revealing and concealing. Thereby the difference between the real and the subject is always maintained.[54] In addition, in mediating one's presence to oneself as subject, the symbolic also mediates at the same time one's absence to oneself. The symbol creates a space between the subject and himself or herself. This space is crucial, however, for it allows the subject to emerge out of the realm of the imagination (that is, a world of the individual's own making in which one can be anything he or she desires) into the real.

It is *from within* this space created in the sacraments that one emerges into his or her identity as a *Christian* subject.[55] It is in the creating of this space in the symbolic activity of the sacraments that there occurs a re-inscription of the *logos* of the cross. But as with everything else mediated symbolically, the *kenotic* outpouring of God which occurs in the symbolic mediation of the sacraments is at one and the same time a mediation of God's presence and absence. To think symbolically, then, is to think *from within* the difference, or even better, to think the difference. It is to let go of one's desires to create one's own world, and in an attitude of "letting-be" or "disappropriation," to allow oneself to be spoken in the sacraments into a new Christian subjectivity.

It is at this third point of convergence, that of new ways of thinking, that the dialogue between Boff and Chauvet becomes most fruitful for the purposes of this discussion. Boff, it is clear, acknowledges the difference between discourse and the real. For him there is no question that although the political and political theology are not to be separated, they are nevertheless not to be reduced to one another. His dialectical thinking is an attempt to respect theology and praxis and the movement between them. From the point of view of Chauvet's theology, however, to identify terms and movement of the dialectic is not to carry the analysis of theology and praxis to its completion, for although Boff's treatment is predicated on the difference between discourse and the real, it has not yet successfully thought *from within* this difference. This is because Boff has not sufficiently attended to symbolic mediation. In retaining a theory of the word and a clear distinction between the real and the known, he has identified the breach between discourse and the real, but has fallen short of understanding the full significance of the breach. By locating symbolic intervention at the level of the theoretical, that is, at the level where it functions to communicate and relate concepts, he misses the function of the symbolic in creating the very breach with which he is so concerned.

It is not surprising that it is difficult to place sacramental practice (as political) in Boff's schema, perhaps because more than many other activities it is *both* word and practice. It is a kind of activity which seems to straddle the breach between theory and praxis. Yet, if one accepts the role of the symbolic in

creating the space between the real and the subject and between the subject and himself or herself, this identifying of sacraments as both word and practice, as both theory and practice, does not erase or fill the breach but in fact opens it and
keeps it open. If Boff contributes to the discussion on credibility by illuminating the complexities of the polarities of theory
and praxis and by calling attention to the dynamism or movement between them, Chauvet contributes by showing how the
sacramental is an integral part of the transformation which the
liberation theologian seeks both to bring about and explain.

Sacramental Theology as Liberating and Credible

In treating the points of convergence in the theologies of
Boff and Chauvet it has been possible to catch glimpses of a
response to the question which motivated this essay: How, if
at all, can I as a theologian of the first world and of the academy contribute to a sacramental theology of liberation? Must
my contribution to sacramental theology always be perceived
as a "going through the church to avoid the poor?" It is now
possible to address this question more fully.

A key insight which emerged in the dialogue is that there is
a difference between discourse and the real, as well as a difference between the discourse of faith and the discourse of theology. What is at issue in the question of credibility is just how
all of these differences come together and yet are maintained
in the one subject called the sacramental theologian. At any
given instance this same subject may be the locus of sacramental activity, of political activity, of the discourse of faith, of the
discourse of a theology of the political or of the discourse of a
theology of sacramentality. The challenge of *credibility* is twofold: (1) to be competent in carrying out the specific activity in
question, and (2) to allow a convergence of these activities in a
single subject which will bespeak the integrity of the subject
and which will command the respect (if not necessarily the
agreement) of the wider Christian community in all its dimensions. The challenge of *contributing to liberation* is to allow the
convergence of these activities to be transformative of the subject and his or her community. Taken together, the challenge
to *contribute credibly to a sacramental theology of liberation* is
nothing less than self-consciously allowing oneself as a subject

engaged in theological discourse to be a locus of God's transformative manifestation.

The dialogue between Boff and Chauvet suggests a principle by which this may be accomplished: maintain the difference. The theologian must respect the fact that to experience and appropriate the transformative manifestation of the divine in an act of theologizing is different from doing so as the subject of other Christian activities such as political activity and sacramental celebration. This difference has an important consequence: there are other transformative manifestations of the divine to which the subject lacks access in the act of theologizing. If these manifestations are to be the topic of specifically theological consideration, they must be so by way of second order reflection, either upon (1) the faith testimony of others or (2) one's own experience as locus of the transformative manifestation of the divine in one's other activities as subject. Simply put, the theologian in service of the transformative manifestation of God in contemporary praxis must seek that manifestation wherever it occurs and must appropriately respect the differences in access to it. This means that the theologian seeking credibility cannot be content simply to theologize. It is necessary also to live fully one's own Christian existence. In addition, it means that theologians must always be suspicious of the claims they make with respect to what God is saying in the churches, especially if their activity as subject is disproportionately that of "subject-as-theologizing."

There is a second sense in which the phrase, "maintain the difference," can be taken, a sense which is perhaps even more important to the sacramental theologian than to others. To maintain the difference is to dwell in the space opened up by the symbolic. It is to immerse oneself in the experience of the sacraments in order to allow oneself to be spoken in a new inscription of the *logos* of the cross. Theologizing for the sacramental theologian is then a "reading" of this new inscription of the Word. This implies that one who seeks to contribute credibly to a sacramental theology of liberation must oneself be living a sacramental life. Moreover, since the symbolic is the most primary mediation of the real to the Christian human person, there is a sense in which it informs all other mediations as well. It is that which is common to all discourses and all human activities despite their very real differences. To dwell in the symbolic is to think *from within* the difference and so to maintain it. For the sacramental theologian, to maintain the difference is to allow oneself to be spoken by a theological language that functions at its most symbolic. It is to regain a sense that the "scientific" language of theology is not that of the social sciences or philosophers with whom one is in dialogue, but the poetic.

So it is that Enrique Dussel's question, "Can we celebrate the eucharist with stolen bread?"[56] is paradigmatic for one seeking to contribute credibly to a sacramental theology of liberation. It is a question born of his experience of the poor, of socio-analytic mediation of the political, of attending to what God is saying in the churches in his sacramental experiences, of the poetic juxtaposition of "eucharist" and "stolen bread." It is a question like the one that arose in me when I met a poor man in an alley between a cathedral and a parking garage, when I filtered the experience through what the social sciences had told about the contemporary experience of the homeless and the poor, when in a poetic word God issued forth in a potentially transformative manifestation: "Is my way of theologizing nothing more than going through the church to avoid the poor?" By forthrightly facing such questions as they emerge, one who seeks to contribute to a sacramental theology of liberation can hope to find credibility.

Notes

1. I recognize the danger of distortion which can come from speaking of "liberation theology" generically or as a kind of abstraction removed from a particular social and historical context. Nevertheless, there do seem to be some presuppositions and methods that are sufficiently common to various liberation theologies to permit a qualified use of the term "liberation theology."

2. The potential fruitfulness of such a method is shown in Roberto S. Goizueta's effort to bring the theologies of Enrique Dussel and Bernard Lonergan into dialogue. See Roberto S. Goizueta, *Liberation, Method and Dialogue: Enrique Dussel and North American Theological Discourse*, American Academy of Religion Academy Series, vol. 58 (Atlanta: Scholars Press, 1988).

3. Clodovis Boff, *Theology and Praxis: Epistemological Foundations*, trans., Robert R. Barr (Maryknoll: Orbis Books, 1987).

4. Louis-Marie Chauvet, *Symbole et sacrement: Une relecture sacra-*

mentelle de l'existence chrétienne (Paris: Cerf, 1987). As far as I know, this work has not been translated into English.

5. Boff, *Theology and Praxis* xxii.

6. This interest, implicit in *Symbole et sacrement*, is clearly articulated in an unpublished address given by Chauvet at the defense of his dissertation (a lengthier version of *Symbole et sacrement*) on 17 April, 1986.

7. See Boff, *Theology and Praxis* 14-17.

8. Ibid. 151.

9. Ibid.

10. Ibid. 6.

11. Ibid.

12. Ibid.

13. Ibid. xxiv, 155.

14. Ibid. 220. Boff is referring here to Gustavo Gutiérrez, *The Power of the Poor in History: Selected Writings*, especially "Theology from the Underside of History" 169-221 (Maryknoll: Orbis Books, 1983).

15. Chauvet, *Symbole et sacrement* 184.

16. For what immediately follows see ibid. 74-77, 542-549. Note that in his treatment of the *logos* of the cross, Chauvet is heavily reliant upon Stanislas Breton, *Le Verbe et la croix* (Paris: Desclée, 1981).

17. See Louis-Marie Chauvet, "Sacrements et institution," in *La Théologie à l'épreuve de la vérité*, ed., Marc Michel (Paris: Cerf, 1984) 211.

18. These reasons are given in a portion of Chauvet's dissertation which was not published in *Symbole et sacrement* but which was graciously provided to this writer by Chauvet. They can be found on page 60 of the text.

19. This is evident in the very title of Chauvet's work. For Boff, see *Theology and Praxis* 139.

20. *Theology and Praxis* 176.

21. Ibid. 272, note 66. Boff summarizes Comte here, noting that throughout its history, human society has variously chosen the "it" to be first God or gods, then being or beings, and now today the world or things.

22. Ibid.

23. Ibid. 312, note 17.

24. Ibid. 45.

25. Ibid.

26. Ibid. 46.

27. Ibid. 44. It is the essence (as opposed to the concrete existence) of faith which concerns Boff here: "On the level of its *essence*, faith can be likened to an absolute *openness* to the Absolute, a real possibility—that is, a demand—for inexhaustible realizations . . . We may say, therefore, that, at the level of its existence, faith is universal, ab-

solute, transcendent, totalizing, and so forth." For a fuller treatment of Boff's understanding of faith, see especially 117-123.

28. Ibid. 48. For further comment on the need for ideo- political vigilance, see 17-19.

29. The need and theoretical justification of what Boff means by socio-analytic mediation is the main concern of the first part of *Theology and Praxis* 1-62.

30. Boff, *Theology and Praxis* 234, note 7.

31. The explanation and justification of this mediation are given in Part II of *Theology and Praxis* 67-153.

32. The relation between theology and praxis is the focus of the third part of Boff's work, 155-220. More will be said about this relationship in the following sections.

33. Ibid. 125.

34. Chauvet, *Symbole et sacrement* 35-37.

35. Ibid.

36. Boff, *Theology and Praxis* 126.

37. Ibid. 291-92, note 86.

38. Ibid. 128.

39. This is admittedly a very big "if." However, given Boff's reference to Plato, cited above, this is not an unreasonable assumption.

40. Louis-Marie Chauvet, *Du Symbolique au symbole: Essai sur les sacrements*, Rites et symbole, vol. 9 (Paris: Cerf, 1979) 196.

41. Chauvet, *Symbole et sacrement* 92.

42. Ibid. 60-62.

43. See the third part of *Symbole et sacrement* 329-461: "L'Acte de symbolisation de l'identité chrétienne."

44. Chauvet is careful to point out that he is not equating Heideggerian "Being" with the Christian "God." *Symbole et sacrement* 68.

45. See the fourth part of *Symbole et sacrement*: "Sacramentaire et christologie trinitaire" 459-566. See especially 542-549.

46. Boff, *Theology and Praxis* 206.

47. Chauvet, *Symbole et sacrement* 14-15.

48. Boff gives a full description of dialectic in his concluding chapter of *Theology and Praxis*, "Dialectic: Its Modes and Norms" 206-220.

49. Ibid. 208.

50. Ibid. 209. Boff also indicates here that the distribution of items listed under "thought" and "expression of the real" is fluid and corresponds to what common sense designates as theory and practice, respectively.

51. Ibid.

52. What follows is a summary of Boff's treatment as given in *Theology and Praxis* 210-213.

53. Ibid. 216.

54. Chauvet, *Symbole et sacrement* 63.

55. Chauvet illustrates this function of symbol by appeal to the legend of Narcissus. Narcissus, seeking to erase the space between himself and his image reflected in the water, falls into the water and drowns. One who fails to acknowledge that one cannot be immediately but only symbolically present even to oneself will be swallowed up and remain a prisoner of his or her imagination. See *Du Symbolique au symbole* 29-30.

56. Enrique Dussel, "The Bread of the Eucharistic Celebration as a Sign of Justice in the Community," *Concilium*, vol. 152, 56-65.

5

She Laughs
at the Days to Come:
Memory and Metaphor

Sally Ann McReynolds, N.D.

LAUGHTER IS THE FACE OF HUMANITY. LAUGHTER ENTICES, INTIMIDATES, liberates, and compels. Laughter derides and laughter cherishes. With laughter racial and sexual allusions become the potent force of bigotry. With laughter a child's tentative smile becomes a household celebration. With laughter African-American slaves shared the struggle and hope for freedom. Laughter isolates and laughter creates bonds of solidarity. Laughter kills and laughter engenders new life. All this, because laughter remembers and laughter forgets.

Memory and laughter are inextricably united. In a disturbing novel, *The Book of Laughter and Forgetting*, the Czechoslovakian author Milan Kundera[1] evokes multiple facets of laughter and memory as they serve or subvert the political task of forgetting. David Power observed to this writer that Kundera's collection of short stories challenges the reader to recognize the ways in which memory itself becomes a kind of forgetting. The contemporary women's movement raises the same concern. It seeks to identify and reclaim the history of women, so that women's stories will foster their authentic humanity and not become another form of forgetting.

Christian theology, liturgical praxis, and preaching have neglected the voices of women.[2] Christian memorial, especially eucharistic celebration, thus has been a kind of forgetting. In order to advance efforts to bring women's experience more directly into Christian remembrance, I explore women's memory as celebrated in the musical drama, *Quilters*, by Molly Newman and Barbara Damashek.[3] It traces the legacy of a mother to her daughters through the memories attached to a quilt pieced from the fabrics of her life.

The play's vignettes, derived from the lives of pioneer United States women, resonate with the tension between life and death expressed in the Markan resurrection narrative. This article proposes a correlation between the resurrection narrative in the Gospel of Mark and women's experiences. Such a reflection seeks to illumine the salvific meaning of Jesus' death, a tragedy become comedy, where laughter and memory unite to forge a bond against laughter and forgetting.

What follows then is an attempt to explicate a relationship between women's memories and the Christian community's remembrance of Jesus. The first of three sections examines memory from two perspectives: David Power's understanding of Christian memory and Milan Kundera's exploration of the interaction between laughter and forgetting. The next presents Paul Ricoeur's theory of metaphoric imagination and its application to the correlation between Markan parables and the Markan passion narrative. The third section examines references from *Quilters* which focus upon childbirth and the attendant care for children. It proposes that women's stories illumine the meaning of the Christian community's memories of Jesus' resurrection. As a "dangerous memory," women's stories celebrate their solidarity and serve a liberating and critical function.[4]

Memory and Laughter

Christian life and worship depend upon a vital interplay between memory, imagination, and desire. In *Unsearchable Riches* David Power reminds us that "to worship is to remember Jesus Christ and God's work in him . . . Jesus asks that his disciples remember him as servant."[5]

Three features of Power's elaboration of Christian memory are especially pertinent to this study. First, Christian memory is an interiorization of narrative, relating one's life story to the story of Christ and the believing community. Particularly important for our attention to women's experience is the awareness that narrative memory connects one's own beginnings to the beginnings of the Christian story. Second, in its form as narrative emplotment, memory presents a creative shaping of past events which anticipates the future. Such anticipation recognizes the presence of the shadow, of what is incomplete, puzzling, harmful, evil in the past, present, and possibly in the future. Desire is stimulated, shaped, and expressed through narrative. Narrative of past events is thus oriented to future action. Third, a generative poetics which maintains a critical function is essential to Christian remembering. Generative poetics incorporates stories and images from a given culture and also finds ways to include other persons' stories in order to continue to narrate the memory of Christ.[6] Generative poetics facilitates the divine invitation to cherish any Other as a human person like oneself. Furthermore, the creative and critical function of generative poetics is necessary to foster mutual critique between Christian memory and the memories and experiences of any age and culture. In the next section we will see that Ricoeur's approach to metaphoric imagination provides a generative poetics which also encompasses the first two functions of Christian memory.

Crucial to the liberative function of narrative memory is the contribution of the creative imagination. According to Power:

> The imaginative is the unifying factor, that which presents a storied and ritualized world in which meaning prevails over data, value over utility, and the inner voice of the Spirit over all that assails us by way of human direction or human coercion. The imaginative frees us from dark forces of alienation in which the human itself is submerged.[7]

From this brief overview of the historical and narrative quality of Christian memory, it should be evident that the believing community must incorporate the experiences of the marginalized and oppressed, in order be faithful to the liberative meaning of God's revelation. If the marginalized and oppressed are to experience Christian community as salvific, then their stories must have a function in interpreting the meaning of the resurrection. Futhermore, their memories and narratives provide a privileged stance from which to evaluate and critique the Christian tradition. The fact that memory itself can falsify and oppress is evident from the history of Christianity. However, the dynamics of memory which can lead it to become a form of oppression and forgetting often elude well-intentioned believers.

Milan Kundera's novel, *The Book of Laughter and Forgetting*, provokes its readers to examine their understanding of memory and its role in their lives. This enigmatic collection of short stories is a novel patterned on musical variations. Each story is a variation of the same theme. And yet that theme deliberately eludes concrete formulation. The novel is not intended to be a clearly constructed journey through an epic world. Rather, in the author's own terms, it constitutes a challenge to journey into the totally inaccessible inner infinity of human existence.[8] Any attempt to delineate the purpose and meaning of the characters, images, and plots would undermine the creative engagement encouraged by the author. In fact, the very characters, images, and plots are presented so as to prevent a ready correlation between specific interpretations and a supposed intent of the author. Here I am solely concerned to draw upon this novel as a resource for examining memory in its relationship to laughter and forgetting.

Forgetting operates on several levels of consciousness and ritualization. It supports both political and private interests. Forgetting is crucial to the efforts of Czechoslovakian communist leaders to control the future. They attempt this by blatantly changing records and photographs. More insidiously, they pursue the goal of forgetting by carefully directing public attention to selected features and events of the past. Forgetting also occurs on the personal level. In Kundera's novel characters cope with guilt or painful memories by denial, selective attention, or refusal to relate the past to the present and future. His primary characters are Czechs, who like himself first embraced communism, became disenchanted, fostered the Prague Spring, and then were ostracized and fled the country. Accounts of rape and sexual orgies and stories of suicide, drowning, and death accompany the persistent and disquieting question of whether Czechoslovakia has been ineluctably swallowed up by Russia. Roles of countries, of landscape, and of persons interchange to challenge the imagination and illumine the power of forgetting at both the interpersonal and social levels.

Laughter attaches itself to memory. Like memory, laughter is multifaceted. It oscillates between the primal laughter of the devil and the derivative laughter of the angels. Kundera opposes the irrationality of laughter to rationally controlled environments. Irrational laughter is the province of devils. It disturbs the goodness and order of the angels. The angels' only power in the face of demonic laughter is to laugh themselves. However, this is a derivative laughter associated with the closed circle, dancing in step, and physical levitation.[9]

Terrifying laughter of angels accompanies the endless sensation of falling which the dissident patriot experiences.[10] For those who dance in step in the closed circle, the same angelic laughter accompanies a joyous upward flight. Demonic laughter has its own unique powers. It transforms memory into a subversion of the stifling oppression of rational order. Laughter is irrational. Demonic laughter is rebellion and salvation.

From *The Book of Laughter and Forgetting* I will treat but two of the many instances of forgetting: the hat and the wife, Tamina. Each is related to the other as the aforementioned variations on a theme.

Clementis, a Czech communist official has been charged with treason and hung. He is airbrushed out of a 1948 group photo and yet his hat persists. On the cold day of the photograph, he had placed his hat on the head of the leader. The widely circulated memorial continues to present Clementis' hat to the people. This hat becomes an expansive symbol of demonic laughter allied with the struggle which memory wages against power. In this context Kundera observes:

> People are always shouting they want to create a better future. It's not true. The future is an apathetic void of no interest to anyone. The past is full of life, eager to irritate us, provoke and insult us, tempt us to destroy or repaint it. The only reason people want to be masters of the future is to change the past. They are fighting for access to the laboratories where photographs are retouched and biographies and histories rewritten.[11]

A hat shows up again near the end of the novel. It comically blows about at a graveside service, finally ending up in the grave itself. All the mourners are silently convulsed by laughter.[12] This memory of the hat in the grave reappears to stimulate the raucous laughter which disturbs a carefully orchestrated sexual orgy. The hat maintains the questioning and revolt which had supposedly been airbrushed out of existence. An attempt at forgetting surprisingly inverts itself to persist as a struggle against power. It does so only through an alliance with disturbing and irrational laughter.[13]

In a more complex fashion, the efforts of the widow, Tamina, to remember her deceased husband actually become a forgetting. In order to reconstitute the exact chronological order of their former vacations and to remember each pet name which her husband had for her, she seeks to retrieve the diaries she left behind upon their escape from Czechoslovakia. In the course of the frustration, which meets her every plan, the memories which she had, albeit not in chronological order, begin to escape her. Yet she was left with her sadness.

Tamina's sadness dissolves at the pleasant and infectious angelic laughter of a young man named Raphael. His invitation to forget her miseries leads her into an idyllic captivity upon a nameless island. Her situation turns grotesque. Her struggle to swim back to the landscape, which mirrored Czechoslovakia, advances her only a fixed distance from the island. There she drowns. Kundera seemingly examines both the power and the pain of memories of those one loves. He relates them to the pain of the dissident who becomes a threat even to his closest friends. At times any invitation to forget the misery seems welcome, especially in the face of the fear that Czechoslovakia may indeed be swallowed up by Russia.[14]

Music, language, stories, naming, memories—all can become instruments of forgetting. Kundera observes that political leaders employ these to keep the youth looking to the past, not to the future. Demonic laughter which upsets the rational order of such planning is necessary so that memory becomes an ally against the rational, the good, the planned.

In the light of this brief exploration of Kundera's theme and variations on laughter and forgetting, we can consider more specifically the role of women's memories and women's laughter in the struggle of Christian faith against the angelic circle, where the select dance in step and levitate above the crowd. In women's stories we have the hat, which has not been airbrushed out of the picture, and a willingness to hold onto memory in the face of sadness.

Memory which is an interiorization of narrative in anticipation of the future can recognize the presence of the shadow. David Power has alerted us to the necessity of a generative poetics which would incorporate stories from a variety of cultures into the memory and retelling of the story of Jesus of Nazareth.

Metaphoric Imagination and
the Markan Resurrection Narrative

Redemptive memory displays an affinity with the notion of demonic laughter. Such laughter disturbs the powerful, celebrates the marginalized, and makes a space for freedom and creativity. Redemptive memory is an expression of a creative and critical imagination. Memory tempts one to think that it is a reduplication of the past, but no form of memory is ever such a stenographic representation. Memory inevitably expresses some relationship, however obscured, to the present and to the future. We next explore Paul Ricoeur's theory of metaphoric imagination in order to illumine further the interaction between memory, metaphor, and laughter.

First, it is necessary to recognize that memory is dependent upon imagination. Memory partakes of the dialectical characteristics of the imagination.[15] From the standpoint of the subject who imagines, imagination possesses a twofold potential: it can criticize or it can be fascinated. In Kundera's book, communist leaders sought to foster a fascinated, controlled memory of the past. Their control was disturbed by the critical memory of a hat. Imagination, moreover, engages its object in a dialectical mode of presence and absence. Reproductive imagination intends an imaginative presence which would represent the absent object. Tamina's efforts to retrieve her diary were concerned with reproductive memory. In contrast, productive imagination indicates an imaginative absence. This embrace of absence acknowledges that it is impossible to re-

produce the past. Memory is challenged to admit its selectivity
and creativity. In this regard Tamina seemingly could not embrace the dimension of absence in her memories of her husband. Eventually even her sadness escaped her.

To this welter of mystification and liberation Ricoeur's theory of metaphoric imagination provides an interpretive approach which engages, evaluates, and enjoys memory. He ex-
plores the metaphorical properties of narrative in order to
identify and unlock the integrative and creative functions of
story. He provides a generative poetics. We are concerned
here to apply this understanding of narrative and imagination
to the critical correlation between the story of Jesus' resurrection and women's stories of childbirth. Ricoeur's contribution
to our understanding of the creative imagination can best be
described by considering how imagination serves the interpretation of the gospel parables.[16]

Parables are narrative metaphors.[17] Like all metaphors they
bring together opposites in a creative tension. They appeal to
the imagination to discover a likeness precisely in and through
differences. Mary Gehrhart and Allan Russell aptly describe
the work of metaphor. They propose that making a metaphor
is like deforming geometric space. Such deformation occurs
when a sheet of paper is rolled over so that it defines two parallel planes. The space between the planes corresponds to the
creative space of the metaphor. The juxtaposition of images
and stories in metaphor creates a new space, the space between the planes. Within this space new meaning appears. The
creative imagination finds similarities precisely in and through
the differences which are joined in the metaphor.[18]

Just as a metaphoric predication yokes unlikes to discover
and create new meaning, so the work of emplotment configures events into a story. Any story, fiction or history, demonstrates the characteristic of metaphoric attribution. Interpreting narrative proceeds according to the dynamics of
interpreting metaphor. For Ricoeur, this interpretation depends on dialectical interactions necessary for understanding
a whole text.[19]

It is the work as a whole which one interprets. What one derives from any text is not conceptual knowledge alone. Rather,
the meaning of the text is a way of being in the world. Inter-

pretation is a matter of praxis, of action. The ultimate goal of interpretation is the appropriation of the meaning of the world of the text. The text projects a world of possibilities within which one understands one's own freedom, into which one can project one's deepest possibilities. Interpretation is even more a matter of imagination and desire than a matter of concepts and analysis. Conceptual thought and critical analysis serve the more fundamental level of desire and action.

Ricoeur's reflections on parable become paradigmatic for his entire analysis of time and narrative. It is in looking at parable that we get an insight, not only into the testimony proclaimed in Scripture, but also into the human configuration of time which occurs in the narratives of a tradition. Parables are metaphors because they link images in a unique and disturbing way which appeals to the imagination. They are also metaphors because they display a narrative function. Parables configure time. The work of emplotment draws upon the metaphoric imagination to link unlikes into a narrative. All narrative, fiction and history alike, involves the selection and arrangement of events and characters. Time is a multi-faceted symbolic reality which comes to expression in narrative. Parables challenge the well-ordered, predetermined, and frequently cyclic time of dominating elites or the status quo.

Parables reveal the extraordinary of the Reign of God precisely in and through the ordinary of everyday experiences. Parables frequently follow a pattern of event, reversal, and engagement or decision. One finds a pearl, sells all one's possessions, then purchases the field with the pearl. This merchandising extravagance is likened to the Kingdom of God (Mt 13:45). Parables appeal to the poetic imagination. They stimulate a new self-understanding in the light of Jesus' proclamation.

Imagination facilitates every step of interpretation. The shock of unlikely combination, the metaphoric impertinence, functions to engage the imagination. The interpreter is helped to abandon preconceived notions and destructive feelings and enter into the possible world of belonging projected by the parable. The imagination then must first exert a certain discipline to distance the interpreting subject from mystifications which fascinate human consciousness. Then imagination opens the subject to the interplay of images and configuration of time presented in the parable. Metaphor stimulates the subject to rethink relationships and to bring images to this emerging meaning. Intellectual explanation and imaginative understanding interweave in this task. One discovers similarities in and through differences. Ultimately, the interpreter appropriates the world projected by the text as a new way of being in the world. Feelings accompany this process and are structured by it to give rise to hope and action.

Thus metaphoric imagination applied to narrative is a form of generative poetics which resonates with the biblical parables. Ricoeur's notion of a whole text as metaphor embraces all of Scripture as the narrative memory of God's liberative activity for humanity. Story is the privileged vehicle for the imaginative link between desire and action. Imagination relates desire and story to conceptual thought. Interpreting Scripture requires a metaphoric imagination attuned to the life stories of those for whom these memories are significant. This dual invitation to creativity and to the stories of the marginalized applies to the scriptural accounts which give testimony to the resurrection.

Remembering the death/resurrection of Jesus of Nazareth should be a dangerous activity. It calls forth not the ordered laughter of the angels but that demonic laughter which unseats the rationality which stifles freedom. Nonetheless, this laughter is frequently not far from sadness. In fact, demonic laughter does not demand that we let go of the sadness which preserves liberative memories. Rather, this laughter embraces remembrance. Because it perseveres, it laughs at the days to come, and may even arrive at hope.[20]

On this note of laughter we turn to the resurrection narrative in the Gospel of Mark. This account is set apart from the other synoptics by its ending in silence, fear, and flight:

> When the sabbath was over, Mary Magdalene, Mary, the mother of James, and Salome bought spices so that they might go and anoint him. Very early when the sun had risen, on the first day of the week, they came to the tomb. They were saying to one another, "Who will roll back the stone for us from the entrance to the tomb?" When they looked up, they saw that the stone had been rolled back; it was very large. On entering the tomb they saw a young man sitting on the right side, clothed in a white robe, and they were utterly amazed. He said to them,

"Do not be amazed! You seek Jesus of Nazareth, the crucified. He has been raised; he is not here. Behold the place where they laid him. But go and tell his disciples and Peter, 'He is going before you to Galilee; there you will see him, as he told you.'" Then they went out and fled from the tomb, seized with trembling and bewilderment. They said nothing to anyone, for they were afraid." (Mk 16:8)[21]

What are we to make of this abrupt ending to the earliest of the canonical Gospels? Some postulate an earlier ending which has been lost. Others protest that the accounts of the appearances were well-known and need not have been repeated.[22]

Both Norman Perrin[23] and Paul Ricoeur[24] propose that the short ending offers profound insight into the meaning of the resurrection. Elisabeth Schüssler Fiorenza joins in this appreciation of the originality of the short ending. However, she cautions against interpretations which propose that the words, "They said nothing to anyone," are intended to mean that the women failed in their mission as disciples. She observes that the description is similar to Jesus' directions to the healed leper, "See that you tell no one anything but go, show yourself to the priest" (Mk 1:44). "Telling no one anything" did not preclude following the command to tell the priest.[25]

For Perrin, Mark's resurrection narrative is to be understood not as an etiological myth but as a primordial myth. The resurrection account is not presented as the foundation of a church but as an expression of the ultimate meaning of the everyday. Perrin claims that the imminent parousia which dominates Mark's Gospel refers not to some other worldly future event, but to the "experience of ultimacy in the experience of the everyday."[26]

According to Ricoeur, the resurrection account displays the narrative yoking of opposites characteristic of a parable. It should be interpreted in the context of the passion account and of the entire Gospel, each understood as an "englobing parable." Mark's account of the passion begins with the anointing of the head of Jesus by the unnamed woman of Bethany. It concludes with the three named women being unable to find the body which they came to anoint. Ricoeur likens the conclusion of fear, flight, and silence to the conclusion of the parable of the murderers in the vineyard where eventually, even the owner's son is murdered (Mk 12:1-8). This tragic death contrasts with the comic conclusion of the parable of the sower and the seed (Mk 4:1-20).[27]

The Gospel of Mark, itself viewed as an overarching parable,[28] sets the parable of the sower in a metaphoric relationship with the parable of the murderers in the vineyard. The death of the son is juxtaposed to the luxuriant growth of the seed that fell on good ground. We are invited to discover similarities in and through the drastic differences. Ricoeur proposes that the phrase "it was necessary" provides a clue to the meaning of Jesus' death. In some way "it was necessary" that the owner's son die that the word (the seed) might grow. In a similar fashion the stark ending of the Gospel is necessary that the word (of God) might grow. The Gospel joins Jesus' death to the growth of the word of God. The resurrection gives witness that Jesus' death is victory and growth.[29]

My intention here is to provide a rationale and basis for relating the experiences of women's lives to the memory of the resurrection. This article cannot investigate the many ways in which meaning of the resurrection accounts have been interpreted. It proposes that those interpretations which connect the resurrection directly with Jesus' death find a particular resonance in the lives of women. The resurrection means that the death of Jesus is ultimately victory and salvation for humanity. How that death is remembered is crucial. Like any memory, the memory of Jesus can represent a fascinated consciousness preoccupied with representing the past. The challenge to the Christian community is to recognize and nurture critical and creative aspects of its memories. A metaphoric imagination fosters this kind of memory.

Memory and Women's Stories

Remembering and reflecting critically on women's lives is necessary in order to interpret the life, death, and resurrection of Jesus as a saving memory. In this section I draw on one specific resource for insight into women's lives and then set this resource in a metaphorical relationship with the Markan resurrection narrative.

The musical drama *Quilters* is an exuberant celebration of

women's memories. Set on the Kansas prairie of the 1800s, it encapsulates the westward journey from the perspective of pioneering white women who traversed the harsh yet promising land. The play is a series of vignettes developed around patterns in a legacy quilt being pieced by the mother, Sarah, for her adult daughters. The memory laden quilt is to be passed from the oldest to the youngest. Each daughter is to keep it for a year at a time and tell the "stories that are in it."[30]

Unlike *The Book of Laughter and Forgetting*, this work does not probe the meaning and distortions of memory. And yet it serves a similar purpose. It displays the role of memory and laughter in the fabrics of women's lives. Women identify, configure, and transform their memories by piecing the patterns of quilts. Evil in the form of personal maliciousness does not make an entrance onto the stage of this production. In this and other ways *Quilters* is necessarily incomplete and subject to the criticism that it also distorts women's experience. Notably missing are the memories of the Native American women, who traversed the same plains and, on occasion, were welcomed into the households described by the play. Despite these limitations, I propose that the interplay of feelings, insight, and ideas engenders fresh ways of appropriating the meaning of the resurrection. In *Quilters* the laughter which bubbles up from the simple incongruities of life is no stranger to tragedy.

For the women of the prairies a complex interplay of emotions and memory is attached to childbirth. Here we explore this one lens onto the complex experience of pregnancy, childbirth, and child care.

The opening scene between mother and daughters links love and laughter, wedding and childbirth in the simple, moving lines of the sung poem: "THIS WAS A PIECE OF / MY WEDDING DRESS / LOVE AND LAUGHTER / AND TENDERNESS / TENDERNESS / AND THIS SPRIGGED MUSLIN / COLOR OF CORN / I WORE RIGHT AFTER OUR JOHN WAS BORN."[31] Dancing and laughter accompany these memories of everyday struggles and delights. From the scattered swatches of lives women piece and stitch the "unspoken emotion" of women's lives.

For many of the women in this play childbirth is a salient memory. The significance of any one birth is shaped by how it is contextualized in the dailiness of the women's lives. It is this celebrated dailiness which compels our attention. Women's work and women's lives are paradoxical. That work is precisely work which "perishes in the usin'."[32] And yet this seemingly ephemeral work is the stuff of music and dance and memory. Sarah's legacy quilt is still unfinished at the close of the play. Her daughters are invited to add the remaining touches. And yet her last line, heralding her own death, proclaims the words from the book of Proverbs: "Give her the fruit of her hands and let her own works praise her in the gates!"[33] Her work has been to stitch the complex of emotions in women's lives.

Six of the sixteen quilt block vignettes concern the mystery of childbirth in its complex emotions of gift and loss, hope and fear. Childbirth is the first of three quilt blocks to receive special attention as a "shadow block." These blocks are dark squares which set the other colorful patterns in clear relief. According to the stage directions, shadow blocks are "nonverbal representations of the darker side of the women's rites of passage. The events depicted are not always tragic, but we should get a sense of the unspoken fears involved and the presence of Mystery and Death."[34] Hushed tones and silences distinguish the shadow blocks from the other blocks. The first shadow block concludes with a voiceless celebration of the baby's birth. The midwife lifts up the baby in thanks as a flute trills a joyous crescendo.

The second shadow block conveys the fears and hopes connected with a near drowning at a young girl's baptism. The last shadow block evokes the desperation at times attached to the experience of pregnancy. After a male doctor has refused her help, womenfolk provide a pregnant and physically depleted mother of eleven with an abortive drink, lest she die or become too sick to care for her children and work alongside her husband.[35]

We next look briefly at three pattern blocks from *Quilters*. These connect emotions welling up from experiences of life and death to the healing labor of piecing and quilting and to memory.

For Cynthia, the earliest memories of quilting date to a poignant episode when she was four. The neighbor's baby has died. The men gather to make the casket, while the women quilt all day to make the lining. Her mother's piece of precious blue silk is carefully taken from storage and made into the "tiny little quilt" to cover the baby.[36]

Lizzie discovers a butterfly quilt block in the tool shed. She is told that Elizabeth is not the name given her at birth. That name is unknown. In the story of the misshapen butterfly, produced from struggling and uneven stitches, Lizzie learns of her birth mother. Shortly after a second child, a boy, was born dead, the young mother was found wandering, sick and delirious. While under the care of some town women, the distraught young mother began a butterfly design for her baby daughter who had been placed in an orphanage. In the few months before she commits suicide, the only words the mother spoke were halting directions to give the quilt piece to the child. An adoptive family welcomes her. Her second mother saves the quilt block for the time when the girl should know, not only of her mother's death, but her mother's gift of the butterfly design. At first, the daughter begins cutting up the quilt piece (an echo of her own mother's disturbed state of mind) but then secretly repairs it, repeating the pattern of stitches made years ago.[37]

Secrecy finds its way into the quilting project Cassie undertakes for her husband. They laugh and dance with delight over the quilt with which she surprises him. A year later she is overwhelmed with grief when his body is brought to her, literally in a basket. After weeks of numbing silence and grief she is barely able to pick up her piecing on a baby's quilt. By sheer effort she finishes the quilt in four months time and her baby is born. Her eyes are able to see again, for as she says, "my hands remembered."[38]

This brief overview is intended to express the profound simplicity of the struggle between life and death, hope and fear, which accompanied the lives of most women of the midwestern plains. In the midst of these struggles there is time for song and dance. There is laughter which is perhaps more akin to the demonic than the angelic. Laughter even preserves quilting itself from becoming a matter of angelic order. The mocking comic design, "The Demise of Sunbonnet Sue," pokes fun at a preoccupation with quilting.[39]

The laughter in this musical drama is subversive. It is women's laughter drawn from women's experiences. It establishes a solidarity among women. It unsettles the world where women's stories have not before been celebrated so forthrightly. The Christian community needs to relate to this celebration. It is possible to enter into a metaphoric space and discover the similarities between the events of women's lives and the gospel record. It is precisely in and through the differences between women's stories and Scripture that similarities can be discovered. Below I sketch a few points of comparison discernable in the drama just reviewed.

In *Quilters* we have the silence of the shadow blocks in juxtaposition with the exuberance of the patterned blocks. We saw that Ricoeur invites the readers of Mark's Gospel to set the conclusion of the Gospel in a parabolic relationship with the rest of the Gospel. He placed the fear, flight, and silence of the women in tandem with the luxuriant growth of the seed. The death of the son is the growth of the word. The testimony that God raised Jesus from the dead proclaims a death that is actually a victory. Insight into the nature of that victory can be gained by reflecting on the intimate connection between birth and death in women's bodies and in the relationships which shape their lives.

The extravagance of the tiny blue silk quilt parallels the extravagance of the unnamed woman who anoints Jesus' head for his burial. In making the coffin, the lining, and the quilt, the gathered neighbors are quietly shaped into a loving people. They become a witness to the meaning of the baby's short life. The three women who approach the tomb on the morning after the Sabbath are similarly united in their appreciation of the meaning of Jesus for them. They have provided us a solidarity which persists through fear and silence to bring forth fruit a hundredfold.

An immediate impulse to destroy a misshapen butterfly is overcome by dedicated effort to repair the pattern. Sadness recognized and accepted has preserved a life-giving memory. The angelic temptation to accuracy and order is overcome.

Memory lives in our bodies. The sheer physical act of picking up the piecing brings the grieving widow to new sight and wholeness. We note here a ritual which carries the individual and communities through disturbing and numbing periods. In the play, the one ritual of quilting serves many diverse functions.

In each of the vignettes where birth and death are intimately connected, death somehow is vanquished. Ricoeur's theory of the parables reminds us that it is in the ordinariness of everyday that the extraordinariness of the Reign of God is made present. It is this relationship of love and justice which Jesus' life proclaimed and his death and resurrection made real. The note of laughter is essential to our remembering. And this laughter is the demonic laughter which knows that it cannot control the past.

* * * * * *

I have proposed that the stories of women's lives must be incorporated into the work of Christian memorial, lest liturgy, theology, and spirituality, themselves become a kind of forgetting. The creative imagination plays a determinative role in this task. The church's mission, to proclaim Jesus as savior, requires a willingness to maintain a critical attitude toward its own memories and a commitment to engage the stories of the marginalized and oppressed in its interpretation of Jesus' life, death, and resurrection. Such willingness and commitment calls for attention to the creative imagination understood as metaphoric imagination. A generative poetics proceeds according to the dynamics of metaphor. This generative poetics serves the interiorization of narrative, understands memory as narrative emplotment, and provides a critical function.

Attending to women's experiences serves these goals of generative poetics. The hopes, desires, struggles, and fears associated with childbirth and the nurturing of young human life helps connect our beginnings with Christian origins. Care must be taken lest even these simple and profound memories become a kind of forgetting. The full and rich diversity of women's lives precludes stereotyping even the common experience of childbirth. The limited accounts reviewed here remind us that women's memories of childbirth itself are shaped by the context of their lives. It is necessary to keep the memories of madness and death as well as the joyousness of the trilling flute.

What *Quilters* celebrates in the laughter of women is their solidarity with one another. The solidarity is expressed in the ritual work of quilting which sustains groups and individuals through painful seasons. Laughter accompanies a vision of work and solidarity which helps prevent memory from becoming a forgetting. To be in the audience and share this laughter is to embrace dangerous memories. Thus does the Book of Proverbs speak of the valiant woman: "She laughs at the days to come."

Notes

1. Translated from the Czech by Michael Henry Heim (New York: Alfred A. Knopf, 1980).

2. For an excellent selected bibliography, see Anne Carr, *Transforming Grace: Christian Tradition and Women's Experience* (San Francisco: Harper and Row, 1988) 245-266. For a succinct examination of women's concerns in relationship to evangelization and preaching, see Mary Ann Zimmer, "Preaching the Gospel to the Whole Creation," *Liturgy* 8:2 (Fall 1989) 81-85.

3. (New York: Dramatists Play Service, Inc., 1986). Based on the book, *The Quilters: Women and Domestic Art* by Patricia Cooper Baker and Norma Buferd (New York: Doubleday, 1978).

4. Johann Baptist Metz in *Faith in History and Society*, trans., David Smith (New York: Crossroad, 1980) critically relates memory, narrative, and solidarity. See Chapter 5, "The Dangerous Memory of the Freedom of Jesus Christ," and Chapter 6, "The Future in the Memory of Suffering."

5. David Power, *Unsearchable Riches* (New York: Pueblo Publishing Co., 1984) 39.

6. Ibid. 121-24.

7. Ibid. 90.

8. Kundera, *The Book of Laughter* 163-164.

9. Ibid. 61-66.

10. Ibid. 76.

11. Ibid. 22.

12. Ibid. 221.

13. Ibid. 222-225.

14. Ibid. 79-115, 162-177, 182-191.

15. The following dialectical analysis of imagination is based on that of Paul Ricoeur in "Imagination in Discourse and in Action," *Analecta Husserliana* 7 (1976) 5-6.

16. Ricoeur's theory of parable is presented in the seminal article, "Biblical Hermeneutics," *Semeia* 4 (1975) 29-148. It is enhanced by his further studies of metaphor and of time and narrative. See *The Rule*

of Metaphor, trans., Robert Czerny with Kathleen McLaughlin and John Costello (Toronto: University of Toronto Press, 1977) and *Time and Narrative*, 3 vols., trans. vols. 1 and 2, Kathleen McLaughin and David Pellauer, vol. 3, Kathleen Blarney and David Pellauer (Chicago: University of Chicago Press, 1984-1988).

17. For an overview of theories of parable, see Norma Perrin, *Jesus and the Language of the Kingdom: Symbol and Metaphor in New Testament Interpretation* (Philadelphia: Fortress Press, 1976). For a comprehensive understanding of parable and current bibliography, see John R. Donahue, *The Gospel in Parable: Metaphor, Narrative, and Theology in the Synoptic Gospels* (Philadelphia: Fortress Press, 1988). Both authors acknowledge the influence of Ricoeur on their thought.

18. *Metaphoric Process: The Creation of Scientific and Religious Understanding* (Fort Worth: Texas Christian University Press, 1984) 95-120. This approach is indebted to the work of Ricoeur who wrote the foreword to the book.

19. An extensive investigation of Ricoeur's theory of metaphor, narrative, and parable is found in my doctoral dissertation "Eschatology and Social Action in the Work of Paul Ricoeur" (Ph.D. diss., The Catholic University of America, 1988) 109-148, 283-371. This article summarizes pertinent features from these pages.

20. Prv 31:25; Rom 8:3-5.

21. *New American Bible with Revised New Testament*, 1986.

22. Norman Perrin, *The Resurrection According to Matthew, Mark, and Luke* (Philadelphia: Fortress Press, 1977) 16-18. See also Sean P. Kealey, *Mark's Gospel: A History of Its Interpretation* (New York: Paulist Press, 1982).

23. Perrin, *The Resurrection* 18.

24. "Le récit intérpretatif: Exégèse et théologie dans les récits de la passion," *Recherches de science religieuse* 73 (1985) 17-38, especially 29.

25. Elisabeth Schüssler Fiorenza, *In Memory of Her: A Feminist Theological Reconstruction of Christian Origins* (New York: Crossroad, 1983) 321-322.

26. Perrin, *The Resurrection* 37.

27. Paul Ricoeur, "La Bible et l'imagination," *Revue d'histoire et de philosophie reliqieuses* 62 (1982) 339-360. Also as "Bible and the Imagination" in *The Bible as a Document of the University*, ed., H.D. Betz, (Chico, CA: Scholars Press, 1981) 49-76.

28. For a careful and creative analysis of this insight, see James G. Williams, *Gospel Against Parable: Mark's Language of Mystery* (Decatur, GA: The Almond Press, 1985).

29. This paragraph is based on the articles listed in notes 24 and 27 above.

30. Newman and Damasheck, *Quilters* 58.

31. Ibid. 7. The first four lines are from "The Quilt" by Dorothy MacFarlane as acknowledged in the text of the play, page 4.

32. Ibid. 9.

33. Ibid. 59. (Prv 31:31).

34. Ibid. 16.

35. Ibid. 26-27, 43-46.

36. Ibid. 15.

37. Ibid. 27-30.

38. Ibid. 51.

39. Ibid. 21.

Liturgy and Spirituality
in a Post-Classicist Age

6

Wounded
in Extraordinary Depths:
Towards a
Contemporary Mystagogia

Richard N. Fragomeni

There is an extraordinary power of revelation latent in the rituals and the symbols and the poetry of liturgical traditions, for
those who would do battle with them, so only those who are
wounded can give testimony to the existence of angels.

David N. Power[1]

RECENT PASTORAL DEVELOPMENTS IN CATECHESIS AND LITURGY HAVE
drawn attention to the importance and necessity of mystagogia.[2] In a volume honoring the life and the difference that David N. Power, O.M.I. has made to the liturgical enterprise, it is
only fitting to offer an essay on this developing field of ritual
interpretation.

This exploration takes its lead from an invitation which
Power himself offers his readers in a collection of commentaries, written by various authors, on the proposed Universal
Catechism. Observing that the starting point of the proposed
catechism's discussion on the sacraments is overly doctrinal

and medieval in its approach, Power argues that a mystagogical method be taken up in the catechism. In this way the texts and experience of the liturgical celebration themselves would be the foundation of sacramental catechesis.[3]

This is not a novel recommendation by our laureate, however, since Power has consistently developed his own liturgical theology by a creative and foundational interpretation of liturgical texts and experience.[4] In a real sense, Power has all along offered an articulation of a mystagogical catechesis. His writings engender reflection and appropriation of the sacramental life of the church by way of a rigorous interpretation of liturgical experience.

The article on the Universal Catechism continues with a brief exposition of the sacrament of anointing, and ends with what might be considered an invitation for mystagogy in sacramental catechesis: "A rethinking of the whole approach seems necessary for a current catechesis. The challenge of a contemporary mystagogia on sacrament remains to be taken up."[5]

It is the goal of this study, therefore, to take up this challenge. It sets forth a modest step in the discussion and development of a contemporary mystagogia by claiming that a significant contribution to the developing conversation about mystagogical discourse in pastoral practice can be found in the writings of David N. Power. His writings interpret the meanings of liturgical experience, offering a sacramental interpretation critically grounded in philosophy, cultural analysis, and theology. While in concert with the characteristics of classical mystagogia, the focus, interpretation, method, and horizon of Power's works are thoroughly contemporary. Furthermore, Power's appropriation of the liturgical tradition is vitally consonant with the purpose of mystagogy: the building up of communities of compassion within the truthfulness of sacramental life.

In responding to this challenge for a contemporary mystagogia, this article make several moves. The first offers a brief overview of the components of mystagogia as it comes to us from the post-baptismal homilies of the early church. Second, we examine Power's own work of sacramental interpretation as a hermeneutical re-reading of the liturgical experience, analogous to the mystagogy of the past. Third, from this examination we will propose several vectors for the discussion and development of a contemporary mystagogia in which Power's work can make a weighty contribution. The concluding step will be a mystagogical offering, a homily-like meditation opening the experience of the Sunday assembly, and encouraged by Power's contribution.

Mystagogia is a promise which can unleash the "extraordinary power of revelation" uttered by the angels of the liturgical eventing. To this end, and to the ongoing discovery of its modes and methods in contemporary retrieval, this article does battle.

The Tradition of Mystagogia

Mystagogia is an ancient pattern of sacramental catechesis. As such, it has recently reentered the parlance of church ministers both academic and pastoral. Its reintegration into the conversation of faith can easily be traced to the promulgation of the *Order of the Christian Initiation of Adults* in 1972.[6]

Attention is given in the rite to the necessity of ongoing formation in faith for the neophytes by way of post-baptismal sacramental reflection.[7] In a period of fifty days following the initiation sacraments, the Easter season or the period of mystagogy, as it is called, the neophytes are allowed the opportunity to come closer to the mysteries of faith by an appropriate sacramental catechesis.[8]

Because the retrieval of this process of initiation has come from the past, and because in recent pastoral practice, sacramental catechesis usually precedes the liturgical experience, an analysis of the components of mystagogy is in order. In a very real sense, mystagogia signals a radical shift of operation and perspective for catechesis and liturgy in contemporary parish communities.

A noted study on mystagogical catechesis in the early centuries of the church is helpful for our discussion. Enrico Mazza, professor of liturgical history at the Catholic University in Milan, has offered an analysis of the constitutive elements of mystagogy in his book *Mystagogy: A Theology of Liturgy in the Patristic Age.*[9] For our conversation we can distill Mazza's interesting discussion by identifying three components of mystagogical theology as it comes to us from the tradition: (1) mystagogy's referent is liturgical experience and its meanings; (2) typology is the constitutive interpretive device for the enterprise; and (3) mystagogia operates within a Platonic world view.

Mystagogia and Liturgical Experience

Mazza claims that mystagogy is a true and proper liturgical theology, the starting point of which is the actual experience of the liturgy. Whereas mystagogy has several meanings as it comes to us from the past, these meanings converge around the centrality of the liturgical experience. Thus, rooted in and connected to the liturgy, mystagogia is more than a simple explanation of rites. It is a mystagogical fashion of doing theology which seeks the understanding and pertinence of the liturgy for the community of faith.[10]

With this as his thesis, Mazza examines the mystagogical writings of Ambrose of Milan, Theodore of Mopsuestia, John Chrysostom, and Cyril of Jerusalem. The conclusion that Mazza draws from his analysis of this mystagogical tradition, in its various forms, is that mystagogical theology seeks to discover the meaning of liturgical experience in the life of the community, and to give the baptized the necessary motivation to live the sacramental life.[11]

Mazza attests to the fact that there are a variety of methods employed in mystagogical theology. All mystagogy, however, in one fashion or another, utilizes typology as the central genre of interpreting the liturgical rites.

Typology and Mystagogy

Mazza employs traditional definitions of typology to speak of mystagogia as a typological method of interpreting the liturgical event. Usually associated with the interpretation of Scripture, typology is a method of deeply reading the First Testament in order to discover within it the understanding of the mystery of Christ. In such a reading, the original context of the scriptural text is changed in order to see the fulfillment of all meaning in the event of Christ.[12] Thus, typology is "a hermeneutical method that is essential for the Christian reading of the Scriptures, for it ensures the unity of the two Testaments."[13] The foundation of this method is the Christian vision which seeks to make a single drama out of the various strands of scriptural texts received by the Christian communities.

Mazza continues to discuss that mystagogia is a typological interpretation of the liturgical life of the community. Thus, typology, having its origins in the reading of Scripture, is transposed to the reading of a sacramental experience. He is clear to state that this typological reading of the liturgy was borrowed from its original use of interpreting scriptural texts. Early mystagogues drew inspiration from this usage and found in the liturgy a new locus for theological reflection both on Scripture and experience.

Mazza concludes that the various forms of typology employed in mystagogia seek to accomplish one common goal: to proclaim the significance of the saving events of the liturgy by acknowledging the corresponding relationships that exist with these liturgical events of the church and the past mysteries of salvation history. Thus, mystagogy sought to proclaim the primordial mystery of God now clearly revealed in Christ. In the Christian sacrament, the events of the new dispensation are seen in the vastness of a continuity with God's activity in the past.[14] The mystery is known and the community's experience is enriched.

The Operational World View of Mystagogy

Throughout his text, and especially at the end of the discussion, Mazza is clear to state that the use of typology in mystagogy is to be understood within the context of the (neo)-Platonic world view. Only within this context can the apparent difficulties with typology be understood.[15]

Mazza summaries the master thread of Platonic thought by distinguishing the two levels of reality that compose it: the sensible, the world of images; and the intelligible, the world of ideas.[16] Within these two levels of reality all activity occurs and humans operate. These two levels of reality are related in ways of (a) *mimesis* or imitation, or (b) of *methexis* or participation, or (c) of *koinonia* or association, or (d) of *parousia* or presence.[17]

The Platonic world view thus is built upon an ontological theory of supra-celestial reality which is employed in philosophical discourse to explain the variety of sensible things and their dependence on the unifying principle of the Idea.[18] Participation in this eternal paradigm became the rule of all life.

Mazza demonstrates that the need of the early church writers to explain the reality of sacramental participation by way of typology was founded within this philosophical system and world view. Thus typology, which allowed for the reading of liturgical experience in continuity with past events and the mystery of Christ, found a reliable home within this horizon of being. Although claiming this interrelationship, Mazza is clear that early writers were not fully conscious of the ontological dimension of their interpretations.[19]

Insights from the Past

From our reading of Mazza's work, several observations can be made about mystagogia. First, mystagogia begins in experience. It assumes a vital and even a robust community ritual. In this, mystagogia is considered a method of doing theology, starting first with the experience of the event of the sacrament itself. Second, as a theology of liturgical experience, mystagogia is an interpretation of meanings. It employs a hermeneutical method to discover the pertinence of the liturgy for the community of faith and rereads the experience from the perspective of Christian belief, linking past and present in the mystery of Christ. Third, mystagogia as an interpretation of liturgy finds itself operating within a philosophical horizon. This world view offers a cohesiveness to the interpretation and gives focus to the meanings proffered in the mystagogia. The world view is perhaps the most significant component for understanding mystagogia, since it is the foundational lens for the interpretation and appropriation of the liturgical experience.

Summary

The tripartite framework of experience, interpretation, and an articulated world view seem important to maintain in the thinking of this author. They offer not only a mode of theological reflection from the tradition of mystagogia, keeping resonance with the past genius of this genre, but also are harmonious with the holistic approaches of theology in current practice. Nevertheless, while maintaining these basic components, the perspective of each must become more comprehensive for any authentic pastoral practice.

For instance, typology, as interpretation, limits meanings of experience and easily gives way to allegory. Such a method begs for an expansiveness of possibilities. Typology is grounded in a world view that is no longer commonly held in western culture and tends to remove the human community from the eventing of history. Contemporary philosophy and cultural studies have already made the turn to the subject, who operates as historical agent. These turns must be attended to in any theology, thus, too, in a contemporary mystagogy. Therefore, while retaining the centrality of liturgical experience in mystagogia, a renewed method of interpretation and a corresponding world view must be admitted. The expansion of these components for an authentic reading of liturgy seems necessary for a contemporary pastoral practice and affords the basic continuity of horizon with the past.

We turn now analogously to the liturgical writings of David N. Power to examine these traditional components of mystagogy. We do this in order to ascertain the contribution that Power's work can make to a contemporary and critical retrieval of this ancient liturgical theology and to the enriching of the components inherent therein.

A Mystagogical Inquiry

To assist our discussion, and to give focus to this analysis, we will give our attention to an article first published by Power in 1978,[20] and now republished in his collection of essays.[21] The essay is entitled "Let the Sick Call." This article is chosen from among Power's many articles because it clearly represents the consistent methodology that Power has been developing over the course of his writings. It clearly portrays his interpretation of liturgical experience as well as demonstrating his operating world view.[22] We first offer a synopsis of this article and then explore the starting point of the theology, its method, and its world view.

A Synopsis of "Let the Sick Call"

Power's essay on the sacrament of the anointing begins with the acknowledgement that contemporary western culture has difficulty facing human limitation, finitude, and death. It is from within this cultural matrix that it then proceeds to discuss the importance of the countersign of the Christian ministry to the sick. Speaking of the anointing as "ode to immortality,"[23] the article can be said to take three significant steps.

A first step, which it makes within the history of the tradition and sensitivity to language, is that an understanding of the sacrament must take into consideration many factors of interpretation. It is not sufficient to appeal simply to the doctrinal tradition of the church for an authentic theology of the sacrament of the anointing. The theologian and Christian interpreter must seek out the "tensive" or evocative quality of the tradition as it can be traced in texts, ritual activities, dogmas, and popular articulations. In this, the article grounds itself in contemporary hermeneutical theory and the richness of experience which emerges from imaginative discourse.[24]

The second and most interesting step for this author is the claim that the sacrament of the sick is not primarily about healing, forgiveness, or preparation for death. Rather, the sacrament centers "on the sick person who through this experience discovers God in a particular way and reveals this to the community. All the other factors enter in, but they are related to this as an organizing center."[25] What becomes obvious is the expansion of meaning that is given to the sacrament, centering it in the phenomenology of sickness within culture.

A third step, which the article makes in a strong way, is an appeal to the centrality of the human person and the power of metaphor and imaginative speech to enliven conversion and awaken the transformation of the human experience of sickness. Such language and experience call for the surrender of the self to the darkness of non-being, most clearly known in sickness. The human person, facing contingency in hope, can come to know the hidden face of Being.[26] Grounding this understanding of human subjectivity and reality in the philosophy of Heidegger and Ricoeur, Power waxes eloquently in translating his metaphysical claims into Christian symbols:

In Christian symbols, the sense of Being intuited through negation is expressed in the awareness of the Father as wholly Other,
experienced by the Son in his abandonment. In other words, the
via negationis of Christianity reaches its climax in the symbol of
the Father as totally other, to whom the Son's self-surrender is
imperative. The fullness of Being which occurs in that relation is
symbolized in the Holy Spirit, in whom the Father and the Son
are united. In the anointing of the sick there is an anointing in
the Spirit. This configures the patient to the Son and asks for
abandonment to the Father, or, in other words, the denial of being, which is at the same time a share in the fullness of Being. To
have reached that point is to have entered into "a silent and all-
absorbing self-surrender to response to God's gift of love."
There, metaphysical language has no more to say.[27]

The human person, carrying sickness in hope, becomes icon
of Christ, fully alive in the paradox of surrender. Standing in
the face of finitude with courage, the sick person is sacrament
of grace.

This synopsis affords us the opportunity to consider Power's mode of operation. We examine the moves and content of
this exposition of sickness and identify Power's field of theological experience, his method of liturgical understanding, and
his underlying world view. Since these are the traditional
components of mystagogia, we make this exploration of Power's work to discover how his writings can assist the contemporary retrieval of this discourse.

Mystagogia and the Work of David N. Power

As we noted, mystagogia is traditionally grounded in the liturgical experience of the community. The interpretive methodology of mystagogia was a varied use of typology applied to
this experience by early church writers. Typology, borrowed
from scriptural interpretation, allowed for the demonstration
of continuity of the Christian sacraments with the creative
mystery of God working in Christ. The significance of the Platonic world view was also noted. This world view informed
the uses of typology and gave them cohesiveness. From the
early writers we realized the importance of understanding the
world view as the necessary foundation for the understanding
of the method of mystagogy. Because of this importance of the

world view in the enterprise of mystagogia, we first examine the understanding of reality from which Power operates in his sacramental understanding of sickness.

Power's World View

A most telling paragraph reveals the core of the operating world view of this text.

> What is needed now is a metaphysical discourse which unearths the realities of being on the basis of the interiority of the subject. Raising the metaphysical question that basis is more likely to facilitate a discovery of the ontological possibilities opened up by imaginative speech and act.[28]

Beginning with this core insight, and drawing from the entire article, several things can be said about Power's horizon of operation. First, it is subject-centered, that is to say, it takes into account the operations of the human person as constitutive of reality. Imaginative, intelligent, affective, psychic, and volitional operations of the person are the foundations of understanding and the roots of being.

Second, there is the possibility of transformation within the subject. This allows the person a fuller participation in the human community and the very fabric of life. Transformation happens when possibilities are awakened in strong narrative, metaphor, and poetry. Such imaginative discourse reveals the sacramental potentiality of human existence in its contingency; thus sickness becomes the opportunity for the transformation of the subject into a witness of grace discovered in the depths of life.

In this article Power speaks of the clash of symbols that sickness evokes. The paradigm of passage is offered from the work of van Gennep[29] to explain the moment of crisis that sickness is. The operations of interiority can enter into and overcome the crisis of sickness, by inhabiting a new orientation in forgiveness, communion, and hope. In so doing the subject accepts the transformation of being and moves away from the side of non-being. Thus, transformation or conversion is a reorientation of the subject and the community into deeper participation with God. This happens in the authentic surrender of the self in hope.

A third dynamic of this world view is the strong appeal to the Christian involvement in history and society. The community which embraces the sick person becomes a counter-sign to the distorted cultural systems of denial and disfunction. Power's world view brings the sick person, who faces the contingency of life with hope, into a new eschatological relationship with others.[30] The image of sickness is given new meanings and the denial of weakness is reversed by the strength of the sick. The sick person, sickness, and those who are well, are all brought to a new reality. Thus, cultural perspectives on weakness are reversed and the denial of death swallowed up in victory.[31]

In summary, Power's world veiw[32] is grounded in the operations of the human subject, who participates in the contingencies of history and is open to conversion and to solidarity involvement in social transformation.

The Mode of Interpretation

As typology cohesively operated within a certain world view as a method for mystagogical theology, Power develops a methodology for his theology of the anointing that resonates with his world view of the interiority of the subject. His lays out this method within the context of contemporary hermeneutical studies with the emphasis placed on experience and the interpretation of texts. Attention to genres and the capacity of imaginative discourse are the cornerstone of this method.[33]

Power offers four postulates which he considers to govern the reading and interpretation of a theological tradition in general. (1) Texts are aesthetically received and must be listened to for their own particular resonance. Not all texts are of equal value as expressions of Christian hope. (2) Every piece of the tradition is related to the entire complexus of symbols, as words are to sentences, sentences to paragraphs, paragraphs to pages, etc. Attention must be given to this interrelationship for an authentic interpretation. (3) The social sciences can be useful for the interpretation of texts and traditions. These sciences can assist by enlightening the intended or unintended but actual meaning of a text. (4) Interpretation always involves the pre-understandings of the interpreter and depends in part on how far the meanings and images of the text evoke an answering imagination.[34]

This method operates with a keen sensitivity to language as meaning. For Power this keen awareness of meaning holds the clue to the ontological potency of a tradition. Thus he offers six rules to govern the inquiry into the tradition of the sacrament of the sick. These rules are offered in summary to demonstrate the holistic and comprehensive nature of this reading of the sacramental tradition. The rules which are offered in the article are an elaboration of the four hermeneutical principles outlined above, directed to the anointing of the sick.

In studying and offering a theology of the sacrament of the anointing several dimensions are required. (1) A conscious differentiation of types of texts, noting that all human discourse is not conceptual. The appreciation of various genres of communication allows for a rich gleaning of the meanings offered in these sources. (2) The reader of texts must stay alert to the on-going process of reading. Meaning is productive of meaning. Certain texts are classics and demand rereading; other texts become period pieces and are consigned to library shelves collecting the dross of centuries. (3) Texts express worlds. The reader is invited to come in touch with these worlds. New possibilities of being-in-the-world are opened up in the everyday reality of the text. This occurs by way of tensive symbols and plot. Thus, puny worlds and rich worlds of meaning are not to be confused. (4) The eschatological perspective of the reader plays a significant role in the appropriation of worlds discovered in the texts. This perspective both negates and affirms moments of reality. (5) Popular religious practices must be considered as having their own classic expression to be considered and interpreted. (6) The church's teaching and dogmatic tradition must be given proper place. The dogmatic tradition must be integrated and reread in context of the entire life of faith.

Several observations can be made about this method of doing theology. First, it is consistent with the world view that supports it because it attends to the nature of the subject who operates in a horizon of language, text, genre, interpretation, and meaning. Second, it is comprehensive in the range of texts it considers, broadening experience in a holistic fashion. Third, it allows for an on-going rereading of the tradition, seeing that every interpretation is historically limited and provisional. Fourth, it attends to the past and the future and calls for a conscious articulation of the reader's own perspectives of understanding. Finally, unlike typology which seeks for correspondence and imitation, this method looks for nuances and possible meanings that can invite participation and involvement in history.

The comprehensiveness of Power's method of theology brings us to the final component of our discussion: the starting point of this theological enterprise.

The Starting Point of the Enterprise

As we have seen, the starting point for the doing of a mystagogical theology is the actual experience of the liturgy, in most cases the initiatory rites of the community. Although Power's work on the sacrament of the anointing has this same starting point, he situates the actual ritual moment of the anointing within the widener meaning of the experience of sickness. He thus expands the field of liturgical experience.

In his essay, the experience that is taken into the theology of the anointing is multi-faceted and allows for the fullness of the meaning of sickness in human life. It includes these salient dimensions.[35] First, it is sickness itself, understood as the premier event of human contingency, culturally denied, that is considered. The experience of illness, with the hardships which it entails, is brought forward. Second, we see that the sick person and his or her relationships to the community is part of the experience of the liturgy. Third, guilt, sinfulness, hurt, separation, and anxiety, are considered as part of the experience which must be read and interpreted. Fourth, the healing process itself, expressed in oil, touch, and prayer are brought into consideration. Lastly, the community which is affected by the sick person's separation and withdrawal is part of the experience.

Consistent with his operative world view, Power offers the starting point of experience and gives these varied contexts for the reading and the interpretation of the sacrament. It would be safe to say that the experience of the sacrament is not only the liturgical moment and rites, but also the cultural, personal, and phenomenological matrix in which the sacrament is celebrated. All dimensions of the experience are to be taken into a theology of sacrament.

Interpreting this breadth of experience and employing the method outlined above, Power deepens the understanding of the sacrament of the anointing. A telling citation from his essay brings focus to his theology within his larger sacramental world view.

> All this suggests that in the sacrament of the sick what is at stake is the sacramentality of sickness itself, or perhaps it would be better to say, the mystery which is revealed in the sick person who lives through this experience . . . To suggest that the core of the sacrament of the sick is the sacramentality of sickness itself, is to take up a particular notion of sacramentality. The sacramental meaning inherent in Christian liturgy is not something added on to nature of human experience. It is drawn out of this; it gives and orientation to the sacramental potentiality which is one with corporeal nature and the human person's presence in this world as an integral part of it.[36]

In this reading of the sacrament of anointing, the sick person is anointed as Christ and prophet for the witness of faith to the community and to the world. Living in hope in the midst of human contingency is the new world which is proffered. This being the case, the understanding of sickness is transformed, and human experience is proclaimed as graced, containing within its limits the presence of mystery.

The experience offered for interpretation is thus cultural, ecclesial, personal, historical, linguistic, Christological, theological, and imaginative of possibilities of being. Power takes this as his starting point and interprets the tradition here, namely, in the comprehensiveness of human existence brought to faith in Christ. Ultimately, historical and cultural transformation, which this interpretation of sickness seeks to engender, is caught up in the hope of a human future beyond repression and denial.[37]

Towards a Contemporary Mystagogia:
Vectors of Discussion

Let us rehearse where we have been in this essay. Noting that mystagogia is of interest in the contemporary pastoral practice of adult initiation, we examined the dynamics and the components of the mystagogical homilies of the early church. Therein we claimed three constitutive components to this doing of theology: the starting point of liturgical experience, the typological method of interpretation applied to the liturgy, and a world view which supported this enterprise.

Our discussion moved us analogously to the work of David N. Power who does liturgical theology. Such a move was made so as to discover how in this author a way of enriching the perspectives of the past could be discovered for an authentic pastoral practice. In our analysis we find that Power does indeed operate out of an articulated world view, employs a specific method of interpretation, and considers a breadth of experience. In each, he articulates a broadening of past perspectives, while retaining the traditional components of mystagogia. The enrichment of these perspectives can be of crucial interest to those who would wrestle with angels, for from them several directions for discussion and development can be identified.

We are now at the point of offering these directions as vectors of conversation about contemporary mystagogia to which the work of Power can offer insight and focus. Three can be identified: mystagogia as theology rooted in experience and interpretation; the formation of mystagogues; and mystagogia as distance and appropriation.

Mystagogia Is a Theology Rooted in Experience and Interpretation

As claimed above, the retrieval of mystagogy must attend to the three components gleaned from the tradition: experience, interpretation, and world view. It thus remains faithful to the past, while seeking a new appropriation of the tradition in the present. It is also clear that neither the world view nor the typological method of interpretation are adequate in a contemporary cultural perspective. The starting point of this mystagogical theology, liturgical experience, continues to be necessary however, if we are to remain intelligent about what we do as Christians. While traditionally interpreting the experience of initiation, the mode of mystagogy can indeed be applied to any liturgical experience of the community by way of extension.

If we take mystagogy, therefore, to be a doing of liturgical theology which interprets sacramental experience within a certain perspective of reality, we clearly see the need for a sensitive broadening of meaning and an authentic horizon for the interpretation of the liturgical experiences of the church. What becomes obvious is the intense discipline that this mode of contemporary mystagogia can be. Mystagogia demands a converting consciousness, an openness to a variety of experience, a playful imagination, faithfulness to the tradition, clarity of purpose, and a social and compassionate involvement with the world on the part of the mystagogue. Thus, the interpretation of liturgical experience must be faithful to contemporary understandings of Christ, the church, the human person, and the evangelical concern for justice.

Mystagogues Create Mystagogia

Mystagogy therefore, while an activity of interpretation, is also the work of becoming a mystagogue, who inhabits a sacramental world in which the incarnate Christ is known at the very center of human contingency and struggle for dignity. Mystagogia may in this case be more than an application of a procedure to an experience, but rather, it becomes a way of being that lives in gratitude and surprise of the possibly possible in human history. The mystagogue becomes a poet, and the interpretation of the liturgical experience itself becomes a liturgy. To paraphrase an old image, mystagogues are made, not born. How such "making" happens needs to be taken up if mystagogia is to deepen in our communities. What is certain in this regard is that the making of mystagogues will be more than passing on a formula or learning a mystagogical drill. It will entail the inspiration of the artist.

Mystagogia Distances and Appropriates

Any retrieval of mystagogia must at the same time be a retrieval of the appreciation of knowing the godly presence
erupting in history and the excitement of discovering new
meanings in life. Ultimately, it seems that the role of mystagogia is to allow for the rereading of the liturgical experience by
distancing from the ritual, by exploring the meanings which
have been uttered, and by the appropriation of those meanings into the life of the person and the community.[38] The goal
of mystagogy is the creation of communities of compassion,
not the amusement of the faint of heart. In other words, mystagogy is a mode in which the community's liturgical experience
is appropriated at such levels of significance that the very nature of the community's being is transformed into the mystery
of Christ.

Towards the discussion and development of these directions, Power's work can offer a contribution of thought in significant ways. First, his liturgical theology attends to the comprehensive quality of experience and invites a sensitive
reading of it. His own writings begin this process and give
both a model and content for a contemporary mystagogy.

Second, the world view that he presents is an authentic one
which demands an ongoing critique of itself, lest it degenerate
into a narrow vision of reality, or a naive allegorization of the
liturgical experience. Authentic mystagogia and mystagogues
must know and attend to the world view from which they operate, thus becoming self critical to any narrowing of perspective.[39] True to the mystery of God's covenant in history, mystagogia can deepen the rupture of hope. Power's writings offer
a classic example of such scrutiny.

Third, the metaphoric twists and insights of Power's texts
awaken expansiveness of consciousness which is the birth-
place of the poetic. The weaving of words and the thinking
they invite make Power's texts more than dense prose. His
own writings can be read as a playful hide-and-seek with the
possibilities of experience. This is the genius which inspires
the formation of mystagogues, past and present.

A Concluding Mystagogical Meditation

To bring this essay to a fitting close, we turn now to a mystagogical meditation. What is offered is an interpretation of the Sunday eucharistic celebration in the Roman rite, as might be shared with a group of adult Christians. This mystagogy is inspired by the enriched perspectives offered by David N. Power in world view, interpretation, and starting place. It operates within the discussion offered above and can be seen as one moment within the mystagogical enterprise of the parish.

It begins with the experience of the gathered community at prayer and presents itself as a meditation, a homiletic piece, not unlike the genre employed by some early church writers. It is a mystagogical reading of the central liturgical experience of the church and an attempt at an appropriation of the vast mystery which we are.

The Word

The community gathers. The silence of prayer braces the assembly to enter into the word of hope, the ancient patterns of synagogue sound again, all are attentive. Weekly, stories weave patterns of meaning, worlds are spun forth from texts of the past. The memory of God's wonderful work is once again ignited. In metaphors, symbols, plots, and vibrant images, the alternative world of desire is given life, to trap the hearts of the hearers and make them burn. Indeed, the proclamation sets forth a new age, regenerated in Christ. Each week the powerful vision, each week a fresh glimpse of what life can be, the magnificent portrait of the reign of God is uttered, energized, and given force.

Those who have eyes to see and ears to hear clamor for the penetrating sense of God. The texts come from the future, while speaking from the past. The enlightenment of the ages is made present, and all will know a godliness of justice, dignity, and human liberation in hope.

God's word is the vitality made flesh in Christ, whose memory is the proclamation. The Christ surrendering in a magnitude of love to the Abba invites the new creation, where boundaries will cease, life will discover creative depths, and the possibility of peace will be born. Ah, such a world, known in hope, and inhabited by the weak ones who can embrace the cross of pain and the cross of life. Deeply living in this world is the alternative being without the falseness of distortion. All will be clear, light has been born. Seek deeply in word, into desire to know life.

The Blessing Prayer over Bread and Wine

The word-vision opens imagination and in deep affect of the heart invites us to a table. Bread and wine gather us in and invitation is given: Lift up your hearts. Let them melt and give praise. Praise, that act of dependency on the greater power. Praise, that act of surrender. Surrender into the world opened by the texts . . . to the new world of one bread, one body. In this surrender we find ourselves united with angels, saints, ministers of the gospel, popes, bishops, the living, the dead. The surrender echoes into cosmos, and we join with stars, moons, black holes, and the limits of the unlimitedness of time. All surrender to the possibility of the regeneration of the flesh. The cross bids surrender to the eons of a world well-nurtured, without distortion and suspicion of any kind. The last, first; the first, last. Such a new world demands surrender. And so to God's new age we unite with Christ, in Christ and through Christ. The community is alive in solidarity with the whole creation, the living sacrifice of praise.

Eating and Drinking Communion

All must be brought into the surrender. All is beckoned. Biology, heart, will, desire. Eating and drinking the death of the Lord, the Paschal Lamb. Eating and drinking rich activity, hearkening beyond to the moments of creation. Eating and drinking: nourishment, celebration, memories of family, refreshment, times of joy, dining, aliveness . . . ah, but at the depth of desires, eating and drinking, survival. Survival, the foundation of desire. Desire to survive . . . held to the fittest, racism, sexism, class struggle, ecology denied, survival of the Aryans, survival: held in eating and drinking, my food, power, earth, money, turf, to find oneself surviving at all costs. And yet we eat and drink to surrender all to the new world, which emerges in the surrender of survival into the desire to be communion, one body healed of division. Eating and drinking the death of the Lord, eating and drinking our own death. Survival by dying: Do you not know that you who have been baptized, have been baptized into his death? The death of the Lord we proclaim, eating and drinking. No one can go hungry. If we eat and drink and do not recognize the body, we eat and drink our own isolation, in judgment of a survival of no one. Eating and drinking, the survival of death. In the embracing of this at the entrails of our bodies, all will be made new, and the face of God will appear in the darkness of hope.

Eating and drinking communion, we survive, not alone, but Christ, in the twinkling of an eye, One.

Notes

1. In his article "Liturgical Praxis: A New Consciousness at the Eye of Worship," *Worship* 61 (1987) 290.

2. Contemporary attempts at mystagogia come under the rubric of "liturgical catechesis." For an overview of this form of interpretation, see Thomas G. Groome, "Catechesis: Practice and Theory," *Modern Liturgy* 18:9 (November 1991) 6-9; and Gilbert Ostdiek, O.F.M., "Examining Liturgical Catechesis," *Modern Liturgy* 18:9 (November 1991) 10-12.

3. David N. Power, "The Sacraments in the Catechism," in *The Universal Catechism Reader: Reflections and Responses*, ed., Thomas J. Reese, S.J. (Harper San Francisco, 1990) 113.

4. The reader need only examine the recent collection of Power's articles which trace his thinking through the years: *Worship: Culture and Theology* (Washington, D.C.: The Pastoral Press, 1990). Power develops an interpretation of the Tridentine doctrine of sacrifice in his own rereading of doctrinal texts from the Council of Trent. This seminal work offers a similar retrieval and cultural appropriation of the liturgical tradition: *The Sacrifice We Offer: The Tridentine Dogma and Its Reinterpretation* (Edinburgh: T. & T. Clark Limited, 1987).

5. *The Universal Catechism Reader* 125.

6. *Rite of Christian Initiation of Adults* (Chicago: Liturgy Training Publications, 1988).

7. Ibid. 151-152.

8. In the pastoral implementation of the rite for the United States, the statutes offered by the national body of bishops shape the development of the catechumenate. These statutes recommend that the

period of mystagogia be extended for an entire year, so as to allow for a more integral appropriation of initiation. See ibid. par. 24, p. 366.

9. Enrico Mazza, *Mystagogy: A Theology of Liturgy in the Patristic Age*, trans., Matthew J. O'Connell (New York: Pueblo Publishing Co., 1989).

10. Ibid. 6. Mazza indicates that while mystagogia as a method of theology is grounded in the liturgy, nevertheless as a term it often signifies various aspects of the liturgy. For instance, whereas today the term can signify catechesis and explanation of liturgical rites, among the early Greek writers it came to have many meanings. "In Cyril of Alexandria, Pseudo-Dionysius the Areopagite, and Maximus the Confessor, mystagogy means the performance of a sacred action; in Theodore of Studios, it means the liturgical celebration; in the writings of Origen and Chrysostom, it means Christian initiation in general. In Epiphanius, Gregory of Nazianzus, and Gregory of Nyssa it also means initiation to the eucharist. In both the Antiochene and the Alexandrian Fathers, it means the oral or written explanation of the mystery hidden in the Scriptures and celebrated in the liturgy. In Cyril of Alexandria, Diodorus of Tarsus, and Origen, for example, it means the explanation of the spiritual sense of the Scriptures; it can also have the broader meaning of an explanation of the figures contained in the Old Testament and fulfilled in the New, or of the eschatological realities announced by the church (as in Eusebius, Cyril of Alexandria, and Maximus the Confessor)" (Ibid. 1-2). In any case, mystagogia retains a connection with the experience of the liturgy and the proclamation of Scripture in the community.

11. See ibid. 165.

12. See ibid. 34-39. A typological reading of the First Testament continues to be employed in the current lectionary used by many Christian Churches. For a critique of this usage, see Gerard S. Sloyan, "Some Suggestions for a Biblical Three-Year Lectionary," *Worship* 63 (1989) 521-535.

13. Ibid. 34.

14. In the course of his analysis of mystagogical texts, Mazza introduces the role of allegory and relationship to typology. Although not easily distinguishable in the early centuries of the church, by the Middle Ages it becomes a method of reading the liturgical experience as a kind of drama of the life of Christ, presenting arbitrary, groundless, and often moralistic interpretations. He sees in this use of allegory the death of mystagogia in the church. See ibid. 13.

15. One of the significant problems with typological usage is the preempting of possible meanings which the First Testament Scrip-

tures can yield. The tendency to see all fulfilled in Christ can easily degenerate into a blatant anti-Jewish stance. See, for instance, Melito of Sardis, *On Pasacha and Fragments*, trans. and ed., Stuart George Hall (Oxford: Clarendon Press, 1979) par. 72-93, pp. 39-53.

16. See Mazza, *Mystagogy* 169.

17. See ibid. Here Mazza quotes from the work of G. Reale, *Per una nuova interpretazione di Platone*. He continues to quote an insightful passage from the text: "The sensible is a *mimesis* of the intelligible because it imitates it, though without ever attaining equally with it . . . To the extent that the sensible achieves its own essence, it *participates*, that is, shares in the intelligible (and, in particular, through the 'sharing' in the Idea the sensible reality is knowable)."

18. See ibid.

19. See ibid. 173.

20. David N. Power, "Let the Sick Man Call," *The Heythrop Journal* 16 (1978) 256-270.

21. See David N. Power, *Worship: Culture and Theology* 243-260.

22. The anointing of the sick seems to be of interest to Power because it demonstrates a unique challenge of interpretation in the limit situation of human contingency. See ibid. 244. He uses the anointing to demonstrate his understanding of imagination and symbolic play in liturgy in his book *Unsearchable Riches: The Symbolic Nature of Liturgy* (New York: Pueblo Publishing Co., 1984) 193-196. The author also takes the cue for the use of this article from Power's own use of the sacrament of the anointing in the example he offers in his commentary on the Universal Catechism.

23. Power, *Worship: Culture and Theology* 243.

24. See ibid. 244-247.

25. Ibid. 249.

26. See ibid. 256.

27. Ibid. 257.

28. Ibid. 253. This world view grounded in a subject-centered consciousness is not only the foundation of this article. One can easily discover it in all of Power's work. In the article "The Sacramentalization of Penance," in *Worship: Culture and Theology*, we read: "An increasingly common way of explaining the sacraments relates them to the symbolic structures of human existence. The human elements are integrated into sacramental structures, not merely juxtaposed to them. The *verbum fidei* transforms the human in its totality . . . Thus a broader symbolism, and human events themselves, are taken into the order of grace and symbolic meaning. The personal intentionality and desire experienced and stressed on these occasions is related to Christ through the liturgy" (pp. 217-218). One can also see it de-

veloped in the article "Human Odyssey in Christ," found in the same collection, pp. 85-101. Perhaps the most complete portrayal of this world view is elaborated by Power in his *Unsearchable Riches: The Symbolic Nature of Liturgy* 180-206.

29. See *Worship: Culture and Theology* 250.

30. See ibid. 255.

31. See ibid. 251.

32. The reader is also directed to Power's essay in this present collection. In this essay, he positions his world view within history, and argues against an understanding of providence which would place us in a supra-temporal world. In this he obviously moves from the Platonic understanding of reality of the early church writers.

33. See *Worship: Culture and Theology* 244.

34. See ibid. 244-245. The reader will no doubt see in this summary what will later be Power's philosophical treatise on the liturgical methodology presented in *Unsearchable Riches: The Symbolic Nature of Liturgy*.

35. See *Worship: Culture and Theology* 247-253.

36. Ibid. 249.

37. One might note that at the close of *Unsearchable Riches* (pp. 213-216) Power offers three criteria for estimating the truth of the sacrament. These criteria give summary to our discussion: fullness of language, adequacy to experience, and celebrations' relation to the orthopraxies of the gospel freedom and solidarity with the suffering.

38. This objective resonates well with the invitation Power offers for the need of a critical and expository form of theological reflection on the liturgy. This obviously needs the critical consciousness of the reflector. See *Unsearchable Riches* 173ff.

39. For instance, I have noticed in the United States a type of mystagogical process where the operative world view is the world of feelings. A liturgy that feels good is what matters. Such a world view, I claim, demands a critical renewal.

7

The Sacraments,
Interiority,
and Spiritual Direction

Stephen Happel

It is only with respect to the available common meanings of
community that the individual becomes [a self].
  B.J.F. Lonergan, "*Existenz* and *Aggiornamento*"

SPIRITUAL DIRECTION ASSISTS INDIVIDUALS IN EXPERIENCING THE JOYFUL
wisdom of the paschal mystery. The process should free both
client and director. But what is the measure for this interaction? To what models should we look to understand the experience? Do all Christians need "directors" to help them live
through the death-resurrection of Christ?

In what follows I have outlined the ways in which the
Christian sacraments affect the relationship of spiritual directors and clients. The first section describes the rhetoric of the
paschal experience. Next we look at various aspects of contemporary religious culture and the way in which spiritual direction has emerged as a part of the needs peculiar to our
modern culture. Then a more technical analysis shows how
the usual "inner" life of the believer is integrally embodied in
the public, "outer" language of the community. Finally, we

look at the ways in which the sacraments become the primary criteria for discerning the way of believers with God.

David Power's theology has always stressed the strength of worship for transforming the Christian community in its mission to the world. His research has argued that worship is an action that both reflects and changes the cultures in which it has lived. The external symbols challenge the church to encounter the triune heart of the world, whether it is through suffering its laments with compassion or celebrating the joy of its transformation. Christ Jesus is a prophetic memory who both provokes Christians into angry resistance at injustices and comforts them with legitimate hope for a different, more generous future.

Liturgical theology, therefore, need never be unrelated to the lives of Christians. Indeed, for David Power, the suspicion of symbols that marks our post-Enlightenment world is simply a way of purifying the tradition of inauthenticity and of preparing it to serve with greater fidelity. It has given the community the opportunity to recover the sermon on the mount's call to poverty of spirit. "Poverty is first the sense of possessing nothing, yet having all. It belongs only to those who know the meaning of gift."[1] To appropriate the gift, Christians must listen to the story, pour the waters, share the bread and the cup; through learning to share these simple worldly goods, they discover the unsearchable riches of the universe. This essay is a gift that was first given in conversation and shared in scholarship with a colleague and friend. It is returned with thanksgiving and praise.

The Paschal Mystery as a Public Process

Human suffering and physical evils are intertwined; like parasitic plants, one does not live without the other. The jungles of material and moral evils do not provide a passive environment in which we dwell, but they entangle and ensnare us, winding their ways into our psyches, banishing peace and fostering resentment.[2] Physical evils make us bear the weight of the world's unfinished goodness. The omissions of others force us to face human failure; our own choices not to build up humanity's store of values make us resent the ideals others put before us. In each case, our basic aversion to climbing outside ourselves keeps us from loving one another. We fear to welcome any other that might compete with our pleasure. Wrapped in our own narcissism, we worship the idols of our own making. The ultimate suffering of evil becomes the pain of isolation, a self-inflicted death to our innate power to love.

The opposite of such death is a love which draws us out of ourselves, a concern which attracts us at all levels of our experience: sensitive, intelligent, and evaluative. We experience the love of others and learn to love through being drawn by others and drawing others to the goods in which we believe. Finally, we wonder if we cannot bear even the suffering of others to help them sustain the pain caused by their lives. And as Christians, we believe this seemingly foolish project to be possible because God chose to carry the crucifixion of our existence in the innocence of Jesus.[3]

Suffering, then, may have many faces, but it always involves the felt imposition of the masks we would not wear if true desire were the first arbiter of life's roles.[4] At the center of Christian experience is the freely accepted suffering and death of Jesus. Letting go of our own suffering to accept the burdens of others authentically imitates his experience. To choose another's suffering liberates the other and declares one's own freedom at the same time. The social surd where narcissism, competition, and ironic distance hold sway give way to genuine altruism, collaboration, and interdependent love.

These brief remarks stress the fact that the mystery of our transformation in Christ is not simply a matter of purely personal import. The transformation of the physical universe from its ways of hurting, maiming, and destroying people is part of the moral responsibility of the converting community of believers. The bearing of others' burdens is at the heart of God's justification of humanity.[5] We are responsible for the aversion of physical evils as well as of moral evils.

But do we need personal spiritual direction to accomplish these tasks of interpersonal responsibility, social and economic change, and international reconciliation? Why (seemingly suddenly) do so many Christians feel the need to seek out spiritual guidance? Feeding the hungry, clothing the naked, and healing the sick are certainly not a religious discovery of our age. In fact, Thomas Merton asserted that only those with some special vocation or mission within the community might need direction—and that for a temporary period.[6] It is worthwhile, therefore, to explore some of the reasons why so many individuals find themselves needing professional religious guidance. We are not the only age to discover religious responsibility. What makes our era so centered upon the development of a Christian identity?

Contemporary Culture and the Search for Spiritual Guides

The suffering of Christ was not a private experience, negotiated between him and a guiding God. Not only was his death a public result of religious defiance, however indirect, but its meaning could only be understood within the available categories of Jewish life. This is true for the individual Christian as well. Each of us takes up our own suffering or accepts the pain of another in the context of public, communal experiences. The social stupidities and public malice of the world determine the shape and size of our sufferings. If we are to meet this suffering with charity and hope, our exemplars must be social and our paradigms public. Beyond the spirituality of my interior life with Jesus loom the concrete patterns of the world Christ died to save.[7]

In classicist Christian culture, public adherence to sacramental life was often the complete criterion of what it meant to be a Catholic.[8] Infant baptism and the duty to receive communion during the Easter season comprised the ordinary Catholic's badge of identity. Professionally religious clerics, monks, and nuns bore the ideal as their goals.

Now, however, the disintegration between the public life of the community and the personal appropriation of faith has reversed itself. The public life of the community has become an occasion for accomplishing some interior process. Yet, if the epigraph is correct, our interior religious lives are determined by the communal vocabulary of the Christian community where the sacraments educate us in bearing one another's burdens with love. The public language of the tradition is the house in which we learn the vocabulary of our Christian identity.[9]

There are no doubt many reasons why the ordinary spiritual life of Christians seems suddenly to require directors. I should like to focus upon several issues: (1) religious conversion; (2) the role of the guide in the shifting religious cultures; (3) the nature of our contemporary cultural shift; and (4) the development of a life-long catechumenate.

Religious Conversion. Older Catholics can recall a time in which "to be Catholic" meant the fulfillment of a number of practices, primarily external, which marked them as believers. These often included not eating meat on Friday, the obligation to Sunday eucharist at sometimes heroic expense (isolated vacation spots, business meetings which began early Sunday morning, and so on), fasting from all food and drink by midnight before eucharist, and a counselled confession before every communion. The stressed points of belonging were not extrinsic, but external.

Few Catholics fail to recognize that there has been a considerable change in the "rules for belonging." Recent homilies and instructions emphasize interior adherence, the personal enactment of external devotions, and the self-involvement required to "make" the external actions "meaningful" or even "true." It is one's conversion to Christ that has become the basis for loyalty to the community of believers. Witness to Christ, attachment to Christ's way now, more so than ever, founds the community of Christian desires. Diocesan rules for baptism, confirmation, and marriage make clear that education must precede celebration of the sacraments to "ensure" some personal commitment.

Role of the Guide. The interiorization of Christian life was never without external mediation. Over the centuries, we can see that what we label conversion, that highest form of our turning toward God, had quite incarnate forms. It is good to trace this well-known history in regard to our need for a "director" of that experience.[10]

At the earliest phases of Christianity, martyrdom was the ideal test for commitment. Loyal Christians disavowed some forms of civil life (the games and circuses, theaters, baths, military service, and so forth) for fear of contaminating their faith. Political and religious symbols were assumed to interpenetrate or interlock in struggle. "Friends of God," whose lives were about to be sacrificed, heard the sins and failures of their co-believers. But with the institutionalization of Constantinian Christianity, some Christians felt the need to flee what they saw as a lax identification between public life and private conversion. They chose to live in the deserts. Others followed them, seeking guidance by word and example. Hermitages and ascetic monasteries of men and women grew in the wilderness, especially in Egypt and Syria. The first experiences of religious and institutional dissonance raised the need for spiritual parents who could aid other Christians in the appropriation of their faith. What was a peer-peer relationship (however based upon admiration for holiness) in the absolution offered by friends of God became a parent-child dependence.[11]

Medieval monastic theology had as one of its primary emphases the personal appropriation of the word. The *lectio divina*, with its daily reading of the religious ancestors and the Bible, encouraged a meditative internalization of the texts which had founded the community. "I believe so that I might experience God," said Bernard of Clairvaux. The effectiveness of this experience depended upon the teacher-disciple relationship, as it evolved in one's monastic life. In partially Christianized cultures, monks became the resident teachers of detachment, a focus for conversion.

But as universities developed, piety and theory seemed to diverge—particularly to monks. Their opposition to the various entries of Aristotelian thought was not to the technical complexities wrought by philosophy, but to their inability to pray in Aristotelian categories. Without the aid of neoplatonist Augustinianism, metaphysicians neglected the life of the spirit. The divorce between symbols and thought threatened the marriage of religion and a particular culture which they loved and through which they arrived at God. Out of the perceived divorce of theory and piety emerged the late medieval mystics, anchorites, spiritual guides with their personal journals, revelations, and books of hours that provided the medium for religious interiorization.[12]

The response in Catholic circles to the Protestant reform produced the broadest emergence of confessors and directors of souls. The reformers changed the rites of Christian experience; within a hundred years, Trent modified the sacraments and solidified uniform practice. Since the crisis of the reformation was in many ways caused by the fact that the symbolic life of the community no longer educated, formed, or transformed, it became necessary to re-acculturate the Christian assemblies. The post-reformation period developed catechetical schools for Catholics, "introductions to the devout life" for believers, and new communities of pious men and women to translate the old symbols into a new personal and public framework.

With the rise of romanticism in the early nineteenth century, we have the final element in an emerging synthesis of spiritual guides. Affective attachment or detachment became a criterion for knowing the truth and/or value of things. The turn to the subject at the beginning of modern thought began to determine the appropriateness of Christian symbols. With the appearance of the techniques of counselling and eventually psychoanalysis, public methods of appropriating internal symbols were articulated.

The convergence should be clear: the emergence of self-appointed, officially delegated, and/or earnestly sought friends of God, counsellors, and "directors of souls" has occurred when it became necessary to provide negotiation between one cultural formulation of religious symbols and another.

Contemporary Cultural Shift. Our lifetimes have seen an acceleration from classicist culture to historical consciousness.[13] Classicist symbols are experienced as uniform all over the earth, eternally fitting the "nature of man," determining the "primitive" cultures into which they are inserted like seeds placed into a neutered soil, voided of its indigenous weeds. Classicist symbols stress their absolutely normative character, their abstract definition in perennial philosophy, and their efficacy in all situations. They have patriarchal roots.[14]

Historically conscious symbols, on the other hand, are quite empirical. Their origins occur in particular places and times; their applications relate to specifically different cultures from which they in turn learn something about themselves. Historically conscious symbols expect to be treated as events rather than as universal things. Where diverse practice in classicist symbols is thought to occur only rarely and in marginal circumstances of crisis, historically conscious symbols are diverse by nature, only analogously similar. The other is experienced as internal to the same; similarity only appears in a conversation of many voices.

It is in this context that the contemporary emphasis upon interiorization of the Christian message has occurred. Because Catholics have found it difficult to assimilate the new cultural context as it attempted to mediate transcendence, translators have appeared. Prior to the Second Vatican Council, spiritual direction was ordinarily relegated to the world of the regular confessor. "His" task was to help Christians to overcome their failures in relation to the established meanings of the symbols and to teach others how to transmit the traditional symbols to communities. As Catholics noted that the new symbols were either desiccated or demanded greater self-involvement, many felt the need to search out an interpreter, a negotiator who could assist them in exercising the claims to meaning in the new symbols or who could help them with the old ones that appeared opaque or confusing.

In earlier ages, such translators may not have been so necessary, not because Christians did not question their attachment to the symbols—but because there was only a single set of meanings seemingly incarnate in the symbols. Now various symbolic meanings clash—and many feel caught. It is conceivable, though unlikely, that were a new Catholic subculture to arise, stable and protected, the need for such translators might disappear. It is unlikely, of course, since spiritual direction in such a unitary context would be experienced as an "already-out-there-now" socialization, a religious imperialism strategically deployed to shape the religious freedom of the individual in a post-pluralist world. It is more plausible to believe that directors and clients would attempt to discover a religious world in which differentiated expressions could be integrated in a variety of ways.

The contemporary situation is, in fact, an extraordinary world. In another, more secure world, the pastor might offer the advice and direction necessary to interpret the word, to gather the community's ministries into prayer, and to challenge people toward conversion. But at present, role decisions (work, love, play, prayer), job decisions (marriage and friendship), leisure-occupations, and so forth require the mediation that will permit the identity of the person to be a publicly available *persona*. Caught in the multiple demands of familial, social, and political life, people experience the need to orchestrate the many selves which jostle for recognition in the public world.

Indeed, this inner pluralism becomes a special contemporary form of human suffering. Avoiding sheer passivity to events, while at the same time refusing controlling hegemony, marks the contemporary situation in which the divine Other is sought and found. The conflicts that emerge between public and private lives, among the various demands of the self thirsting for personal authority in the world become the material for negotiation of transcendence, both one's own and God's. The life of interiority becomes the root metaphor disclosing human and divine interaction. The decisions for a role within the larger history of the world and the flash-points of one's own development seem to require the weighing and testing which another voice can offer.

A Life-Long Catechumenate. In essence, what has begun to appear in this attempt to negotiate symbols is a new period of instructive interiorization for Christians. A fundamental shift in the focus for transcendence has occurred. This shift is not necessarily a turn toward the narcissism of the present, but a recognition that a self-consciously appropriated intersubjective interiority can be a symbol of the divine. In the developing history between a director and the client, intersubjectivity does not appear as a egoism for two, but as the confronting presence of a God who addresses both.

In the process the director helps clients find their authentic desires: in projects for the world; in affective attachment to, or detachment from, others; in moral enthusiasms and repulsions. These are the threshold situations of a person's interiority, the locations of religious desire. Thus, where Aquinas ended his treatise on sacraments with their analogous relationship to the life situations of believers, contemporary understanding of sacraments begins. The congruity or incongruity between the public and private exercise of the sacraments reveals the religious life of the individual.

Interiority is the creative fulcrum on which the Christian symbols and the public world are integrated. The sacraments are not just occasions through which personal religious life is promoted, nor are they the moral gestures through which God invites us into communion. They are not just an entry into a socialized religious tradition which announces fact and moral demand. They are the enactment of ongoing redemption within the believing community. Lukewarm sharing in the sacramental life of a community not only appears as an incongruous anomaly in an individual's life; the communitarian origin and confirmation of sacramental life are a requirement for determining, understanding, and fostering the religious life of Christians. The sacraments must always remain as the yearned-for expression of our religious desires. The public experience of communitarian life will have different meanings in the ongoing passages of people's lives. Even if we were to take some relatively simple schema of the adult journey,[15] the director and client would see that Christian life between fifteen and twenty-seven years will focus upon those liminal experiences which charter the individual's fundamental psychic, social, and religious talents. Between twenty-five and thirty-five, while the client is becoming his or her own person, the sacraments which relate to public tasks in the world or personal satisfaction in role identification (orders and marriage) should be significant. Between thirty-six and forty-two or forty-five, important mid-life transitions may take place such that earlier seemingly solid adult formulations may need reexamination.[16] If the more aggressive and constructing side of the personality has been dominant during the early to middle adult phase, the second half of life may well focus upon the more intuitive, reflective, and contemplative aspects of existence. The public symbols of communion, penance, and nurturing others will emerge as important. Between sixty and eighty, participation in eucharist may become part of the yearning for solitude and an authentic aloneness with the one significant other. The sacraments have different functions at various points of interiorization to the varying age groups. It is crucial to determine what engages the client in the exterior world; this means investigation of the public symbols of ecclesial attachment.

There have always been blatant examples of dissonance between the private life of believers and their public participation in ecclesial activity. Where the dissonance is due to ecclesiastical limits on participation (divorce and remarriage, non-ordination of women or married men, etc.), then it is crucial to develop the public roles that will enrich the particular community. But the problem becomes particularly acute when the director finds inauthenticity between public avowals and personal life. Every director can probably offer a case in which a believer claims a deep ongoing contact with God in prayer—only to discover in time that there has been and remains little external expression of this extravagant inner life. What seemed like an exciting conversation with God from the client's point of view was largely a self-deception in which ethical, sacramental and affective interpersonal success had disappeared.[17]

In closed environments in which both director and client are involved participants, this may become obvious early in the relationship. Then part of the question raised by direction turns on how much of the director's external observations can enter the conversation as explicit matter for discussion.

Generally, it seems that, although directors cannot help but function on what they know, it is unlikely that such knowledge can become explicit matter for discernment until clients begin to discover the dissonance for themselves. What is often the case is that the same conflicts that emerge in the public world, though studiously ignored by the client, will regularly appear in the relationship with the director. Such conflicts should be encouraged, or at least permitted to take place, precisely because they allow for the emergence of the interchange between "inner" and "outer" religious life to appear. No client, no matter how "contemplative," should assume that his or her inner life can be unrelated to the public life of the community, even if the community in this case is comprised of only a single individual—the director.

The Public Nature of Interiority

Becoming a subject in Christ is not a solipsistic enterprise painfully achieved only by silent, non-ritualizing hermits. On the contrary, conversion to Christ is always experienced as a tending toward God in the world. Even though the affective life of individuals has often become the place in which God is disclosed, that interiority is framed and shaped by familial history, education, fantasies and the experiences of submission and dominance.[18] Upon occasion, some individuals come to God through their intelligent self-discovery and a genuine eros of the mind about the world—but rarely. Philosophical mystics are unusual. It is also true that some find God in the painful moral heroisms of their lives; there is surely an ascent to God through praxis. But more often, the "stuff" of self-transcendence attempts to achieve a focused subjectivity, a self-recognized agency through which the client can negotiate the multiple demands of a complex world. Rather than adding another "ought" to their experience, believers hope that religion will enable them to get clear the world they already know so ambivalently.

The director must help clients discern where in their experience the authentic otherness of God appears. The goal of the religious journey is to love the other in and for the sake of the other, rather than for what that other can do for oneself. As a result, movement that always exceeds or transcends the present self is necessary. In any public situation in which there is posturing, that is, self-idolization (a cessation of the process of moving toward the other), then there is ambiguous motivation for loving God. The public life of individuals plays a constitutive role in their pursuit of God.

Conversion and Imagination

Throughout this essay, I have been describing the public character of the religious imagination.[19] There is no way to discern with clients their way with God without the public areas of imaginative formation that have constituted their identities. One must ask what images of God are operative—and exceptionally pious answers (such as "God is my covenant-maker") should make directors uncomfortable. Such answers might have conceptual content, but little affective energy; they may even have affect, but remain unconnected to sources in public discourse. Directors should listen to the way in which clients speak of parents, siblings, lovers, spouses, friends, and dependents. One should recall the words of Mauriac's Monsieur Calou: "If we want to know in what relation we really stand to God, we cannot do better than consider our feelings about other people."[20]

The investigation into a client's governing life images or root metaphors will disclose both the resentments whose angry reenactments block appropriation of love of God and the possible and probable avenues that encourage the journey forward.[21] Images are a liminal, tensive vocabulary of religious life. Part of the director's task is to help the individual see that it is not possible to "hide" from misreadings of the self and God by participation in ethical and sacramental deception.

Catholic Christians find their root metaphors in the sacraments—birth and belonging and their relationship to water, light, oil, and clothing; guilt and failure and its expression in a personal avowal of sinfulness and merciful embrace; a common table of thanksgiving with sinners, the less fortunate, the unwanted and ugly; the promise of affection to a beloved as a pledge of love to the community of believers; and so forth. In each case, we have public images of threshold—of possible change, revival, and/or doom. There are certain nodal points in every story, such that if one enters the room a certain way or closes the door in a particular fashion, the tale is directed in a particular way and not in another.[22]

The director's discernment of how clients share in these liminal metaphors permits their continuing authentic self-appropriation. The language discloses insight into the concrete dramatic patterns of human experience. Just as artists develop their style through various paintings, musical compositions, or choreographic works, so clients ascertain their religious style by celebrating sacramental life. The director carefully attends to what clients say and do in the life of the community, determining through this how God is speaking to the interiority of the individual.

The sacraments are the standard discourse of the community. By participation in their activities, Christians incrementally become what they enact in words and rituals. The sacramental symbols embody an orthopraxis that gradually accomplishes an interpersonal experience of agape. As a result, for the converting community, they also set forth the dissonance between the melodies of religious life and the eschatological harmonies yet to be realized.[23] Clients who feel paralyzed between guilt and duty will find the public life of the church judgmental and demanding, rather than merciful and encouraging. Testing how Christians feel their way through the sacramental thresholds is a constitutive part of spiritual direction.

The Inner Word of Love and God's Revelation

One way of explaining how the sacraments and spiritual direction are related is to see the nuanced description one contemporary theologian provides. Bernard Lonergan has reflected on what Christian tradition has called the "inner" and "outer" word.[24] The theological notion dates from Justin Martyr (d. 165) who used it to distinguish the way in which the word of God was immanent in the divine from eternity, yet offered God to humanity "in these times and in various ways" (Heb 1:1). Augustine developed the notion into a human analogy for triune life revealing itself in time and celebrating divine glory. Aquinas provided the Aristotelian epistemological and metaphysical framework to clarify what it meant to speak of this pattern in human beings as an image of God.

When Lonergan uses this distinction to specify his notion of language, personal appropriation, and the presence of God in religious experience, it should not be assumed that he means the words as though "inner" meant the "already-inside-me-now-real" feeling and the "outer" the "already-out-there-now-real." Expression in words and gestures is not a secondary adaption of some interiorly determined concept. Languages are not external tools "ready-at-hand" to the inwardness of mind.

The interpenetration of linguistic expression (the "outer") and the knowing insights (the "inner") invests our words with meaning.[25] Lying is possible because speakers are reserving to themselves "other" concepts or judgments with which they could supplant the deception.[26] Words have their meanings not simply through formal comparison of independent, individual signs, but through their function within discourse in which subjects and predicates are mutually implicated. The basic unit of language is actually the sentence.[27] We spend our lives hunting for the sentences which will disclose the world. "What is known, what is meant, and what is said, can be distinguished; but the distinctions point merely to differences of aspect in what inevitably is the same thing."[28]

When Lonergan states that linguistic expression is instrumental, he does not mean that language is a secondary invention—expendable, unnecessary for understanding oneself or the world or God.[29] Rather, expressions are either adequate or inadequate to communicate the subject matter. Through comparison with previous expressions, one becomes clear whether the present language embodies the central meanings well or poorly. Through adequation with the tradition of language, one's present words take on their credibility or incredibility. One handles the instrument better or worse depending upon one's intellectual development, which in its turn is incarnate in its linguistic expression.

Why then postulate an "inner word"? Why not speak of our life in language? There are two reasons. The first is the recognition of deception. People lie, and they do so not by mistaking what they mean in their words, but by choosing to "hold back" what they know to be the case from those who have a right to know it and can understand its truth. This must mean that there is some inner intention which can be distinguished, but not separated from external communication.

But secondly, the inner word is more. It is not a conceptually formulated word which linguistically precedes our verbal sentences. We are not limited to the sedimented speech which our native tongue gives us. We discover things and ideas; we probe beyond what others have said and create new words to communicate our insights. If lying makes it clear that there must be some inner self-possession, then discovery of the new sharpens the notion. The "inner word" is the very operation of mind itself. Prior to our gestural or verbal expression, there is the preconceptual act of the mind itself which is the condition for all expression. This interior world is not available except through expression, for we would not know that objects we perceive had an "inside" if they did not originate some self-expressive behavior. But the "inside" is an ontologically prior condition, an originating self, the one who quests, who searches for truth, value, and God. Expression is not an optional adjunct to interior life. To say that we are limited to our ready-made expression would be to neglect the possibility and fact of human discovery, the reality of the new which in turn begins to appear in language.

Just as in the case of lying in which we must postulate the possible non-coincidence of what I mean to say and what I do in fact say, so in new discoveries we must recognize the difference between an expression that is odd, ill, or genuinely illuminating. In each case, the pivot that distinguishes the healthy discovery embodied in a new expression from the crazy formulation or the deceptive from the authentic self-expression is the operation of the inner word. It is the activity through which expression comes to fruition. When this intentionality is satisfied, then we cease questioning conceiving, judging and deliberating.

But if this seems too technical, too philosophical for our purposes, let us look at the religious reference for the union of the inner and outer word. There is one point in which the inner development of love expresses itself perfectly in outer life, where God's love discloses itself completely in external words and gestures—in Jesus of Nazareth. Here is the true interpenetration of inner and outer word; between question, judgment, and expression; between desire for value and right action. In Christ's sinlessness and preaching, there is never a dissonance between public and private existence. Christ is precisely the authentic word, the external self-communication of the inwardness of God's truth and love and the public embodiment of God's opaque compassion for creation. Jesus is neither deceptive nor crazy in his announcement of the new. In him the inner words of love are disclosed in outer words; and in an outward human historical development, the authenticity of inner intentions becomes manifest. By comparison, ordinary Christians must struggle for the same authenticity.[30]

In Aquinas and Lonergan, the existence of the world of interiority was recognized in the context of a religious proclamation and faith. Jesus's holiness of will and sinless truth of intellect were gratuitous, sheer generous gift. This truth and love, so perfectly expressed, need not have been spoken. The word that God speaks in Christ might have remained forever within the divine. If it had, we human beings would have been left with only our finitude and guilt, our incomplete expressions and deceptions. The only way in which we know the truth about ourselves, that we can be good and holy, is because God has chosen to reveal the divine self, to utter an "outer" word. Thus inner and outer are intertwined in our faith in such a way that they cannot be separated. We need the public, exterior, created expressions to know the "interior" disposition of God toward us and the power to tell the truth and to love, gifts that are ours by birthright and sold into sin.

In sum, this lengthy analysis states that we cannot understand our inner religious life without external expressions for both philosophical and theological reasons. Authentic religious experience has its issue in ecclesial expressions, and the church's public acts disclose the religious style and identity of a community. The genuine barometer of that life is the sacraments. They are the place in which the inner word is awakened to what is authentically Christian; they are the test as gift within the community for determining both self-deception and sickness. Those who love God without loving their neighbor cannot claim they do the former. The community provides a developing expression, proportional to the growing inner life of love and truth. The appropriate expressions for this ongoing interior transformation are the Christian sacraments.

How Do We Know We Are Bearing Someone's Burdens?

No one loves anyone "all at once." Just as betrothal, wedding, honeymoon, and marital life follow the initial *coup de foudre*, so in loving God, there emerges a discernment of actions and words. In this article I have wanted to find the basic role for the sacramental symbols in spiritual direction, the quotidian expression of our love for God. Too often, direction is seen and experienced as a private counselling relationship, separated from the common life of the church.[31] But loving God cannot be accomplished by focusing solely upon one's own "private" feelings about God. These are always intertwined with the public language of the community.

Spiritual directors will spend time helping clients understand their intimate loves, whether familial, friendly, or sexual. There must be the study of clients' philanthropy and ministerial generosity; they can so easily be, in professional caregivers, a sign of guilty resentment or anger at personal powerlessness. Although it is true that the love for God must be differentiated from other loves, that love will appear most clearly as the inner word of the public loves which encompass a client's life.[32]

A critical touchstone of these loves will remain the sacramental life of the clients' community. How does the client share the eucharist? What does public prayer mean to the client? Does the client seek public opportunities to express the desire to pray? Perhaps there is an avoidance of communitarian religious expression. Why? The sole criterion for authentic religious development is not interior feeling. Such introspection can simply cater to cultural narcissism. More concretely, the gestural and verbal dimensions of the sacraments provide the liminal language for a developing life with God. Baptism and its metaphors of belonging, cleansing, and strengthening bring people into contact with both the religious and non-religious meanings of water and oil. How do we treat the waters made holy by Christ's passage through the Jordan river?[33] Do we know how to cleanse the wounds of sin in our world? The symbols of eucharist (the community of the Body, the sign of peace, bread and wine, the stories of the tradition) ask clients to reflect upon their own ongoing insertion into Christian charity, about their ability to coexist with diversity and otherness.[34] Does the offering of bread at the table of the Lord recognize the responsibility for offering one's food to the needy? Does Jesus' self-commitment to the fragile crumbling bread of passover and the bloody wine of sacrifice contrast with our need to memorialize ourselves in consumerist acquisition and monumental self-elaboration? And what of the honest avowal of sin? Can we face another, the friend of God who is a sinner as well, and admit not just mistakes of judgment but offenses against our beloved?

The human suffering which rummages through the interiority of our lives is never isolated quiet desperation. This is the case for two reasons: (1) in the sacramental life of the community, believers assume the burdens of each other's lives through accepting the suffering of Jesus' story; and (2) when this interconnected story is shared with the director, Christians permit one other person to share that suffering in an intimate fashion. Of course, the director's understanding is not a substitute for the collaboration in redemption which occurs at the public level. Rather, the director is there to help the individual negotiate the "worldly" life of the believer.

As the director determines how clients "suffer" the rites

themselves (dutifully? joyfully?) from time to time, he or she learns how Christians are growing through their presence to the "outer word" of God's love. The pain which many feel is measured, controlled, and expressed in the experience of the sacraments. The ability to "take on" the various narrative structures of the community's life is the practical religious competence which clarifies for the director the stages of religious growth. As individuals pass through ritual experiences, they distinguish their own roles within the church.[35] As they gradually assume responsibility, find themselves cleansed by the sometimes abrasive events of public prayer, they relate their own stories of suffering to those of Christ and the community. Through the ongoing relationships of ritual, Christians discover the means whereby and the fact that they do love another.

Lonergan remarks about human love that two people know that they are in love "by making the discovery that all spontaneous and deliberate tendencies and actions regard the beloved."[36] Loving God takes place in the same way; or so C.S. Lewis would have it in one of his stories for children:

> And don't mention it to anyone else unless you find that they've had adventures of the same sort themselves. How will you know? Oh, you'll "know" all right. Odd things, they say— even their looks—will let the secret out. Keep your eyes open.[37]

By discovering the common concerns, the direction of common desires for the world, the value of some common judgments, and the world's need for redemption, we become aware that we are in love with God. In participating in the sacraments, we learn God's concern; we suffer God to shape us, without worrying about the cost. Bearing the "burden" of ritual should mean carrying the pain of our brothers and sisters; sharing the life of the community should become carrying the suffering of Jesus who bore our pain.

My hope is that the relationship of sacramental life, the role of the spiritual director should no longer appear extrinsic or simply parallel to some internal spiritual process. Neither director nor client should assume that the only materials for discussion are the client's emotions, the quality of the directorial relationship, or the private prayer life of the client. A great deal more is entailed by religious self-appropriation.

Bernard Lonergan's understanding of religious experience shows us how serious thought about our religious identity can contribute quite practically to issues facing the contemporary church. His understanding of the relationship between interiority and communal religious expressions can indicate how the sacramental world of our common religious meanings has an intimate role to play as an interpretation, a diagnosis, and a fulfillment of our religious life.

This may help understand how our Christianity can find a new home in a quite different world than the Jewish and Graeco-Roman worlds in which it was born, or the medieval, renaissance, and reformation worlds in which it evolved. The previous common sense and former theories of Christian experience require a new basis in the interiority of the human subject—but that subject as public, working and loving in the world. Spiritual direction uses this basis to "link the experience of the transcendent with the world mediated by meaning."[38] In this ongoing process are the warrants for authentic religious knowledge, the conditions which must be fulfilled to make discernments between self-deceiving victimization and generous self-giving, between mental illness and the authentic discovery of God. The only way directors can help clients ascertain whether they are in contact with the originative love of a triune God is if there is some shared sacramental experience of how both God and humanity participate in a community of believers.

Notes

1. David N. Power, *Unsearchable Riches: The Symbolic Nature of Liturgy* (New York: Pueblo Publishing Co., 1984) 209.

2. For the basic distinction between moral and physical evils, see Bernard J.F. Lonergan, *Insight: A Study of Human Understanding* (New York: Philosophical Library, 1967) 666-668; for some comments, see Stephen Happel and James J. Walter, *Conversion and Discipleship: A Christian Foundation for Ethics and Doctrine* (Philadelphia: Fortress, 1986) 29; and George Carlson, "Spiritual Direction and the Paschal Mystery," *Review for Religious* 33 (May 1974) 532-541.

3. See William P. Loewe, "Lonergan and the Law of the Cross: A Universalist View of Salvation," *Anglican Theological Review* 59 (1977) 162-174.

4. For Sebastian Moore's current interpretation of the way in

which desire is fundamental in the quest for salvation, see *Jesus: The Liberator of Desire* (New York: Crossroad, 1989) 9ff., 51ff.

5. Thomas Aquinas, *Summa Contra Gentiles*, 158,7; see Bernard Lonergan, *De Verbo Incarnato* (Thesis decima quinta ad decimam septimam), 3d ed. (Rome: Pontificia Universitas Gregoriana, 1964) 510-513.

6. Thomas Merton, *Spiritual Direction and Meditation* (Collegeville: The Liturgical Press, 1959) 13.

7. Matthew Lamb, *Solidarity with Victims: Toward a Theology of Social Transformation* (New York: Crossroad, 1982).

8. Stephen Happel, "Conversion: From Common Problem to Common Resolution," *Ecumenical Trends* 10 (Nov. 1981) 155-158.

9. Elinor Shea, "Spiritual Direction and Social Consciousness," *Way Supplement* 54 (Fall 1985) 30-42; see the minimal social context in Robert Morneau, "Principles of Spiritual Direction," *Chicago Studies* 26 (Aug. 1987), 135-136.

10. Basic data may be found in Kenneth Leech, *Soul Friend: The Practice of Christian Spirituality* (New York: Harper and Row, 1980).

11. See Raymond Studzinski, "The Minister of Reconciliation: Some Historical Models," in *The Rite of Penance: Commentaries*, ed., Nathan Mitchell (Washington, D.C.: Liturgical Conference, 1978) 50-61; note that a parallel argument is made in the emergence of a hierarchical model of church from the "discipleship of equals," in Elisabeth Schüssler Fiorenza, "The Biblical Roots for the Discipleship of Equals," *Journal of Pastoral Counselling* 14 (1979) 7-15.

12. For a splendid collection of edited texts and commentary, see Elizabeth Alvilda Petroff, *Medieval Women's Visionary Literature* (New York: Oxford University Press, 1986).

13. See Happel-Walter, *Conversion* 85-101; and Stephen Happel, "Classicist Culture and the Nature of Worship," *The Heythrop Journal* 21 (1980) 288-302.

14. I have not sufficiently stressed the gender-determined issues in classicist culture. See Marjorie Procter-Smith, *In Her Own Rite: Constructing Feminist Liturgical Tradition* (Nashville: Abingdon, 1990).

15. See Daniel Levinson et al., *The Seasons of a Man's Life* (New York: Ballantine, 1978); and Carol Gilligan, *In a Different Voice: Psychological Theory and Women's Development* (Cambridge, MA.: Harvard University Press, 1982).

16. See Raymond Studzinski, *Spiritual Direction and Midlife Development* (Chicago: Loyola University Press, 1985).

17. William A. Barry and William J. Connolly, *The Practice of Spiritual Direction* (New York: Seabury, 1982) 81-82.

18. William M. Shea, "Imagination and Prayer: Outline of a Theo-

ry," *Review for Religious* 39 (1980) 743-44; see John W. Dixon, Jr., "Form and Spirituality: The Role of Art in the Inner Life," *Studies in Formative Spirituality* 4 (Fall 1983) 33-46.

19. This essay interconnects at various points with two previous analyses. See Stephen Happel, "Whether Sacraments Liberate Communities: Some Reflections upon Image as an Agent in Achieving Freedom," *Lonergan Workshop*, V, ed., Fred Lawrence (Chico, CA: Scholars Press, 1985) 243-261, and idem., "The Sacraments: Symbols That Redirect Our Desires," in *The Desires of the Human Heart: An Introduction to the Theology of Bernard Lonergan*, ed. Vernon Gregson (New York: Paulist Press, 1988) 237-254.

20. François Mauriac, *The Woman of the Pharisees*, trans., Gerald Hopkins (New York: Carroll & Graf, 1988) 169.

21. See Paul Ricoeur, *Interpretation Theory: Discourse and The Surplus of Meaning* (Fort Worth: Texas Christian University, 1976) 63-69; and Power's use of root metaphor in *Unsearchable Riches* 154-158.

22. Roland Barthes, "An Introduction to the Structural Analysis of Narrative," *New Literary History* 6 (Winter 1975) 2, 237-272, esp. 266ff.

23. Stephen Happel, "The 'Bent World': Sacrament as Orthopraxis," *CTSA Proceedings* 35 (1980) 88-101.

24. Bernard J.F. Lonergan, *Verbum: Word and Idea in Aquinas*, ed. David Burrell (Notre Dame: University of Notre Dame Press, 1967) 1-46; idem, *Method in Theology* (London: Darton, Longman & Todd, 1971) 70-73, 86-90, 112-115; Frederick Crowe, *Theology of the Christian Word: A Study in History* (New York: Paulist Press, 1978) 104-43; see the questions raised by Thomas F. Torrance, "The Function of Inner and Outer Word in Lonergan's Theological Method," in *Looking at Lonergan's Method*, ed., Patrick Corcoran (Dublin: Talbot Press, 1975) 101-126.

25. Lonergan, *Insight* 554.

26. Sissela Bok, *Lying: Moral Choice in Public and Private Life* (New York: Pantheon, 1978) 13-31.

27. There is a parallel between the way Paul Ricoeur focuses upon the sentence in discourse (see *The Rule of Metaphor: Multi-Disciplinary Studies of the Creation of Meaning in Language*, trans., Robert Czerny with Kathleen McLaughlin and John Costello [Toronto: University of Toronto Press, 1977] esp. 65-172 and a briefer statement in idem, *Interpretation Theory* 6-23) and the way Lonergan focuses upon judgment (see *Insight* 271-316), though there appear to be differences concerning the primordial nature of language and in the conditions necessary for predication. For both, however, the issues include "how" language and judgment refer to the way the world is.

28. Lonergan, *Insight* 555.

29. Ibid. 556. In "Whether Sacraments Liberate Communities (see note 19 above), I have tried to show how "image" is primary for Lonergan and how the experience of language is equi-primordial with the operation of consciousness.

30. Lonergan, *Method* 119.

31. This is not so true of the classical manuals in the field of spiritual direction in this century. See, for example, Reginald Garrigou-Lagrange, *The Three Ages of the Interior Life: Prelude of Eternal Life*, vol. 2, trans., M. Timothea Doyle (St. Louis: Herder, 1947) 263: "A soul that is increasingly incorporated in our Lord by Holy Communion should in its turn serve somewhat as the bread of the souls which surround it, following the example of our Lord who wished to be our bread." See also Jean Leclercq, *The Interior Life*, trans., Fergus Murphy (New York: Kenedy, 1961) 3-6, 46-93; Louis Bouyer, *Liturgical Piety* (Notre Dame: University of Notre Dame Press, 1957) 251-252. However even in Barry and Connolly, *Spiritual Direction* 53, 60, 69 the public life of the client is only a situation for discovering the "privileged places" for becoming aware of the "emotional facts" of interior life.

32. See this principle applied to the way personal prayer is determined by the social context in Stephen Happel, "The Social Context of Personal Prayer in Seminaries," *Review for Religious* 39 (1980) 846-854; George Schemel and Judith Roemer, "Communal Discernment," *Review for Religious* 40 (1981) 825-836.

33. Power, *Unsearchable Riches* 178-180, 206-210; David L. Kertzer, *Ritual, Politics and Power* (New Haven: Yale University Press, 1988) esp. 77-124.

34. See Bernadette Roberts, "The Eucharist, a Christian Path," *Studies in Formative Spirituality* 8 (Nov. 1987) 343-353; Tissa Balasuriya, *The Eucharist and Human Liberation* (Maryknoll: Orbis, 1979).

35. See Mark Searle, "The Pedagogical Function of the Liturgy," *Worship* 55 (1981) 332-359; Roger Grainger, "Sacraments as Passage Rites," *Worship* 58 (May 1984) 214-222.

36. Lonergan, *Insight* 698.

37. C.S. Lewis, *The Lion, the Witch and the Wardrobe* (New York: Collier, 1970) 186.

38. Lonergan, *Method* 114; see Hilda Montalvo's use of Lonergan's transcendental imperatives in "The Spiritual Director as Mediator of Meaning," *Spirituality Today* 40 (Summer 1988) 128-134.

8

Devotio Futura:
The Need for
Post-Conciliar Devotions?

Regis A. Duffy, O.F.M.

THE DISAPPEARANCE OF MOST DEVOTIONS AND PARALITURGICAL SERVIC-
es in the post-conciliar Roman Catholic Church in the United
States has often been noted, and sometimes bemoaned. The recent spate of writing on popular religion also raises the question of whether devotions are part of a larger sociological process. In contrast to *devotio moderna* (the sixteenth-century call
to personal reform through Christian inwardness), I employ
the term *devotio futura* to indicate a liturgically grounded piety
which also finds personal and ecclesial expression in non-
liturgical prayers and actions. For the sake of clarity, I use the
term "devotion" in its singular and plural forms. Devotion is
understood here as the affective dimension of faith. Spiritual
writers characterize feelings of gratitude, wonder, love, and so
on as components of certain types of prayer and meditation
(e.g., the affective dimension of the Ignatian exercises). Such
writers also insist on the deepening commitment to the gospel
life as a test of genuine devotion.

Some of this meaning carries over into the plural form of
the word. Devotions or popular devotions usually refer to

prayer forms which foster affective attitudes and which may give the impression of a more efficacious response to personal needs than liturgical prayer: "As contrasted with the official liturgy of the times in which they were composed, they [devotions] express, cater to, and foster devotion—precisely the religious feelings and affections disenfranchised in the official services."[1] There are instances where private devotions have eventually found liturgical expression (e.g., the feast of the Sacred Heart).

The purpose of this article is to ask what ecclesial advantages there might be to the restoration of devotions in the American Catholic context. This question will be developed in several stages. First, a comparison of the contemporary American situation with the teaching of Vatican II will be made. A second section will sketch some of the historical background of the American church on the subject of devotions. A final section will offer some observations on the possible ecclesial advantages and dangers of a *devotio futura* in the American situation.

The Contemporary American Scene

In the American Roman Catholic Church of the pre-Vatican II era, popular devotions were forms of prayer that seemed to provide some immediate access to God in contrast to the removed character of the Latin liturgy. Often enough a devotional rather than a moral type of preaching was heard at novenas or a holy hour. Every American parish usually had an ongoing Miraculous Medal novena, as well as benediction and holy hours as a regular feature of their schedule. October and May were occasions for increased Marian devotions (e.g., rosary and benediction, May crownings, etc.), and June brought the Sacred Heart novena. Some devotions were privately celebrated in a public liturgy (e.g., the first Fridays and later, the first Saturdays). Lenten devotions usually included the stations of the cross or a sermon and benediction.

In the aftermath of Vatican II, such parish devotions were a less prominent part of parish life or seem to have disappeared. While it appears that most parishes no longer offer popular devotions to the extent that they had before Vatican II, private devotion to the saints is still surprisingly vigorous. The recent

Gallup survey of a broad spectrum of practicing and non-practicing Catholics noted that the rosary remains a more popular form of religious expression than reading the Bible, attending a prayer meeting or a spiritual conference, and that the recitation of the rosary has increased from thirty-six percent (1977) to thirty-eight percent (1986).[2]

The Notre Dame Study of Catholic Parish Life (NDS) questioned its participants (non-hispanic practicing Catholics) as to whom they prayed. Not surprisingly, sixty-three percent of the respondents prayed to Jesus, forty-six percent to Mary, twenty-eight percent to the Father or to the Lord, and six percent to St. Jude (followed by St. Joseph and St. Anthony). When this data is viewed in terms of age and parish involvement, the results are more helpful: "Younger parish-connected Catholics are far more likely to address the Father, Son, and Holy Spirit alone; less than a majority pray to Mary or a saint."[3] Older Catholics are more likely to pray to Mary and the saints in addition to a member of the Godhead. Even more revealing is an analysis of the same data according to regions of the country. Catholics of ethnic parishes of the Northeast or the upper mid-West are far more likely to address Mary and the saints than Catholics south of the Mason-Dixon line or west of the Mississippi River. Further, in areas where Catholics predominate, devotion to Mary and the saints is more likely than in areas where Protestants are in the majority.[4]

The council itself had not forbidden such popular devotions, but did mandate that they conform to the norms of the church, should harmonize with the liturgical seasons, and should accord with and in some way derive from the liturgy, and lead the people to it.[5] But as Paul VI noted some years later, this conciliar guideline has been difficult to apply, especially in regard to devotion to Mary. He points to two attitudes in pastoral practice that frustrate the direction of Vatican II on this matter. Some have completely suppressed popular devotions and have thus created a vacuum. A second group combines popular devotions and services of the liturgy into a "hybrid" celebration (e.g., parts of a novena incorporated into the eucharistic celebration). The result is a liturgy that is subordinated to popular devotions. Paul VI reiterates the instruction of the council in this way: "Wise pastoral ministry sets out clearly and explains the inherent nature of liturgical services; it extols and promotes popular devotions in such a way as to adapt them to the needs of individual ecclesial communities and to direct them toward contributing to the liturgy."[6]

But Paul VI does not limit himself to warnings about mistaken pastoral practice in regard to Marian devotions. He proceeds to give an excellent example of how a devotion might be celebrated within the larger mission and liturgy of the church. Marian devotion directly touches on the ecumenical concerns of all the churches. While the Orthodox have always retained this devotion and the Anglican communion has given a place to Mary in its theology, serious differences between the churches remain on the question of Mary's role in the work of salvation and thus, the type of veneration that should be given her. With great sensitivity he also notes the feminist critique of some attitudes toward Mary as woman. In response to these concerns, Paul VI offers a practical guideline: "As the Church surveys the long history of Marian devotion, it rejoices at the correspondence between the cultus and its own era."[7] In other words, each cultural and historical period expresses its devotion in ways appropriate to its situation. Ultimately, a true devotion to Mary should move Christians to a more committed gospel life.[8] These last two remarks provide guidelines which we will return to shortly.

Devotions are not only of interest to theologians but also are discussed by historians, cultural anthropologists, and sociologists. These disciples contextualize devotions within the larger movements and concerns of a particular culture and age. Aron Gurevich has sketched the medieval mentality about the function of saints and how they were to be dealt with. Of particular interest is his demonstration of how the reactions of medieval peasants to their saints are grounded in some of the social expectations of the time.[9] In a similar effort, Rosalind and Christopher Brooke look at the devotions to the saints through the examination of buildings and artifacts to uncover some of their political and social contexts.[10] Robert Orsi has taken a particular devotion to the Madonna in Our Lady of Mt. Carmel parish in New York City from 1880 to 1950 and shown it to be a microcosm of the Italian immigrants' world and their social mores.[11] The interest of such research for the theologian is that it invites a more broadly structured analysis of popular devotions and their ecclesial function within the particular socio-cultural setting of the United States. Before attempting such an analysis, we must briefly look at some of the historical contexts of devotions in their early developments and in the American church.

The Devotional Church

Peter Brown has transformed the discussion about the cult of the saints with his penetrating studies of its historical and cultural contexts.[12] He contrasts the restrained and even critical attitude of Augustine toward some aspects of the cult of the saints with that of his contemporary Ambrose, who knew how to use the cult of the martyrs to strengthen his episcopal role.[13] During this period (the end of Latin Christianity) these cults were made to carry an important public as well as spiritual meaning.[14] Another important cultural factor is the classical pagan emphasis on an invisible companion who acted as patron and protector. Christian piety knew how to shape this belief to its own purposes. Brown offers the example of St. Paulinus' relation to his patron saint: "He [the saint] is far more than a distant intercessor before the throne of God; he is a guardian of Paulinus' identity . . ."[15] This relationship also explains the later custom of giving Christian names of saints who were to form the neophyte in his or her new-found faith.

These dynamics behind the cult of saints in late Latin Christianity, it must be remembered, still function as a rule within the fairly healthy liturgical life of Christian communities of the fifth and sixth centuries. Although there were abuses associated with the graves of the martyrs and the family dead, there was also creative pastoral transformations of these cults that helped to connect ecclesial and social life of Christians.[16] While Brown also gives examples of misplaced devotional piety in this period, what emerges from this complex picture is a very creative use of the cult of the saints to forge or to renew ecclesial belonging and to anchor these devotions to the larger liturgical life of the community. The cult of the martyrs which eventually develops into that of non-martyr saints has its origins in a strong ecclesiology in which the witness of some (martyrs) is to strengthen the faith of the whole community. The celebration of the eucharist at the tombs of the martyrs connected the vision of faith in the community with the liturgical discipline of that community.[17] These remarks prepare us to look at devotions in the American church.

It is precisely the socio-cultural and historical contexts of nineteenth-century American Catholicism that explain the intense devotional life of parishes. I will briefly discuss three broad periods in the American story of devotional piety: the republican period (up to 1820), the immigrant period and its aftermath (1820 to Vatican II), and the post-conciliar period.

The Republican Period

During the republican period, the style of worship in American Catholic churches was fairly simple. It centered around the sacraments. After some initial experiments with the use of the vernacular in the liturgy, John Carroll and his fellow bishops reverted to the Latin liturgy.[18] Even the architecture and furnishings of colonial Catholic churches were more likely to reflect the conservative republican taste in such matters. In areas where a priest made a circuit to a number of otherwise priestless parishes over a period of time, not only Mass but confessions, marriages, and prayers for those buried in the priest's absence (as well as catechism) had to be celebrated during his short stay.[19] There was, therefore, no great emphasis on additional external devotions under such circumstances.

On the contrary, John Carroll's own training as a Jesuit and his knowledge of the classics of English spirituality (J. Gother and R. Challoner) had helped to form a genuinely liturgical spirituality. Following the lead of Gother and Challoner, he understood the liturgy as the basis of personal piety. His Jesuit training, for example, had inculcated a devotion to the Sacred Heart. Carroll not only encouraged personal devotion, but as early as 1793 he also asked the Propaganda for permission to celebrate the Mass and office of the Sacred Heart in the colonies.[20] Joseph Chinnici emphasizes the way in which Carroll understood this devotion:

The devotion focused attention away from needless external

practices and toward identification with Jesus in the ordinary
activities of life . . . Devotion to the Sacred Heart was one of the
chief means by which Carroll came to appreciate the humanity
of Christ.[21]

Carroll also actively promoted the Ignatian method of meditation as an important help to the laity in continuing their Christian conversion. Once again he encouraged his people to develop a sense and practice of inward prayer that would give
direction to the other activities of their lives. Carroll even
urged American Catholics to set aside several days for a personal retreat each year, if this were at all possible. Obviously
the church on the east coast under Carroll's direction already
had an active liturgical life in the understanding of that period. In contrast to a later emphasis on popular devotions, the
laity were invited to develop a prayer life with the classical
means of spiritual reading, prayer, and meditation on the mysteries of Christ.

The Immigrant Church

It is difficult to measure the pastoral impact of nineteenth-
century immigration on the American Roman Catholic
Church. The Irish immigration had already begun in earnest
well before the potato blight and famine. During this same period there was a heavy influx of German immigrants. Late in
the century, Italian, Polish, and French Canadian immigrants
also began to swell the cities of the East and Mid-West.[22] Suddenly there were large numbers of Catholics without enough
priests or parishes to accommodate them. But the usual terri-
torial approach to establishing parishes would not work with
immigrants who were intent on preserving the familiar customs and language of the old country in their worship. The solution, national parishes, did permit the first generation of immigrants to hear sermons and be ministered to in their own
language. As Jay Dolan has richly documented in the case of
the Irish and German parishes in New York City during this
period, an active "social Catholicism" was also an important
part of the pastoral strategy. These parishes had to deal with
the urgent problems of poverty, terrible housing, widespread

sickness, and a lack of health care. The existence of national parishes also created a number of pastoral problems that were to persist into the twentieth century.

National parishes, however, were only one part of the new pastoral strategy adopted by the bishops in the face of these massive, century-long waves of immigration. As already noted, many of these people needed to be evangelized in their faith. The parish mission, a pastoral success in Europe, was to provide an important means for evangelization and renewal of parish life on the frontier as well as in the city. And an equally important purpose of the parish mission was to instill a devotional piety and encourage membership in the multiple devotional societies of the parish as a practical way to continue the beneficial effects of the mission. The Redemptorist Fathers' *Mission Book*, already successful in Europe, was but one example of this new genre of parish renewal literature in the United States. It provided a convenient summary of Tridentine teaching and a vademecum of devotional piety.[23]

Ann Taves has researched these nineteenth-century American Catholic devotions and the prayerbooks that fostered them.[24] Several characteristics are common to this devotional literature and practice. First, there is usually a strong emphasis on the graces and favors to be received from such devotions. Catholic magazines of the time, such as *Ave Maria* and *The Messenger of the Sacred Heart*, regularly published accounts of the favors granted.[25] A second characteristic was an affective approach to prayer. This emphasis, already apparent in Francis de Sales, Alphonsus Liguori, and Frederick Faber, was shown in the strong emotional overtones of the wording of the prayers and in the method of meditation taught.

A third characteristic was the growing influence of indulgences in the choosing of confraternities to join and pious devotions to use. After a period of benign neglect, indulgences became an important part of Pius IX's pontificate. Publishers immediately saw this trend as a persuasive marketing device. As Taves shows, American prayerbooks in the latter part of the nineteenth century were regularly advertised for the number of indulgenced novenas and prayers they contained.[26] A fourth characteristic was the tendency to emphasize sin in devotional literature (e.g., the Sacred Heart devotions).[27] Dolan maintains that "in a culture of sin, the system of devotional Catholicism made sense, and the more help, that is, devotions, were available, the better the chance for victory."[28] Finally, these devotional groups and prayers were part of the "romanization" of the American church in the nineteenth century:

> Once taken up and approved by Rome for use throughout the church, a practice was generalized, and in this sense "romanized" . . . Those who supported it viewed Roman attempts to standardize practices as a means of making the church truly catholic . . .[29]

The American bishops, faced as they were with overwhelming administrative problems because of the immigrant explosion, still expended a great deal of pastoral energy on the questions of worship and prayer. Chinnici has given a detailed picture of one such prelate, John Hughes, archbishop of New York. Hughes explained the practice of the liturgical year as a way of reenforcing the economic system of the work week with days of rest and worship: "Through the celebration of its liturgical year and the enforcement of Sundays and holy days, the church could insist on the benefits of spiritual self-interest and counteract the selfishness prevalent in society."[30] As Chinnici notes, the American economic system influenced the explanation of the Mass and prayer by Hughes and his fellow bishops, and this same influence can be found in prayerbooks of the time where financial metaphors ("contract," "pay," "salary") pervade their pages.[31]

In contrast to the earlier republication period where an inward prayer life was encouraged, devotionalism became a major pastoral strategy to overcome the divisions of rich and poor, of native and immigrant within the church community. The devotional emphasis for bishops like Neumann, Spalding, and Hughes reflected both the European experience of crushing famine and poverty and the Irish and German churches' response of intense prayer and sacrifice, and the pastoral conviction that a more personalistic approach to Christ and the saints would make religion more accessible to the poorly educated and traumatically displaced immigrants.[32] The result was a proliferation of devotional confraternities of perpetual adoration, the passion of Christ, the

Holy Family, sodalities of the Blessed Virgin, and associations dedicated to particular saints.[33]

The social corollaries of devotional piety in the lives of the immigrants have only recently begun to receive the study they deserve. Robert Orsi has done a model study of the feast of the Madonna in the Italian Harlem section of New York City (1880-1950).[34] He draws a careful picture of Italian immigrants whose living and working conditions are unimaginably hard, the territoriality of the Italian neighborhoods, and the local clubs as representing towns in Italy. Orsi sums up the four major problems of Italian Harlem as urban pathology, neighborhood isolation, degradation in the view of outsiders, and the persistent poverty.[35] Through the initiative of the people of Italian Harlem, a feast of the Madonna was celebrated in the courtyards of the tenement houses.

To appreciate the importance of the feast, Orsi summarizes the pervasive influence of the family (domus). This factor explains, among other things, the Italian immigrants' distrust of diocesan priests, the place of a saint as part of the domus, the eating of traditional foods as the "sacrament" of the domus, and the belief that the domus is the source of conflict.[36] Against this complex background, Orsi then shows how the feast of the Madonna, in this situation, was a recapitulation of these immigrants' experience, and the efforts of the people to make the long journey from New Jersey and Brooklyn to the feast in uptown New York City reminded them of their immigrant journey from the old country.

> The statue itself was a link between Italy and East Harlem. The festa served as a powerful antidote to this fundamental moral and sensory anomie, assuring the immigrants that the world still turned on its axis and that they were still human beings, who could taste things and who could be good people.[37]

The feast ritually condensed the value system of the domus and provided time for reconciliation, renewal, and remembrance.[38] The prayers and rituals of the feast centered around the needs of each domus and thus, were not as individualistic as they might first appear. As Orsi insists, the celebration of the feast effectively, if temporarily, overcame the isolation of the neighborhood by opening up its festivities to those who were not parishioners.

The importance of Orsi's analysis is that it challenges any superficial assessment of devotional piety. These Italian immigrants had brought with them a strong anti-clericalism in regard to the diocesan clergy (though not against religious orders of men or women). But this anti-clericalism, as Orsi demonstrates, is a corollary of their domus-centered lives. Rather than being individualistic, their devotion to the Madonna is an expression of the domus and the neighborhood. It provides a point of social and personal identity for the people that the parish church does not. The efforts of the Pallotine Fathers to have the statue placed in the church shows an awareness on their part of the function of the feast in the larger community. One wonders if there would be any possibility to build up an ecclesial sense in such a community without the help of such devotions.

Toward the Twentieth Century

As American church historians have often noted, the major ecclesial transition of the nineteenth century was from a national church (in John Carroll's sense) to a "romanized" church. This was probably inevitable. The pastoral emphasis on pious confraternities and public and private devotions did provide a more accessible form of prayer to many immigrants as well as play a role in making the American church something of a carbon copy of the European church. There was some opposition to this trend but it had little effect.[39] And so, the American church came into the twentieth century resembling the European church in its liturgies and devotional life.

Chinnici, in describing the American church in the first decades of the twentieth century, points to its understanding of the eucharist as indicative of its attitude toward the Body of Christ with its separate identities of priest, lay people, and women. The Priests' Eucharistic League, at one point, had half the priests in the United States enrolled. The League, in turn, urged priests to encourage their parishioners to more frequent communion, to the monthly holy hour, and to frequent visits to the blessed sacrament. Women, as reminded by Leo XIII, could have no place in celebrating or serving the eucharist or even touching the sacred species. But the Archconfraternity of Perpetual Adoration urged women to frequent reception of the eucharist and to a more active assistance of priests in their work. But the overriding emphasis of this eucharistic activity was individualistic and did not initially seem to be able to draw out the social and political corollaries of eucharistic participation. By the 1930s, however, Catholic Action had finally begun to make the connections between the eucharist and the mission of the American church to the world.[40]

The connection between liturgy and participation in the ecclesial mission of the church was to receive its major impetus from Virgil Michel in his editorship of *Orate Fratres* (later, *Worship*) and in his influential writings, and in the pastoral implementation of the liturgy by Martin Hellriegel. Michel connected the papal social teaching with prayer and worship of the church. In many ways, he repeated one basic message: liturgy is the necessary basis of Christian social regeneration. Michel pointed to American individualism as one of the major obstacles to a more honest participation in the eucharist. On the other hand, it is liturgy that rebuilds a Christian social order as it forges a more credible witness of the Christian community.[41]

Martin Hellriegel demonstrated the pastoral viability of a relevant liturgy in his parish in St. Louis. Even within the restrictions of the pre-Vatican II church, he enabled his parishioners to participate actively in the eucharist and other sacraments as well as pray some of the hours of the office. Like Michel, Hellriegel believed in the building up of the Body of Christ through prayer and worship and in the vocation of the community to live the social message of the Gospel. He did not so much displace devotions in his parish as substitute devotional customs and rituals that were inspired by the liturgy and that led back to the liturgy.

In the thirty years before the council, there were individuals and small enclaves in this country who responded to the work of Michel, Hellriegel, and others with great enthusiasm. The practical sign of this response was the growing number of people who took part in the annual Liturgical Conference where not only the reform of the liturgy was called for, but where the questions of racial prejudice, rural life, unionism, collective bargaining, Catholic Action, and social reconstruction were addressed as part of the ecclesial responsibility of all the baptized. What must be kept in mind, however, is that most Catholic parishes in the United States were never touched by this movement. Up to Vatican II, most seminaries continued to give a devotional spirituality to future priests and to teach them rubrics rather than liturgy. Parish missions continued to appeal to the devotional life as a practical continuation of their work. Those who were particularly zealous might take part in the St. Vincent de Paul Society or in the Young Catholic Worker movement. But these efforts remained marginal to the institutional concerns of the American church.

In this historical overview, we have seen that the initial attempts in the republican period to construct an ecclesial life and worship that would benefit from the American culture were short-lived. The immigration period put an end to such attempts. Devotional piety became an important part of the pastoral strategy of the American bishops in attempting to deal with large numbers of immigrants. This type of piety seemed to assign a passive liturgical role to most of the baptized within an institutional ecclesiology. (I shall qualify this interpretation below.) Devotional life had apparently become a substitute for an active participation in the liturgy and in the mission of the church.

Before jumping to such conclusions, however, we might take into account some of the influential observations of Timothy L. Smith in his article "Religion and Ethnicity in America." He notes that the immigrant experience (because it caused a loneliness and separation difficult to appreciate) often became a theologizing experience, as in the Exodus event. The immigrant had to decide not only how to deal with the "host" culture but also with the competing subcultures and their values. In reaction to the deterioration of some immigrants' values, there was, often enough, a reaffirmation of ethical action: "The immigrant's religion needed both rule and transformation of rules, both the law and the prophets."[42] The practical result was an invitation to become more involved in one's religious community and its practices.

But Smith points out that this renewed commitment to one's religious community often resulted in old rituals assuming new meanings for their new situations (e.g., the Irish resistance in this country to the stricter clerical control of wakes). These reappropriated rituals and customs, he argues, should not be interpreted as individualistic. Rather, "though they made faith a profoundly personal experience, their aim and outcome was to bind individuals to new communities of belief and action."[43] I believe that this explanation might be extended to include, in some cases, devotions as used by the immigrants. Smith's insight would restore the possibility of an ecclesial dimension to some devotions, a dimension that is usually lacking in the discussion of liturgy and devotions. Robert Orsi's work might serve as an example.

Certainly Orsi has demonstrated that the devotion to the Madonna of 115th Street took on the new meanings of the Italian immigrant experience. Although the procession of the Madonna through the streets of Italian Harlem might seem a devotion, detached from ecclesial and liturgical meaning, it might also be interpreted as the only way in which a domus (family)-centered people might integrate this socio-religious experience of immigration in a communal context. Since the liturgies of baptism, marriage, and funerals were already reduced to a domus-event among these immigrants, this devotion to the Madonna remained the one viable way to re-evangelize them in this new situation. If it is argued that this devotion to the Madonna of 115th Street did not result in a deepened ecclesial commitment, I would reply that this may be as much the fault of a church or parish community that has a petrified and institutional ecclesiology as of those who seem to have no authentic ecclesial bond. Such a community seldom perceives the need to use bonding processes of a group that is marginal to or even outside the "church" boundaries.

In other words, if we examine some of the devotions that have acquired a classical standing (such as the Christmas crib, the stations of the cross, the devotion to the Sacred Heart), their original inspiration seems to have been a response to a certain religious or ecclesial indifference or distortion of some belief. In addition to the affective dimension of these devotions, there was a reaffirmation of the importance of the humanity and passion of Christ (as well as a response to the Jansenist distortions by means of the Sacred Heart devotions). The ways in which these devotions are derived from and lead back to the liturgy are indeed crucial. (The feast of the Sacred

Heart, for example, is a better interpretation of the devotion, I would suggest, than the reasons given for the practice of the "Nine Fridays" in honor of the Sacred Heart.[44])

In reviewing the popular devotions discussed above, things may not always be what they appear to be. Praying part of the office, as well as private prayer and meditation, as advocated by John Carroll and others, was possibly the best pastoral option available, given the situation in the colonies at the time. (On the other hand, this approach presumes a fairly literate and educated community. Carl Dehne's observation should also be kept in mind: early devotions usually arose "when the received monastic office was becoming inadequate as a means of worship for the monks, and that most of the real communal prayer of the medieval monasteries took place during the devotional offices rather than the adjacent canonical hours").[45] In any case, it would be hard to disagree with Chinnici's assessment that Carroll tried to encourage a "genuinely liturgical spirituality" within the understanding of the time.[46]

The immigrant situation and the pastoral solution of the nineteenth-century American church are more difficult to evaluate. As already argued, "belonging to the church" in the ecclesiology of that century with all its institutional emphasis was an important context for the proliferation of devotional practices in American parishes. When people "belong to" but are not considered to be the church, then the distanced character of the liturgy accurately reflects the praxis ecclesiology of such a community. These popular practices also represented an affective dimension which uneducated people did not always perceive in liturgical celebrations. Some devotions, such as the stations of the cross and benediction of the blessed sacrament, were certainly more understandable to such people than their liturgical counterparts of Holy Thursday and Good Friday celebrations (or even the ordinary celebration of the eucharist) in their preconciliar form.

Furthermore, in the decades immediately preceding the council, the liturgical movement in this country was viewed by many as an elitist concern. The movement did have some positive effects in eucharistic participation (such as the "dialogue" Mass) and in bringing about the religious music and texts for both the liturgy and devotions. But without the reform of the liturgy and its implicit ecclesiology, the reform of devotions in any thorough fashion was not possible.

"Devotio Futura"

Twenty-five years after Vatican II, the reformed liturgies are, more or less, a normal part of American parish life. The Notre Dame Study of Catholic Parish Life has confirmed the general impression that the implementation of these reforms has been one of the more successful outcomes of the council. Philip Murnion and his staff reported to the American bishops in *Parish Life in the United States* that "the intent of Vatican II's reforms, which emphasized intelligibility of the rite and participation of the people, has been remarkably achieved and is being furthered by continuing efforts."[47] Renewal programs and parish retreats during this period offered parishioners explanations of how the liturgy was the prayer of the "people of God." Parishioners were invited to share in liturgical ministries of the lector, the cantor, or of the eucharist. The practical corollary of this postconciliar activity was the decline, though not the disappearance, of popular devotions. But John Coleman and other astute observers of the American scene have wondered if this devotional vacuum is a positive sign. To respond to such legitimate questions, I shall examine a celebration that might objectively be considered liturgical, at least for some participants, but is more probably considered devotional by many of the participants.

Rather than employ traditional distinctions of liturgical and paraliturgical, "sacrament" and "sacramental," I will briefly examine a postconciliar celebration that has enjoyed a degree of pastoral success in this country, namely, the communal anointing of the sick. I suggest that this celebration might serve as a paradigm for devotions that lead from and to the liturgy. For those who qualify as "sick," this celebration is obviously liturgical. But for many people who are not, strictly speaking, "sick" but who enthusiastically crowd into such celebrations, this ritual brings a great deal of meaning to their lives and potentially renews their ecclesial vocation.

The usual plan for such a celebration is simple: there is a liturgy of the word with appropriate readings and homily, penitential prayers and prayers of intercession, the blessing of the oil, and the anointing. When celebrated correctly, such a celebration: (1) evangelizes people on central Christian themes (e.g., suffering, a sense of time linked to vocation, eschatological hope, etc.); (2) includes a penitential concern (e.g., care and concern for the sick, the responsible care for one's health, awareness of shunned diseases such as AIDS, etc.); (3) introduces a strong ecclesial dimension in which people become vividly aware of the vocational needs of their brothers and sisters; (4) affords the Christian community a practical lesson in eschatological awareness in which the promise of God's future challenges their use of the present for the sake of the reign of God.

Such a celebration complements the ecclesial dimension of all liturgical celebrations. The communal celebrations of the anointing of the sick continue the evangelization of the community in specific and important ways. The American culture of the twentieth century consistently tends to avoid areas of human living where finitude and mortality are encountered. This celebration, on the other hand, draws positive and countercultural lessons of hope from such situations. David Power has evocatively developed this point in speaking of blessings:

> The fundamental meaning of blessing, whatever form it takes, is that God's power redeems the powerless. Earliest Christian communities, sects to the prevalent religion and temporal cultures of their time and place, could see themselves made powerful in Christ. They found their way of dwelling on earth and using among themselves the things of the earth by reason of their strength in Christ. This depended on the strength of being a community in him.[48]

Such a celebration also directly examines and challenges the cultural assumptions and religious values of the community. Our American culture permits us to tolerate widespread disease and sickness, especially among the poor, in the midst of affluence. But the Christian perspective on sickness and healing insists on God's original purpose in creation (the Garden of Paradise myth) and its retrieval as "the new creation" in Christ. The honest celebration of the anointing of the sick by the community will inevitably raise prophetic questions about the witness and service that the community gives to the suffering and outcasts of its social world.

Such a celebration always helps to redefine and clarify the mission of the ecclesial community. The practical problem that parish communities have in calling out the gifts and ministries of their people is the result, in part, of our advanced post-technological culture in which it is difficult to gather people and even more difficult to invite them to share their limited time with others in some form of service. Participation in such celebrations, however, does enable the Christian community to reassess its priorities and does provide an occasion for individuals to reassign their use of time and health in view of the needs of their particular world. This type of celebration seems to follow the spirit of the conciliar reform: "For well-disposed Christians the liturgy of the sacraments and sacramentals causes every event in human history to be made holy by divine grace that flows from the paschal mystery."[49]

The phrase "well-disposed," however, is key to concluding our discussion of devotions. I assume that this description includes not only the moral attitudes of the Christian but also those qualities of liturgical participation that the council described as "full, active, and conscious" and "communal."[50] I would further argue that none of these descriptions are adequately understood apart from the affective dimension of all integrated human actions.

> When people cease to represent reality by picturing and so differentiate between images and symbols, not only their world of conceived meaning is touched but also their affective relationships, their dispositions of belonging, awe, and respect and their sense of personal wholeness and oneness with the world.[51]

Moreover, as David Power notes, affective wholeness also confronts the darkness that accompanies symbolic awareness.[52] In brief, affectivity is a necessary component of authentic liturgical participation.

In contrast to their Tridentine predecessors, the liturgies of Vatican II actively invite an integrated response that includes the affective. This means that *devotio futura* should model itself on this integrated approach that the postconciliar liturgies demand. When this liturgical criterion is consulted, it is obvious that affectivity has nothing to do with the maudlin. Affectivity in liturgy and devotions enables the participants to discern God's redemptive action in the whole of their lives. This ongoing discovery invites new praise, wonder, and gratitude. What is said of proper liturgical dispositions should also be true of popular devotions:

> But in order that the liturgy may possess its full effectiveness, it is necessary that the faithful come to it with proper dispositions, that their minds be attuned to their voices, and that they cooperate with divine grace, lest they receive it in vain.[53]

Paradoxically, it is the discussion of the affective which brings us back to the crucial ecclesial dimension of popular devotions in the American context. It is the unique strength of liturgy that it connects the personal with the communal, the subjective with the objective. To the extent that people are able to integrate their own acculturated experience into their devotional and liturgical worship, they discover more fully their gifts and roles in the community of Christ. *Devotio futura*, then, in whatever form it takes, should clarify the current vocation of individuals within their ecclesial community. But that vocation is never fully understood apart from their own cultural as well as personal situation. When the stations of the cross, for example, are celebrated by a hispanic parish in the drug-ridden streets of Newark on Good Friday, it is the cultural context which clarifies the text of the passion of Christ. When the mark of Ash Wednesday is worn publicly in the successful and affluent business world of Chicago or New York, then there is always the strong possibility that prophetic actions may replace folkloric customs. In brief, the genius of the American cultures and the specific mission of the American church may well contribute to expressions of popular devotion that speak to the people of a new generation.

Notes

1. C. Dehne, "Devotion and Devotions," in *The New Dictionary of Theology*, eds.. J. Komanchak, M. Collins, and D. Lane (Wilmington: Glazier, 1987) 283-288.

2. G. Gallup, Jr. and J. Castelli, *The American Catholic People: The Beliefs, Practices and Values* (Garden City: Doubleday, 1987) 30-31.

3. M. Searle and D. Leege, "Of Piety and Planning: Liturgy, the Parishioners, and the Professionals," *Notre Dame Study of Catholic Parish Life* (NDS), Report no. 6 (1985) (Notre Dame: University of Notre Dame, 1985) 6-7; see also J. Gremillion and D. Leege, "Post-Vatican II Parish Life in the United States," NDS, Report no. 15, p. 8.

4. NDS 6, p. 7.

5. *Sacrosanctum Concilium* 13, in *Documents on the Liturgy 1963-1979* (Collegeville: The Liturgical Press, 1982) 13 (henceforth DOC; numbers in the DOC refer to sections, not pages).

6. DOC 3929.

7. DOC 3934.

8. DOC 3936.

9. A. Gurevich, *Medieval Popular Culture: Problems of Belief and Perception* (Cambridge: Cambridge University Press, 1988) 39-77.

10. R. and C. Brooke, *Popular Religion in the Middle Ages: Western Europe 1000-1300* (London: Thames & Hudson, 1984) 31-45.

11. R. Orsi, *The Madonna of 115th Street: Faith and Community in Italian Harlem 1880-1950* (New Haven: Yale University Press, 1985).

12. Peter Brown, *The Cult of the Saints: Its Rise and Function in Latin Christianity* (Chicago: University of Chicago Press, 1981).

13. Ibid. 37-39.

14. Ibid. 48.

15. Ibid. 56.

16. For an excellent example, see ibid 46-47.

17. P. Jounel, "Le culte des saints," in *L'Eglise en prière: Introduction à la liturgie*, 3d ed. (Paris: Desclée, 1965) 789.

18. J. Dolan, *The American Catholic Experience* (Garden City: Doubleday, 1985) 114; see also J. Chinnici, *Living Stones: The History and Structure of Catholic Spiritual Life in the United States* (New York: Macmillan, 1989) 16-17.

19. Dolan, *The American Experience* 209-210.

20. Chinnici's treatment of Carroll's attitudes in this area is quite detailed, and I am indebted to his work on the subject; see Chinnici, *Living Stones* 26-36.

21. Ibid. 31.

22. See Dolan, *The American Experience* 127-157 for an extended discussion.

23. Dolan, *The Immigrant Church* (Notre Dame, University of Notre Dame Press, 1983) 150-151.

24. A. Taves, *The Household of Faith: Roman Catholic Devotions in the Mid-Nineteenth-Century America* (Notre Dame: University of Notre Dame Press, 1986).

25. Ibid. 54-63.

26. Ibid. 27-28.

27. Dolan, *The American Experience* 226-228.

28. Ibid. 228.

29. Ibid. 115.

30. Chinnici, *Living Stones* 63.

31. Ibid. 64-65.

32. See Chinnici's detailed discussion, ibid. 68-69.

33. Jay Dolan and Jeffrey Burns, who directed the Parish History Project at the University of Notre Dame, provide the data for the development of parish organizations (1800-1900). Out of the 151 such organizations founded between 1800 and 1860, 72% were devotional, and of the 1328 organizations that emerged between 1800 and 1900, 60% were devotional. See Taves, *The Household of Faith* 17-18.

34. Orsi, *The Madonna of 115th Street*.

35. Ibid. 44-45.

36. Ibid. 75-106.

37. Ibid. 169.

38. Ibid. 171.

39. Taves, *Household of Faith* 116-118.

40. Chinnici, *Living Stones* 146-154.

41. R. Duffy, "The U.S. Catholic Contribution to Liturgy," *New Theology Review* 1 (1987) 30-52.

42. T.L. Smith, "Religion and Ethnicity in America," *American Historical Review* 83 (1978) 1155-1185.

43. Ibid. 1179.

44. Karl Rahner's careful analysis of the Sacred Heart devotion must be acknowledged, though I do not find his treatment of the "great Promise" of the Nine Fridays theologically convincing; see his *Theological Investigations*, vol. 3 (New York: Crossroad, 1972) 321-352.

45. Dehne, "Devotion and Devotions" 285.

46. Chinnici, *Living Stones* 27.

47. P. Murnion, *Parish Life in the United States* (Washington, D.C.: National Conference of Catholic Bishops, 1982) 33.

48. D. Power, "On Blessing Things," *Concilium*, vol. 178, 33.

49. DOC 1716.

50. DOC 14; also 432-433.

51. D. Power, *Unsearchable Riches: The Symbolic Nature of Liturgy* (New York: Pueblo Publishing Co., 1984) 73.

52. Ibid. 73-74.

53. DOC 11.

Ecclesiological Issues

9

The Roman Catholic Response to *Baptism, Eucharist and Ministry:* The Ecclesiological Dimension

Geoffrey Wainwright

AT LIMA, PERU, IN JANUARY 1982, THE FAITH AND ORDER COMMISSION OF the World Council of Churches (WCC), after fifty-five years of remote and fifteen years of proximate preparation, finally released its text on "Baptism, Eucharist and Ministry" (BEM) in the unanimous conviction that the work was now sufficiently "mature" for consideration by the churches.[1] The churches were respectfully invited to make their responses "at the highest appropriate level of authority." The Roman Catholic Church is not a member of the WCC, but since 1968 it designates twelve Catholic members to the Commission on Faith and Order, who "participate by personal title, as full voting members in the Commission." In August 1987, the Roman Catholic Church sent to the Faith and Order Secretariat in Geneva its response to BEM.

That response is printed in the first forty pages of the sixth volume of *Churches Respond to BEM.*[2] The process for arriving at the response had been coordinated by the Secretariat for

Promoting Christian Unity; it had included consultation with the conferences of Catholic bishops throughout the world, solicitation of opinions from Catholic theological faculties and academic societies, and collaboration with the Congregation for the Doctrine of the Faith.

The Roman Catholic response is one of the most detailed made by any church. Its general tone is positive. It makes the most of agreement and convergences between BEM and the faith and practice of the Roman Catholic Church. It is sensitive to factors which have led to certain formulations in BEM that are not familiar to Catholics and yet are congruent with the Catholic faith. It also indicates quite openly those points where BEM appears inadequate to, though scarcely ever contradictory of, the Catholic faith, and where further work needs to be done.

A constant theme in the Roman Catholic response to BEM is ecclesiology. It is recognized that ecclesiology was not a primary focus of BEM. Yet much that is said on baptism, eucharist, and ministry inevitably has ecclesiological implications and consequences. Therefore the Catholic response repeatedly asks for the further development of the topics of BEM in an ecclesiological framework.

The response itself suggests four focal points of ecclesiological interest: (1) the nature of sacrament and the sacramentality of the church; (2) the structure of the church both in its local assembly and in the relations among local churches, as far as the universal level; (3) the location of pastoral and doctrinal authority within the church; (4) the nature and means of the apostolic tradition. The last two points are related in a particularly close way by the Roman Catholic response. It is there that it becomes especially evident that theological descriptions of the church are intimately bound to the concrete identification of the church; and I shall therefore add a fifth focus, namely, the question of mutual "recognition" among claimants to ecclesiality, which surfaces several times in the Catholic response and is in any case inevitable in any move towards the realization of Christian unity. My method will be, in each of these five areas, to listen first to the Catholic text; then, to indicate whether the Catholic concerns are being taken up in post-Lima projects of Faith and Order or elsewhere; and finally to address some comments and questions of my own, as an individual theologian, back to the Catholic response. In conclusion, I will return to the nature and identity of the church.

It is, therefore, time that I declare my own interest in these matters. Between 1976 and 1982 I was heavily engaged in the process of turning the Accra text on "One Baptism, One Eucharist and a Mutually Recognized Ministry,"[3] in the light of intervening comments from many sources, into a version that would come to the meeting of the Faith and Order Commission at Lima; and then at Lima I chaired the definitive redaction of the BEM text. As soon as the responses of the churches started to flow in, I again became involved in the preparation by Faith and Order of "Baptism, Eucharist and Ministry 1982-1990: Report on the Process and Responses."[4] Concurrently with my membership in the WCC Faith and Order Commission and its steering group on BEM, I have been since 1983 a member, on the Methodist side, of the Joint Commission between the Roman Catholic Church and the World Methodist Council.

The Sacramentality of the Church

While observing that BEM, particularly in the sections on baptism and ministry, rarely uses the term "sacrament," the Catholic response recognizes the text as "affirming the principal features of baptism that the word sacrament has served to express"[5] and including "the essentials of a sacramental understanding"[6] in its description of ordination. The section on eucharist uses the term sacrament rather more freely and so finds its language positively appreciated on the Catholic side without further comment in this regard. The Catholic response is sensitive to the fact that the word "sacrament," "because of its complex history, needs a great deal of explanation in interchurch conversations."[7]

For its part, however, the Catholic response wants the whole church as such to be understood in sacramental terms. Commenting particularly on the ministry section of BEM, the Catholics write:

Further reflection will be needed in the Commission on Faith

and Order, in order to put the ordained ministry in clear perspective. As an illustration, one essential dimension of the
church that remains obscure, although it is of the greatest importance for understanding and valuing the authority of the ordained ministry, is the sacramental aspect of the whole church,
at work in a particular way in the ministry, in its teaching office, in the administration of the sacraments and in its governing. *In a real and effective sense the church is an icon of the presence
of God and his kingdom in the world.* This is always because of
God's actual and constant faithfulness to his promise in Jesus
Christ. The basic ministerial structures participate in that sacramental dimension. Further ecumenical dialogue will have to
deal more fully with that spiritual and sacramental dimension
of the church and its ministry.[8]

Now the sentence I have emphasized fits rather well with the
opening paragraphs of the ministry section of BEM on "The
Calling of the Whole People of God," which the Catholic response approves[9] and which reads in part: "The church is
called to proclaim and prefigure the kingdom of God. It accomplishes this by announcing the gospel to the world and by
its very existence as the body of Christ. In Jesus the Kingdom
of God came among us . . . Christ established a new access to
the Father. Living in this communion with God, all members
of the church are called to confess their faith and to give account of their hope . . . In so doing they bring to the world a
foretaste of the joy and glory of God's kingdom."[10]

The sacramentality of the church is in fact the most comprehensive category behind the approach finally taken by Faith
and Order in the difficult study it has been engaged in for
over two decades on "The Unity of the Church and the Renewal of Human Community." There the theme appears as
"The Church as Mystery and Prophetic Sign."[11] Although the
two poles of "mystery" and "prophetic sign" do not quite correspond to Vatican II's "sign and instrument," there is a very
considerable similarity to the description in *Lumen Gentium* of
the church as "a kind of sacrament, that is, the sign and instrument of communion with God and unity among people."[12]

Behind Vatican II stood the writings of Henri de Lubac (already in his *Catholicisme* of 1938 he concluded that "if Jesus is
the sacrament of God, the church is for us the sacrament of

Christ"), Otto Semmelroth (*Die Kirche als Ursakrament*, 1953), Edward Schillebeeckx (*Christus, Sacrament van de Godsontmoeting*, 1957), and Karl Rahner (*Kirche und Sakramente*, 1960). Protestants have been quite receptive to the notion of Christ himself as the original sacrament (the idea is found as early as Luther's treatise *On the Babylonian Captivity of the Church*), but they have been very wary of extending the notion to the church. Most jejunely, they have objected that such an extension upsets their own (scholastic) definition of a sacrament. In a more sophisticated way, they have feared an intrusion of the church between Christ himself and his direct operation in the dominical sacraments (so Peter Brunner,[13] Eberhard Jüngel[14]). Most subtly of all, they have indeed recognized that the church is in some sense God's "instrument" but questioned what they take to be Catholic teaching concerning this *activity* of the church (André Birmelé[15]). By now, however, a real convergence is discernable and could in fact be achieved if both sides were willing to accept a certain leeway in the interpretation of, say, the formulation made by the second Anglican/Roman Catholic International Commission in *On Salvation and the Church* (1986): the church is both "evangelized and evangelizing, reconciled and reconciling, gathered together and gathering others."[16] The church "is called to be, and by the power of the Spirit actually is, a *sign, steward*, and *instrument* of God's design. For this reason it can be described as *sacrament* of God's saving work."[17] The church is sign, steward, and instrument—"of what it has received."[18]

This may be the best perspective in which to tackle a question which the Roman Catholic response twice remarks that BEM did not treat, namely, the necessity or otherwise of baptism for salvation.[19] The Catholic text appropriately notes that the church's confession of "Christ as universal Saviour" has its context in "universal human sinfulness" and "the universal need for salvation."[20] In the "further common study" which is called for, it will be interesting to see whether Catholics follow Karl Rahner in the "copernican revolution" which he saw himself completing after Vatican II. In *Kirche und Sakramente* his thought had substantially followed the sequence of God, Christ, the church, the sacraments, and the life of Christians in the world; in a couple of late essays, however, the direction of his argument moved rather from God's presence in secular human life to the sacraments and to the church itself, so that the sacraments and the church become the symbolic manifestation of what God is already salvifically doing in the world.[21] I should myself want to affirm that both movements are dialectically necessary: the movement from church to world is a baptismal movement and justifies the continuance of evangelization, which the more Hinduistically inclined among Christian theologians appear content to abandon; the movement from world to church can be eucharistic, where Christians are able to discern and give thanks for the work of God also beyond the institutional church.[22]

The Structure of the Church, Local and Universal

The Roman Catholic response recognizes that the BEM section on ministry is attempting to face "a fair question"[23]: "how, according to the will of God and under the guidance of the Holy Spirit, is the life of the church to be understood and ordered, so that the gospel may be spread and the community built up in love."[24]

The place of the ordained ministry in the Christian community shows itself to be a crucial matter for ecumenical agreement. The Roman Catholic response welcomes the fact that BEM mentions "two complementary forms" of the ordained ministry's "representative" character: "the representation of the people of God, and the representation of Jesus Christ."[25] With regard to the latter, however, further development is needed in order to make it clear that "through its relation to the Archetypos Christ, the ordained ministry is in and for the church an effective and sacramental reality, by which a minister acts *in persona Christi.*"[26]

The best formulation I know of the representative character of the ministry comes in a composite, though not (I hope) distorting, quotation from David Power:

> The needs of the church and of its mission are what determine ministry . . . The office-holder, through the service of supervision and presidency, represents back to the church that which in the faith of the ordination ceremony it has expressed about itself . . . Because [the eucharistic president] is empowered to

represent the church in this vital action, to represent to it its own very ground of being, we say that he is empowered to represent Christ . . . The role of the ordained minister is to represent in the midst of this community its work for the kingdom, its eschatological nature, and its relationship to Christ . . . The validity of ministry, to use the word loosely, is not assessed on the ground of its ecclesiastical provenance, but on the ground of its benefit to the church.[27]

Such a vision allows also for the overcoming of the ill-formulated alternative from Trent and Vatican II that the Catholic response to BEM repeats yet again, namely, that the "common priesthood of the faithful and the ministerial priesthood . . . differ from one another in essence and not only in degree."[28] Precisely as *representatives* of Christ and his church, the ordained ministers are *distinct*, but *what* they represent is *not other* than the character and mission of the whole church, which is itself nothing other than participation, by the grace of the Holy Spirit, in the ministry of Christ the savior and head of the church.

It is encouraging that the Catholic response should also say perhaps more than it knows when it refuses to "exalt [the minister] above [the community]."[29] The way is thereby opened for seeing the Christian community as structured on a more "horizontal" plane, rather than the "laddered" notion of a ministerial scale from layperson to deacon to presbyter to bishop that BEM itself had been careful to avoid in its depiction of a threefold ordained ministry within the church. The new vision is close to the liturgical constitution of Vatican II with its normative description of "the full, active participation of all God's holy people . . . in one prayer, at one altar, at which the bishop presides, surrounded by his college of presbyters and his ministers."[30]

At the moment, little ecumenical work is being devoted to furthering agreement on the place of the ordained ministry in the church. This is perhaps due to the blockage over the question of women's ordination, even though the Catholic response to BEM opines that differences on this matter "should never become prejudicial to further reflection upon the ordained ministry within the ecumenical context."[31] In the Roman Catholic/World Methodist dialogue, Msgr. Kevin McDo-

nald keeps reminding us that the matter of women's ordination becomes vital only when, and precisely because, we are
coming closer to agreement on the nature of ministry. Recipro-
cally, it may be that reflection on women's ordination will in
fact help in the attainment of greater clarity, and (one may
hope) agreement, on the nature of ministry.

Gently and tactfully, the Catholic response to BEM asks
whether reflection on "the personal expression of a 'focus of
unity' in the universal church" might not be "a logical result
of the reflections started upon a representative service of over-
sight, continuity and unity in the church."[32] When, at Lima, an
Anglican member of the Faith and Order Commission asked
whether a paragraph should not be inserted on the petrine
ministry, some Orthodox and Baptists were quickly on their
feet to call such a proposal premature. Meanwhile, several bilateral dialogues have begun to treat this question, notably the
Anglican/Roman Catholic International Commission in its *Final Report* (1982) and the Joint Commission between the Roman Catholic Church and the World Methodist Council in its
Nairobi report, *Towards an Agreed Statement on the Church*
(1986); and these had been importantly anticipated by the national Lutheran/Roman Catholic dialogue in the United
States. This very specific theme, however, requires greater attention to the wider context of our next two, and closely related, sections, namely, "authority in the church" and "apostolic
tradition."

Authority in the Church

The Catholic response to BEM declares that the Lima text
raises for Catholics the question of "the constitutive elements
of authority and order in the church."[33] BEM itself had stated
that "the authority of the ordained minister is rooted in Jesus
Christ, who has received it from the Father (Matt. 28:18), and
who confers it by the Holy Spirit through the act of ordination."[34] The Catholic response makes the further precision that
the bishop "by his ordination to the episcopacy . . . is commis-
sioned to exercise leadership in the community, to teach with
authority and to judge. All other ministries are linked to his
and function in relationship to it."[35] Furthermore, "bishops

represent and symbolize in their person their local church and relate it, in communion with the other churches, to the universal church. The ecumenical council becomes thus a representative image of the universal church, because it is a meeting of the college of bishops around the bishop of Rome who, according to the Catholic Church, is the head of this college."[36]

The Catholic response notes that the Vancouver assembly of the WCC in 1983 recommended as a step towards unity the "quest for agreement on common ways of decision-making and teaching authoritatively."[37] While some bilateral dialogues have considered these matters, it must be confessed that they have received little consideration in Faith and Order in terms of theological principle since the exploratory report "How Does the Church Teach Authoritatively Today?"[38] The matter remains on the agenda.[39] Meanwhile, the very processes by which churches have produced their official responses to BEM provide some incidental empirical evidence as to how churches make decisions on matters of some doctrinal importance in an ecumenical context, although of course more formal steps would doubtless be necessary when it came to creating new relationships with other churches.

At several points, the Catholic response raises the (formal) question of authoritative decision-making precisely in connection with the (substantive) question of a pastoral and magisterial ministry. Thus it notes that among the questions raised for Catholics by BEM are these: "What is the nature and role of decisive authority in the discernment of God's will as to the development of ministry in the church in the past and with regard to the present needs of the church? . . . Does the threefold ministry belong to the constitutive being of the church as rooted in God's will for the church, or only to the ecumenical wellbeing (*bene esse*) of the church? How is this decided? With what authority?"[40] Again, the BEM text needs to be "ecclesiologically deepened by examining whether the text [of Ministry, 22] means that [the threefold] ministry belongs only to the ecumenical wellbeing (*bene esse*) of the church, or rather to its constitutive being, rooted in God's will for the church *as it has been discerned by the authority of the church*. Therefore one has to distinguish between the fundamental and constitutive core of the threefold ministry, as the institutional expression of what was involved in the message of the New Testament, and the historic form, style and organization it has inevitably assumed and will also assume in the future. An *ecumenical discernment* is needed to see what belongs to the constitutive structure of the church and what to the contingent social organization."[41]

At the moment it appears that there is a certain tension between the two phrases I have emphasized, for an "authoritative discernment" has already (according to Catholic teaching) taken place, while an "ecumenical discernment" is still needed. Other parts of the Catholic response in fact make plain that Catholic bishops have "discerned" (which can only mean "decided") that the historical development and continuing exercise of an authoritative episcopate—and indeed in communion with Rome—is at the constitutive core of the church. Can, then, other churches be persuaded by this circular move? Clearly it is important to see what the Catholic response to BEM says about apostolic tradition.

Apostolic Tradition

The Catholic response to BEM notes that, in dealing with the "historic evolution of ministry," the text "frequently gives special weight to an argument from antiquity."[42] This is welcomed as far as it goes, but more is said to be needed:

> The attention given to origins and "antiquity" certainly meets a concern of many churches. But this approach in the document still remains incomplete because too often it involves only a statement of fact and is insufficiently supported by theological reflection on the normativity of such antiquity. In other words, it must be completed by considering also the role of the decisive authority in the discernment of such developments in the past, as well as in regard to the present needs of the church and the ecumenical situation today.[43]

Taught by bishops whose ordination to the episcopate allows them "to teach with authority and to judge," the Catholics go on to speak about "the unique importance of the episcopal succession for the edification of the church through the ages":

> Through the episcopal succession, the bishop embodies and actualizes both catholicity in time, i.e. the continuity of the

church across the generations, as well as the communion lived in each generation. The actual community is thus linked up through a personal sign with the apostolic origins, its teaching and way of living.[44]

And regarding ordination: "The competent minister of the sacrament is a bishop who stands in the authentic apostolic succession and who acts in the person of Christ. We therefore ask the Commission on Faith and Order to reflect on the ecclesiological meaning of the episcopal succession for ordination. We believe that its necessity is due to the fact that the episcopal succession signifies and actualizes the sacramental link of the ministry—first of all the episcopal ministry itself—with the apostolic origin."[45] And, repeating the deliberately strong "we believe": "We believe that ordained ministry requires sacramental ordination by a bishop standing in the apostolic succession."[46]

Now BEM had made a deliberate distinction between episcopal succession and the apostolic tradition:

Apostolic tradition in the church means continuity in the permanent characteristics of the church of the apostles: witness to the apostolic faith, proclamation and fresh interpretation of the gospel, celebration of baptism and the eucharist, the transmission of ministerial responsibilities, communion in prayer, love, joy and suffering, service to the sick and the needy, unity among the local churches, and sharing the gifts which the Lord has given to each.[47]

Within this broad context, "the succession of bishops became one of the ways . . . in which the apostolic tradition of the church was expressed."[48] The Catholic response recognizes that episcopal succession belongs within the broader reality of apostolic tradition, but asks of BEM:

Is there not the tendency here to be content with a listing and a juxtaposition of items which all have to do with the apostolic tradition without showing sufficiently how they have their own function within the totality and how they are related among themselves?[49]

The request for greater precision is, in my view, legitimate. The closest BEM comes is the declaration that the episcopal succession "was understood as serving, symbolizing and guarding the continuity of the apostolic faith and community."[50] BEM's suggestion that episcopal succession is "a *sign* of the apostolicity of the life of the whole church"[51] is accepted by the Catholic response: "We agree that the 'episcopal succession' is of the order of the sign that can signify, through the image of historic transmission, the fact that the church is rooted in the apostolic church around Christ and therefore shows its fundamental apostolicity."[52] Importantly, however, a preference is immediately expressed for the earlier text from Accra, which had spoken of an "effective sign." In fact, the Catholic response then goes on to contradict the view expressed in BEM on behalf of some "churches which have not retained the episcopate" that episcopal succession may be appreciated "as a sign, *though not a guarantee*, of the continuity and unity of the church."[53] The Catholic response asserts:

> Episcopal succession can rightly be called a *guarantee* of the continuity and unity of the church if one recognizes in it the expression of Christ's faithfulness to the church to the end of time. At the same time it lays upon each individual office-bearer the responsibility to be a faithful and diligent guarantor.[54]

There, for one whose church does not claim episcopal succession in the Roman Catholic sense, is the rub. Looking from the outside, one wonders what account Roman Catholics can, on those terms, give of the Orthodox (or vice-versa), when each side claims episcopal succession and yet the two bodies appear to be in schism from each other. The language of "guarantee" depends logically on a Cyprianic ecclesiology, whereby only the bishops of one's own community afford the guarantee, while bishops in schismatic bodies are at best dubious. Or how, as a Protestant, could I hold that the medieval western bishops were guaranteeing the substantive apostolicity of the church? When the Reformation failed to take effect throughout Western Christendom, it could even be argued that a *break* in succession on the part of the reformed provided a valuable, if regrettable, sign of the return to the apostolic Gospel.

BEM's location of episcopal succession within the broader apostolic tradition opens the door, I would suggest, to a more adequate account of the relationship between the episcopate and the apostolic faith as an internal dialectic. The bishops become the *servants* of that faith; but because there are other manifestations and vehicles of that faith (the Scriptures, the sacraments, testimonies from previous generations, the whole Christian life of believers . . .), there are also *criteria for discerning* when bishops are satisfactorily serving the preservation and proclamation of the faith and when they are failing in their responsibilities. One might then consider bishops and their succession to be a sign of the apostolic Gospel and faith *as long as they remain faithful to it.* That is saved from being a tautology by the fact that bishops are subordinated to the Gospel itself, to which there are also other witnesses that, in an admittedly complex way, hold the bishops to account. Or one might view episcopal succession as a kind of sacrament which does not always produce its full fruits but is nevertheless not thereby rendered quite ineffective; its efficacy depends on the degree to which it is celebrated and received in (the true) faith. That account is prevented from being a tautology by the productive power of grace, which nevertheless respects the liberty of human beings to "pose obstacles." According to the Nairobi report, "Methodists . . . can regard a succession of ordinations from the earliest times as a valuable *symbol* of the church's continuity with the church of the New Testament, though they would not use it as a criterion."[55] I myself might prefer to say "as an independent criterion," either necessary or sufficient.

With this last discussion we are coming very close to the question of mutual recognition.

Mutual Recognition

The constitutional purpose of the WCC and of Faith and Order is to help the churches towards "visible unity in one faith and in one eucharistic fellowship." The Catholic response to BEM welcomes the maintenance of the "visible unity of divided Christians" as the goal of the ecumenical process.[56] Regarding unity in faith and in eucharistic communion, it says (in regard to the question of interim sharing in the sacrament):

> The policies of the churches and ecclesial communities differ in regard to eucharistic sharing. In our view, the problem of eucharistic sharing has an ecclesial dimension and cannot be resolved in isolation from an understanding of the mystery of the

church as well as the ministry. In this regard, for Catholics, it is unity in the profession of faith that constitutes the core of ecclesial communion. Because the eucharistic celebration is by its very nature a profession of the faith of the church, it is impossible for the Catholic Church presently to engage in general eucharistic sharing. For in our view we cannot share in the eucharist unless we share fully in that faith.[57]

We have already seen that for Catholics, belief about the ministry is integral to the faith itself: "We believe that ordained ministry requires sacramental ordination by a bishop standing in the apostolic succession."[58] "It is necessary now to work towards unity in faith *on this central ecclesiological issue*."[59] And "for us it is not only agreement on the question of apostolic succession, but also being situated within it, that is necessary for recognition of ordination."[60]

It is obvious, therefore, that "recognition of the ordained ministry" forms "a crux in the endeavours towards Christian unity"[61] in "one faith and one eucharistic fellowship." The Catholic response evaluates the present situation in this way:

It must be clear that the recognition of ordained ministry cannot be isolated from its ecclesiological context. The recognition of the ordained ministry and of the ecclesial character of a Christian community are indissolubly and mutually related. To the extent that it can be recognized that communion now exists between churches and ecclesial communities, however imperfect that communion may be, there is implied some recognition of the ecclesial reality of the other. The question that follows is what does this communion imply for the way we perceive the ministry of the other? This perhaps is one question that should be taken up when attention is given to the fundamental ecclesiological dimension of the problem of recognition of the ordained ministry.[62]

The further theological work is to take place within a practical context: "We hope that a growing fraternal solidarity of collaboration, common reflection, prayer and service between churches and ecclesial communities, and particularly their ministries, can reach a point of seeing whether, or in what terms, an ordained ministry recognized by all might become possible."[63] This is to occur within "mutual respect" and "dimensions of fellowship . . . reflecting the levels of communion that now exists."[64] The Catholic Church should "find ways of expressing" and deepening "its recognition of the real bonds of faith and life in Christ that exist between communities which celebrate baptism authentically."[65] While the desire for "mutual respect" is evidently sincere, it seems that when it comes to a question of "recognition," and especially the recognition of ordained ministries, the main concern for Catholics is less for "mutuality" as such than for how *they*, for their part, will be able to recognize others.

By dominical promise, there is an infallible church, against which the gates of hell will not prevail, and its members constitute the communion of the saints. Whenever non-Catholics come into dialogue with Catholics, they are confronted by the question of whether, in order to be a part of that church, one must, or may (have) be(en) in communion with (a bishop who is in communion with) the bishop of Rome. In internal Catholic terms, the question may be framed in terms of the meaning and interpretation of the *"subsistit in"* of Vatican II: "This [sole] Church [of Christ] subsists in the Catholic Church, which is governed by the successor of Peter and by the bishops in communion with him."[66]

We thus face again the nature and identity of the church.

Conclusion: The Nature and Identity of the Church

The Catholic response to BEM concludes that "the goal of the unity of divided Christians [cannot] be reached without agreement on the nature of the church."[67] The Nairobi Report of the Joint Commission between the Roman Catholic Church and the World Methodist Council cautions that "as we reflect on a reunited Church, we cannot expect to find an ecclesiology shaped in a time of division to be entirely satisfactory."[68]

At its Budapest meeting in 1989, the Faith and Order Commission instigated a major ecclesiological study that would extend over several years and include a world conference.[69] From examination particularly of the churches' response to BEM, it appeared that the following could serve as a theological structure for a "convergent vision on the nature, unity and mission of the church."[70] If such a description were to succeed, the various communities claiming to be Christian would then have the chance of asking themselves, for the purpose of concretely identifying the church, whether their own body, and which others if any, match such a description.

The draft project places itself under the rubric of *"koinonia* (communion/participation/fellowship)" in a way that might meet, without using the word, the Catholic desire for a sacramental understanding of the church in a comprehensive sense:

> *Koinonia* in the life of the Father, the Son and the Holy Spirit (cf. John 14:17; 1 John 1:2-10; 2 Pet. 1:4; 1 Cor. 1:9; 2 Cor. 13:13) is the life centre of all who confess Jesus Christ as Lord and Saviour. They share and participate in the gospel and in the apostolic faith, in suffering and in service (2 Cor. 8:4; Rom. 15:26; Acts 2:42). This *koinonia* is lived in Christ through baptism (Rom. 6) and the eucharist (1 Cor. 11) and in the community with its pastors and guides (Heb. 13). *Koinonia* means in addition the participation in the holy things of God and the communion of the saints in all times and places (*communio sanctorum* in the double sense of the word). Each local Christian community is related in *koinonia* with all other local Christian communities with whom it shares the same faith. In this *koinonia* they live the catholicity of the church. To say it with the words of the Lima document: "Witness to the apostolic faith, proclamation and fresh interpretation of the gospel, celebration of baptism and the eucharist, the transmission of ministerial responsibilities, communion in prayer, love, joy and suffering, service to the sick and the needy, unity among the local churches and sharing the gifts which the Lord has given to each" (M 34). Such a *koinonia* is not an inward-looking group of believers, but a missionary community sent into the world to bear witness to God's love for humanity and creation.[71]

By the time of its *Final Report* (1982), the first Anglican/ Roman Catholic International Commission discovered that *koinonia* had been its latent leitmotif all along; and the second Commission entitled one of its agreed statements *Church as Communion* (1991). The same notion provided the headline for the 1986 Nairobi report of the Joint Commission between the Roman Catholic Church and the World Methodist Council, "Towards an Agreed Statement on the Church"; and this same commission worked under the rubric of *"koinonia* in time" as it prepared its 1991 Singapore report on "The Apostolic Tradition." There appears, therefore, to be an ecumenically promising atmosphere for this approach to the WCC Faith and Order study on ecclesiology.

After the general description of *koinonia*, the Faith and Order sketch then lists four more particular "key conceptions and images which have been especially emphasized by different Christian traditions." The hope is that they will prove to be "complementary." Since ecumenical theologians will be working with these notions for several years ahead, it may be useful to conclude this chapter with the full quotation of these four:

> *The church as gift of the word of God (creatura verbi).*
> The *koinonia* of the church is centred and grounded in the word of God testified in the scriptures, incarnated in Jesus Christ and visible among us through the living voice of the gospel in preaching, in sacraments and in service. All church institutions, forms of ministry, liturgical expressions and methods of mission should be submitted to the word of God and tested by it. The *pleroma* of God's creative word is never exhausted in the churches' institutions.

> *The church as mystery or sacrament of God's love for the world.*
> The church as *koinonia* is the church of the living God (1 Tim. 3:15), not a human association only. It lives in permanent communion with God the Father through Jesus Christ in the Holy Spirit and is not merely the historical product of Jesus' ministry. Because of its intimate relation with Christ himself as the head of the body, the church is to be confessed according to the apostolic faith as one, holy, catholic and apostolic. Therefore the visible organizational structures of the church must always be seen in the light of God's gifts of salvation in Christ. The word and the sacraments of Jesus Christ are forms of God's real and saving presence for the world. As such they express the church's participation in the mystery of Christ and are inseparable from it.

> *The church as the pilgrim people of God.*
> A third aspect of the understanding of the church as *koinonia* stresses the provisional and incomplete character of the church in its present form, its hope and despair, its suffering and compassion, its shame and glory, its being still a mixed reality of sinners and saints. The church is a community of justified sinners in search of the kingdom of God, struggling as they serve the world to be obedient to the commands and promises of Christ as expressed in the sermon on the mount. It is a commu-

nity of pilgrims who have already received a foretaste of that fulfillment for which they are longing.

The church as servant and prophetic sign of God's coming kingdom. The church is also a servant people for God's coming kingdom, "the sign held up before the nations." As a first-fruit of the kingdom the church takes sides with the weak, the poor and the alienated. This is for the sake of involving all its members in a personal appeal to seek first of all the kingdom of God by being itself, as a collective whole, an instrument for the liberation of people in distress. An ecumenically conceived ecclesiology, therefore, must not be self-centred, triumphalistic or complacent, but should direct the churches' service to the world, to justice, peace and the integrity of creation.[72]

The implicit questions put to the Roman Catholic Church (and, *mutatis mutandis*, to the other churches) by such a text, with its partly overlapping and putatively complementary aspects, are these: How far are you able to recognize in it a satisfactory theological description of the church? To what extent does your own community then measure up to it? How far do you see its being met by other communities which claim to be church?

Notes

1. *Baptism, Eucharist and Ministry* (Geneva: World Council of Churches, 1982).

2. Max Thurian, ed., *Churches Respond to BEM*, vol. 6 (Geneva: World Council of Churches, 1988).

3. *One Baptism, One Eucharist and a Mutually Recognized Ministry* (Geneva: World Council of Churches, 1975).

4. *Baptism, Eucharist and Ministry 1982-1990: Report on the Process and Responses* (Geneva: World Council of Churches, 1990).

5. *Churches Respond* 10.

6. Ibid. 34.

7. Ibid. 10.

8. Ibid. 26.

9. Ibid. 28.

10. BEM, Ministry 4.

11. See *Faith and Renewal: Reports and Documents of the Commission on Faith and Order Stavanger 1985 Norway*, ed., Thomas F. Best (Geneva: World Council of Churches, 1986) 192-207; and *Church, Kingdom,*

World: The Church as Mystery and Prophetic Sign, ed., Gennadios Limouris (Geneva: World Council of Churches, 1986).

12. *Lumen Gentium* 1, also 9, 48, 59. See already *Sacrosanctum Concilium* 5 and 26, and further *Gaudium et Spes* 42 and 45, and *Ad Gentes* 1 and 5.

13. Peter Brunner, "Zur katholischen Sakramenten- und Eucharistielehre," *Theologische Literaturzeitung* 88 (1963) 169-186.

14. Eberhard Jüngel, "Die Kirche als Sakrament?", *Zeitschrift für Theologie und Kirche* 80 (1983) 432-457.

15. André Birmelé, *Le Salut en Jésus-Christ dans les dialogues oecuméniques* (Paris: Cerf, 1986).

16. *Salvation and the Church* (London: Church House Publishing/ Catholic Truth Society, 1986) 28.

17. Ibid. 29.

18. Ibid. 27.

19. *Churches Respond* 6, 12.

20. Ibid. 12.

21. Karl Rahner, "Considerations on the Active Role of the Person in the Sacramental Event," *Theological Investigations*, vol. 14 (New York: Seabury, 1976) 161-184; "Zur Theologie des Gottesdienstes," *Schriften zur Theologie*, vol. 14 (Zurich: Benziger, 1980) 227-237.

22. See already BEM, Eucharist 22.

23. *Churches Respond* 28.

24. BEM, Ministry 6.

25. *Churches Respond* 29.

26. Ibid. 29.

27. See David N. Power, "The Basis for Official Ministry in the Church," *The Jurist* 41 (1981) 314-342; and *Gifts that Differ* (New York: Pueblo Publishing Co., 1980).

28. *Churches Respond* 30.

29. Ibid. 29.

30. *Sacrosanctum Concilium* 41.

31. *Churches Respond* 30.

32. Ibid. 32.

33. Ibid. 9.

34. BEM, Ministry 15.

35. *Churches Respond* 33.

36. Ibid. 31f.

37. Ibid. 8.

38. *Ecumenical Review* 31 (1979) 77-93.

39. Thomas F. Best, ed., *Faith and Order 1985-1989: The Commission Meeting at Budapest 1989* (Geneva: World Council of Churches, 1990) 296.

40. *Churches Respond* 9

41. Ibid. 31, (italics added).

42. Ibid. 27.

43. Ibid.

44. Ibid. 33.

45. Ibid. 35.

46. Ibid.

47. BEM, Ministry 34.

48. Ibid. 36.

49. *Churches Respond* 32.

50. BEM, Ministry 36.

51. Ibid. 38.

52. *Churches Respond* 33.

53. BEM, Ministry 38, emphasis added.

54. *Churches Respond* 33, emphasis original.

55. *Towards an Agreed Statement on the Church* (Lake Junaluska: World Methodist Council, 1986) 31, emphasis original.

56. *Churches Respond* 4, 37.

57. Ibid. 25; see 38.

58. Ibid. 35.

59. Ibid. 36, emphasis added.

60. Ibid. 38f.

61. Ibid. 35.

62. Ibid. 36.

63. Ibid. 35.

64. Ibid. 39.

65. Ibid. 38.

66. *Lumen Gentium* 8.

67. *Churches Respond* 40.

68. *Towards an Agreed Statement* 22.

69. *Faith and Order 1985-1989: The Commission Meeting at Budapest* 293, 296.

70. *Baptism, Eucharist and Ministry 1982-1990: Report on the Process and Responses* 151.

71. Ibid. 150.

72. Ibid. 150-151.

10

Partnership:
A Challenge to Clericalism

Warren Kinne, S.S.C.

THE CHURCH IS IN DEEP CRISIS. THIS IS SEEN IN A PRONOUNCED WAY IN its cross-cultural missionary exchange. In the following pages I hope to show that the root of some of the difficulties is exemplified in our language, and especially in the dichotomies of clergy/lay and sacred/secular. But fundamentally, I consider that a redefinition of ordained ministry is demanded if there is to be partnership between baptized Christians, whether ordained or not, for cross-cultural mission. The context to resolve these issues is an understanding of the church as "communion" which is demanded in a world that is ultimately interconnected and interdependent.

Our Language Exhibits Our Difficulties

Language is more than mere words. It exhibits a mind-set. Our language betrays us in as much as there are presumptions behind the categories we use. Through language we communicate with people, and in that communication we mirror and reinforce social relationship; we display our prejudices; and our discriminatory use of language reflects and supports hierarchical relationships.[1]

In this time of great cultural and religious change, the problem of our language becomes acute. I experience this both as a missionary and as an ordained minister in as much as I am deeply unhappy with such images as "priest" and "missionary." These images carry the burden of the history that shapes the way we think and the way people understand us.

Clergy/Laity Dichotomy

The term "laity," which originally encompassed the whole people of God, now rests on a negative definition referring to those who are not clergy. Although we champion equality through baptism, in the next breath we are defining the majority of Christ's faithful as non-clergy.[2] To talk of laity is to use priesthood as the point of reference.

While there may indeed be a specifically clerical viewpoint, usually we refer to the "lay person" in contrast to the one with the real knowledge and power. So when we speak about the vocation and mission of the church, the distinction clergy/laity puts one group, namely, the laity, at a disadvantage.

Yet baptism, which marks our membership in the church, is the basis of our equality in Christ, and from it comes our vocation and common call to mission.[3] The community of all the baptized carries the responsibility for the proclamation of the Gospel. Everyone has to live the Gospel and to celebrate this in the eucharist. In this regard there is nothing exclusive for one group. A unique domain for one group is not conceivable.

This belonging to the church and commitment to its mission has, in official church documents, been seen in terms of the "threefold and yet unique moment of the announcement of the Word, of the celebration of the sanctifying worship and the service of humanity in the charity of Jesus Christ."[4] Yet I am aware that there is a language problem here too in this division into the prophetic, priestly, and kingly roles. What could a royal character possibly mean to people in the church as it exists today in non-regal societies? Also, in practice the prophetic potential of the laity has not been realized. There is the need to broaden the meaning of magisterium to include involving the laity in the consultative process toward what would be the magisterium of the church. This would certainly be wider than that of the bishops. There is an immediate need to reduce the gap between a teaching church and a learning church toward one church—which learns from the Spirit.[5] The theological language in general does not match the reality and the imagery is inappropriate.

Sacred/Secular Dichotomy

According to the Second Vatican Council, the ecclesial condition of the laity is inseparably defined in their baptismal state and their secular state.[6] I find this description, widely used in official church documents, to be problematical.

Pope John Paul II, in *Christifideles Laici*, recognized the need to speak about the vocation and mission of the lay faithful in positive terms rather than the predominately negative ones of the past. Yet he too uses the words of Vatican II to describe the lay faithful's unique character as in a special way to "seek the Kingdom of God by engaging in temporal affairs and ordering them according to the plan of God."[7]

He sees this secular character of the laity as not "only an anthropological and sociological reality, but in a specific way, a theological and ecclesiological reality as well."[8] He goes on to say that the gospel images of salt, light, and leaven, "although indiscriminately applicable to all Jesus' disciples, are specifically applied to the lay faithful."[9] This, I believe, is a distortion and an arbitrary form of reductionism. Is "the vast and complicated world of politics, society and economics, but also the world of culture, of the sciences and the arts, of international life, of the mass media . . ." merely the field of evangelizing activity of the laity?[10]

Whereas the "secular character" of the vocation and mission of the laity is true from a particular point of view,[11] the division is ultimately untenable. The sacred is a dimension of reality; the spirit permeates all reality. There is no such thing as the purely secular.

As Vatican II acknowledged:

> The split between the faith which many profess and their daily lives deserves to be counted among the most serious errors of our age . . . Let there be no false opposition between professional and social activities on the one part and religious life on the other.[12]

Of course the council also upheld the distinction between

sacred and secular.[13] But is not the task of transforming the temporal order too fundamental to the Christian vocation to be confined to the specifically lay state?[14] The whole church, ordained or not ordained, is involved in the evangelization of the one world, blessed by God and in need of redemption. As David Power has said:

> One can wonder whether the distinction between sacred ministry and secular involvement even settles the practical concerns which it is intended to meet, let alone the theological problem.[15]

"New" Context

I propose that the context for a discussion on the future shape of ministry, in a church of equal opportunity, is best constituted by the insights from ecology and the model of church based on the image of "communio."

I have become increasingly conscious of the interconnectedness of all reality: its interdependence. This is partly a spiritual and partly an ecological awareness. At the level of church, we believe in the same pattern of interconnected life or communion.

Church as "Communion"

Situations of dominance in the world and in the church are not tenable. In this regard, the World Council of Churches has come up with some thoughtful affirmations at its covenanting ceremony at Seoul in March, 1990. The Council stated that "all forms of human power and authority are subject to God and accountable to people." The Council pledged to "*resist* any exercise of power and authority which tries to monopolize power and so prohibits processes of transformation toward justice, peace and integrity of creation."[16]

Likewise, Pope John Paul II, quoting from the 1985 Synod of Bishops,[17] said that "the ecclesiology of Communion (koinonia) is a central and fundamental concept in the conciliar documents."[18] He used the parable of the vine and the branches as a backdrop and an exposé of this ecclesiology of communion. There is, he said, a sign of the time—the human longing for participation in all levels of life: women and men desiring "to be creators of a new, more humane culture."[19]

The church in the past was often preoccupied with power and dominance, as is still mirrored to some extent in the church of today. But in today's church there should be communion, an interrelationship and interconnectedness for mission, based on discipleship.

Baptism, common to all members of the people of God, forms the very root of Christian vocation and dignity. As the *Lineamenta* for the Synod on the Laity stated:

> There is a common dignity of members deriving from their rebirth in Christ, a common grace as children, a common vocation to perfection, one salvation, one hope and undivided charity. In Christ and in the Church there is, then, no inequality arising from race or nationality, social condition or sex . . .[20]

There is no doubt but that there has been too much identification of the mission of the church with the function of the hierarchy. The laity was seen as the bridge between the church and the world. But the laity *is* church. I therefore join those who hope that we have seen the final essay on a theology of the laity, in as much as every attempt to deal seriously with the topic reveals an inadequate ecclesiology based on the premise that:

> the non-ordained constitute a special segment of the Body of Christ whose vocation, dignity, and mission are somehow regarded as a limited aspect of the total vocation, dignity and mission of the Church.[21]

Indeed, much of the theology of the laity is devised by clerics about lay people in order to explain the role of the laity. It is not a theology by lay people, but rather about them.[22] A methodological starting point for a theological reflection might be the experience by the laity of their vocation and mission in the world. There should really be no *particular* vocation for laity *in* the church, and there should theologically be no need for a quest for lay identity, since ultimately a lay person does not "belong to the church," nor does a lay person "have a role in the church."[23] Through baptism and in union with Christ, a lay person's mission is the mission of the church itself.

The laity/clergy dichotomy obscures the fact that there is

one fundamental vocation but a diversity of different roles and ways of living this out.[24] Teresa Pirola ably points out that in the family model the fundamental distinctions between family members are made on the basis of relationship bonds, not on the basis of jobs or functions.[25] She notes that:

> We are so ingrained with the clergy-laity distinction that it will take some concentrated practice to get into the habit of viewing our faith family as having one basic vocation and (five) unique ways of living this out.[26]

She sees this in contrast to the commonly accepted two unique ways: priests and religious on the one hand, and laity on the other. She perceives, in her context, five ways: married people, priests, religious, singles, and youth.

Pope John Paul II's "The Vocation and Mission of the Laity" notes the fact of diversity and complementarity in the church shown in the diversity of ministries and charisms given by the Spirit for communion and mission.[27] Also an important emphasis is placed on "collaboration, dialogue and discernment"[28] as the best way for all in the church to realize genuine communion and to participate in the mission to evangelize.

If there is an outstanding, but interim, theology of the laity, it will be directed to ecclesial restructuring.[29] As a point of departure, there will be a move from the juridical to a sacramental understanding of the church as announced in the Dogmatic Constitution on the Church at the Second Vatican Council. This is a vision of the church as community prior to being hierarchical institution; the organizational model is collegial rather than monarchical; and the mission results from baptism, confirmation, and personal charisms.[30]

There is an urgent need for a declericalized church. a church concerned with serving; a church from the roots; and a democratized church.[31] The ecological insight concerning the interconnectedness of reality confirms this.

Ecological Perspective

In order to nurture and to sustain the world's life, the World Council of Churches recently committed itself to work, and to engage its churches to work, for an "indispensible reversal of thinking"[32] that is necessary for our survival. They covenanted to personally witness through a lifestyle that would promote and facilitate an ecologically-sound life. This involves, they said, joining in global, local, and personal efforts to safeguard the world's atmospheric integrity and quality, and to resist globally the causes of atmospheric destruction.[33]

This group of the World Council seeks ways to live together in harmony with God's creation. To this end they wish to deepen their biblical understanding; to rediscover old traditions such as the patristic teaching on creation; and to develop new theological perspectives concerning creation and the place of humanity within it. They also saw the need to promote a spirituality in their church communities which embraces the sacramental character of creation.[34] This would involve protecting and celebrating God's gift of creation and sharing resources. Also they will reject and fight against hierarchical thinking which puts one race above another and men above women.

Today we see a general change in attitude taking place toward the natural world, a change that is truly a sign of the times. People are becoming more devoted to the natural world and are coming to see the human as a species among species. The eco-system supports all the manifestations of life including human beings. We need to become more earth-centered. Indeed there is a sense in which all human activities must be judged by the extent to which these foster a mutually enhancing human-earth relationship. This has ramifications for all our life and thought and inevitably affects our theology and liturgy.

For too long we have been blighted with the idea of progress at the expense of the natural world. Our western philosophies and theologies have been anthropocentric and overly-fascinated with the human. Our lust has been to control matter, to conquer nature. We do not still adequately commune with nature, and we lack an emotional rapport with the natural world. We must, for our survival and psychic well-being, let nature teach us that a community of life is essential.

This communion should bring about a fascination with life and a zest for living that will give psychic energy. It is our nature to create communion and to bring people to the moment of insight about the interrelatedness of all things. In this context, our notion of church as the sacrament of communion has particular significance.

God's world is one of diversity, harmony, and continuous transformation. This is a law of nature. With *awe* we need to celebrate these realities, in communion with everything past, present, and yet to be.

Notes toward Redefinitions

It is sociologically a fact that all groups need some form of leadership to survive, and presumably the church too needs it. However, we have to defer fully understanding what leadership should be in the church until we first come to a more adequate rediscovery of the mission and vocation of the Christian in the world. This is liturgically celebrated in baptism. Basically, this vocation of the Christian is to nourish among people the perception of the world in terms of the Gospel.

What Is Ordained Ministry?

Although ordination is associated with the charism of leadership, it nevertheless basically means whatever service of the Gospel demands in a particular context. The core determinant is living out the Gospel in a way that is Good News for the poor. In this sense, it has no fixed meaning and generally our fixed meanings are invalid.

David Power notes that the present day thrust for grassroots community, "while it does not threaten to wipe out the sacrament of order, places ordination is another perspective, one which makes it clearly auxiliary to the common mission rather than determinative of it and its modalities."[35]

Power also believes that too much is made of baptism as a rite or ceremony and not enough of the great realities of initiation into a faith community. In like manner he says that we focus too much on priesthood or the sacrament of order. He states that "order itself has been mysticized as the source of power and authority almost without considering the faith and charism of the person ordained." The demysticization or demythologization of these two sacraments will be part of a process to retrieve their true significance for the church and its mission.[36]

The presbyter is, I consider, best described in the context of the whole people gifted for mission. As such, this minister is a coordinator and animator of charisms that are in the community.

The presbyter is also the symbol of the unity, catholicity, apostolicity, and wholeness of the community. When we focus on the meaning an ordained minister (who must always be considered as part of a group) brings to the Christian community, we see that this person has a role that preserves and fosters responsibility for what the church is and should be—for its unity, holiness, apostolicity, and catholicity.[37]

The ordained minister symbolizes the thrust for unity in the church: that they may be "one mind and heart"; where leadership is to reconcile and mediate, while respecting legitimate pluralism. Also this person should strive to live the church's holiness, inasmuch as the ordained minister, like the community, should be imbued with the Spirit. As a part of the presbyterate, the ordained minister should also be a window to other communities. The church should be a communion of churches, and there is the need of openness to how the Spirit is operating in other communities, which we call a concern for catholicity. The apostolicity of the church is symbolized by the ordained minister being part of the one sacrament of order stretching back through time. This minister sacramentalizes the community's gospel and apostolic tradition and roots. One may also note a missionary dimension to ordination which Karl Rahner says is foundational, in as much as the minister is ordained to proclaim God's word.[38]

The heart of the matter for any ministry is the building of a gospel community in freedom. The ordained person coordinates the charisms that are given by the Spirit to members of the community for its edification. Not that the community is an end in itself, but it should be seen in the context of its service to the world. And that is all that there is! People mistakenly suspect there is a lot more. But the role of the presbyter in the Christian community is that of *unifying spiritual leadership*.[39] The presbyter signifies and represents the headship of Christ: to inspire, to direct, to encourage, to foster initiatives, and to help charisms develop.

> *Both priesthoods* [of the laity and ministerial] have their christological basis in the Christian discipleship, even before or prior

to any configuration to the "headship of Christ." Exaggerating the headship of Christ in the ministerial priesthood, and ignoring the fundamental and proper discipleship of Christ, brings about a false ontologism of status.[40]

Values that motivate this type of leadership are ones that will promote participation, co-responsibility, and dialogue. Here teamwork is necessary. And the authority of this leadership is based on one's degree of discipleship, and is not primarily a juridical reality.

Presidency of community and presidency of the eucharist require the charism of leadership. They fittingly go together, and history suggests that it was one suited to the former who in fact assumed the latter.[41]

David Power states that in looking for the meaning of order in the church, it is necessary to leave behind the theological and canonical system which had its point of departure in the hierarchy. He says that we should "look instead to the reality of the unit which is the people of God in Christ, and locate grace and discernment in that body."[42] In fact, the primary form of priesthood is that of the baptized. And the heart of ordained ministry is an intensification of baptism. But it is also closely tied up with leadership.

Word and Sacrament

To reduce ordination only to leadership of sacramental celebration is to trivialize ministry. Indeed, many people have a cultic view of ordained ministry that has no basis in Scripture. Images of ordained ministry that were in the course of history taken from Old Testament models and used in a metaphorical sense were later literalized, to the detriment of an adequate understanding of ordination.

The ecumenical debate has helped develop a theology of the relationship between word and sacrament. In my reading of the documents of the Second Vatican Council, and especially *Presbyterorum Ordinis*, ordained ministry is seen in the light of the prophetic rather than the cultic function. It is stated that ordained ministers have as their "primary duty the proclamation of the gospel of God to all."[43]

This ministry of the word is carried out in many ways, according to the various needs of those who hear and the special gifts of those who preach.[44]

Sacraments intensify the word and help make what the word proclaims happen. Also in the words of Vatican II, the "eucharist shows itself to be the source and apex[45] of the whole work of preaching the gospel."[46] It is the high point of proclamation.

Part of the present tunnel-vision is that in the Catholic tradition sacramental celebrations have become the exclusive focus for an understanding of ordained leadership. However, what ordination means is much broader than this. The focus on the ordained minister, understood as a priest, had for a long time been as the confector of the sacrifice. But the eucharist stands quite distinct from the sacrament of order. Here it is the community that stands responsible. I do not consider that one can get primary specification for the sacrament of order from the liturgical context. Sacramental leadership simply follows from the patristic principle that it is fitting that the church leaders should also preside at liturgy.

There is a valid insight from the symbolism inherent in the sacramental action that considers the priest as necessarily distinct from the people. The logic of the liturgy demands that its presider at times be seen to symbolize the radical gift of God. But this role of the ordained minister in liturgy does not throw light on the nature of ministry in the church. An extrapolation of this role outside liturgy can give rise to a dominatingly hierarchical view of church.

Sacrificing Priest?

The notion of sacrificing priesthood is part of the problem here. Many of us who are ordained have an inadequate self-understanding. What does it mean to consider ourselves as "priests offering sacrifice"? Here there is an emphasis on what the priest does, rather than on what the people are.

Sacrifice in the New Testament is a term that denotes an offering in spirit and in truth. The focus is on the community: "A chosen race, a royal priesthood, a consecrated nation, a people set apart to sing the praises of God."[47] The sacrifice of

Jesus was his life lived in the truth. Our sacrifice is our lives—of faith, good works, and living the truth—joined to his. This is the real sacrifice of Jesus, and ourselves in him. The death on the cross is a symbol of his life as lived. It is a consequence of his living the truth. As a sacrifice it must not be understood in a crass way separated from the context of his whole life.

The eucharist is the high point of the proclamation of this truth—the Good News that triumphs over evil. The story in memory of him nourishes us with hope and meaning.

Liturgy and Life

There is a sense too in which liturgy is not good news, but celebrates it. Jesus' death was not in itself liturgy. It was a secular event—an execution.

In our liturgy, in the context of the story of Jesus, we celebrate and remember our lives. And ultimately, the quality of our liturgy depends on the quality of our lives: on our commitment to the mission of Jesus, for liberation and freedom.

There is a sense too in which liturgy does not mirror our actual world. Indeed, it is often the opposite of our experience of a world shaped by the forces of death. Liturgy puts us in touch with the truth of life that may be denied in the circumstances of our lives.

We can have aesthetic liturgies—fine choirs, rich vestments, beautiful stained glass. But real celebration must be about the transformation of our lives outside the boundaries of the sanctuary. This is the meaning of the incarnation and in liturgy we give thanks by proclaiming God's redemptive acts in our midst. God is at work in the world, and we see the liturgy in our life and celebrate our life in our liturgy.

The Missionary Vocation of All the Baptized

For any missionary, lay or ordained, there is but one goal: to preach the Gospel in a cross-cultural situation. This gift that drove Paul on his missionary journeys has in every age driven other people, men and women, lay and ordained, across the boundaries of geography, culture, language, and religious experience in the name and in the power of the Spirit of the Risen Christ. Not all are called to leave their own land and to go to another in the name of Christ. This is the special calling of the foreign missionary who lives in another land and among other people for the sake of communion. As is stated in *Christifideles Laici*:

> Communion and mission are profoundly connected with each other, they interpenetrate and mutually imply each other, to the point that communion represents both the source and the fruit of mission; communion gives rise to mission and mission is accomplished in communion.[48]

Challenge for Missionary Societies

Many missionary congregations and societies are on the brink of extinction. Vocations as we have known them are on the wane. Often their vision of mission, as seen in the constitutions and the acts of their general assemblies, is adequate, but their membership is narrowly defined, and there is no adequate model for partnership with others. The imagery too that is employed is inadequate: "mission," "priest," "laity." But until there is a change of thinking at the center of the church, missionary groups on the periphery will probably not flourish.

For these groups, more resources are being used in maintenance and in care for the aged. The world view at the time most of these groups came into existence is essentially Eurocentric, dominating and superior, and permeated by a paternalistic/donor mentality. There is little sense of the need of the other, of the mutuality of giving and receiving. But the kingdom cannot be furthered by any group working out of a *power* position. The relationship between evangelizer and evangelized, and the partnership between lay and ordained who are concerned for evangelization, must be one of strict equality, and there is the need of continuous conversion toward this goal.[49]

We need forms of innovation for this *partnership*, which like a conscious sense of *communion*, should be the way of the future. This is a communion with all animate and inanimate reality: communion within congregations, between and among congregations and religious traditions; and between men and women, married and single. This is the call of the future.

The only authentic meaning of being Christian is to be in service of the world in which we live. Hence the new description of religious congregations and societies dedicated to missionary activity might be to facilitate this universal charism of mission, and not to pre-empt or control what equally belongs to others. Hence there is a need for "professional" missionary groups to re-define themselves into this facilitating role. It will demand a radical breakdown of clerical structures so as to facilitate awareness of the universal vocation to mission of all Christians and to help them to be liberated from whatever prevents them from taking responsibility for their baptismal missionary vocation. And a recovery of the concept of *ministry* may well be the basis for understanding the relationship between ordained and other forms of service in the work of mission.[50]

* * * * * *

The church faces many difficulties. The long period in which the common priesthood of the faithful was downgraded has given rise to passivity of the laity. At the same time, we do not understand the implications of the oft-spoken words of Vatican II about sharing, dialogue, and co-responsibility. Even when there are clergy and laity, with a clear grasp of the Vatican II vision, who are willing to work together in partnership of brotherhood and sisterhood, they do not know how to go about living this model of church.

Another problem today is that so much potential and real gift for leadership in the church is not officially recognized by the church. The ecclesial recognition that we call ordination, by which one is incorporated into the one sacrament of order is, for example, withheld on the basis of sex, and only for those with the gift of celibacy. This is discriminatory and does not serve the mission.

Also, we have a difficulty in regard to models of leadership in the church. As Bishop Claver of the Philippines has observed:

Most experiments in training lay leaders in the Church end up forming clericalized lay leaders. It is an inevitable outcome since the only model of leadership in the Church is clerical.[51]

In short, the biggest block in the church and in specific

groups in the church is clericalism. This comes from our education, our theology, and our experience. I am a member of a missionary society whose median age is rising, and as such it is finding it psychologically and logistically more difficult to undergo radical change. But the challenge is to transform ourselves to meet the demands of mission for the future. We ought to experience partnership. People must be empowered, not overpowered! Yet, while there is good will for experiment, there is not much energy for it.

This is a time when I see many lay people trying in extraordinary ways to live out their missionary vocation generally without adequate official church support. As one of them, now married and on mission in Brazil, has said:

> Being "lay" is one form of preferential option for the poor. To remain lay is to seek the path of poverty in the church! Being lay, being without hierarchical status doesn't then imply that one does not possess theological, pastoral, intellectual or administrative expertise. The state of life of the laity brings no perks, but still there is no limit to the number of charisms the Holy Spirit may give the individual.[52]

Both clergy and laity need a commitment to deepen and nourish their fundamental Christian vocation, and this in partnership with each other. But true partnership is between equals. A necessary move toward such equality would be the affirmation of the true ecclesial identity of lay Christians.[53]

Notes

1. See Camille Paul, "Christifideles Laici": A Feminist Response," *Australasian Catholic Record* 66 (October 1989) 414.

2. See Teresa Pirola, "Laity: A Block to the Mission of the Church?", *The Australasian Catholic Record* 66 (October 1989) 422-431.

3. See John Paul II, *The Vocation and Mission of the Laity* ("Christifideles Laici," 30 December 1988) no. 33 (Dublin: Veritas, 1989).

4. Lineamenta, "Vocation and Mission of the Laity in the Church and in the World" no. 29 (Homebush, Australia: St. Paul's Publications, 1985).

5. See "The Teaching Authority of Believers," *Concilium* (August 1985), ed. J.B. Metz and E. Schillebeeckx.

6. See Lineamenta no. 22.

7. "Lumen Gentium" no. 31, in *The Documents of Vatican II*, ed., W. Abbott (London: Geoffrey Chapman, 1966); as in John Paul II, *The Vocation and Mission* no. 9.

8. Ibid. no. 15.

9. Ibid.

10. Paul VI, "Evangelii Nuntiandi" no. 70 (Homebush, Australia: Daughters of St. Paul).

11. Presuming the validity of the distinction and given the reality of most people's lives.

12. "Gaudium et Spes" no. 43, in *The Documents of Vatican II*.

13. "Lumen Gentium" no. 31.

14. See Pirola, "Laity: A Block" 426.

15. David N. Power, *Gifts That Differ: Lay Ministries Established and Unestablished* (New York: Pueblo Publishing Co., 1980) 49, also see 130.

16. World Council of Churches, Final Document, "Justice, Peace, Integrity of Creation," Document no. 19, Seoul, Korea, 6-12 March 1990, Affirmation 1, p. 9.

17. The Second Extraordinary General Assembly of the Synod of Bishops (1985), "Ecclesia sub Verbo Dei Mysteria Christi Celebrans pro Salute Mundi."

18. Ibid. Relatio Finalis, II, C, 1, quoted by John Paul II in "Christifideles laici" no. 19.

19. See John Paul II, *The Vocation and Mission* no. 5.

20. Lineamenta no. 16 (part quoted from "Lumen Gentium" no. 32).

21. Richard McBrien, "A Theology of the Laity," *American Ecclesiastical Review* 160 (1969) 73.

22. See Raphael Gallagher, "The Synod on the Laity: First Proposals," *The Furrow* (February 1986) 74.

23. See Leonard Doohan, "Contemporary Theologies of the Laity: An Overview since Vatican II," *Communio* 7 (1980) 241.

24. See Pirola, "Laity: A Block" 424.

25. Ibid. 428-429.

26. Ibid. 430-431.

27. John Paul II, *The Vocation and Mission* no. 20; see also Gerry Kelly, "Communion and Mission: The Idea of Church in Christifideles Laici," *Australasian Catholic Record* 66 (October 1989) 387, 393.

28. John Paul II, *The Vocation and Mission* no. 25.

29. See Y. Congar, *Ministères et communion ecclésiale* (Paris: Cerf, 1971) 31-49.

30. See Doohan, "Contemporary Theologies" 236.

31. See K. Rahner, *The Shape of the Church to Come* (London: SPCK, 1974), chapters 3 and 4 of Part II, and chapters 3 and 4 of Part III.

32. World Council of Churches, "Justice, Peace," Part III, no. 4, p. 25.

33. Ibid. Part III, nos. 2-3, pp. 24-25.

34. Ibid. Part III, no. 1, p. 23.

35. Power, *Gifts That Differ* 114-115.

36. Ibid. 115-116.

37. For the eschatological nature of these notes which shows that unity is not possible in history, but that we are in the process of overcoming the roots of disunity, see Moltmann, *Church in the Power of the Spirit* (London: SCM Press, 1977) 337-361.

38. K. Rahner, "What Is the Theological Starting-Point for a Definition of the Priestly Ministry?", *Concilium* 3:5 (March 1969) 43-46.

39. See "Asian Colloquium on Ministries in the Church (Hong Kong, 27 February - 5 March 1977)" in *Cardinal Bea Studies*, vol. 7, ed., Pedro S. De Achútegui (Manila: Ateneo University Publications, 1977), Conclusion, nos. 103, 48.

40. S.J. Emmanuel, "Contemporary Catholic Thought on the Vocation and Mission of the Laity in the Church and in the World," *FABC Papers* 44 (1986) 22.

41. Power, *Gifts That Differ* 127.

42. Ibid. 116.

43. "Presbyterorum Ordinis" no. 4, from *The Documents of Vatican II*.

44. Ibid.

45. "Source and apex" is perhaps overstated. Most proclamation is in fact a form of witness outside the context of liturgy. Whereas celebration is essential to the nourishment of life, liturgy is related to that wider involvement in life; regarding "witness," see "Evangelii Nuntiandi" no. 41.

46. "Presbyterorum Ordinis" no. 5.

47. 1 Peter 2:4-9.

48. John Paul II, *The Vocation and Mission* no. 32.

49. See Brendan Lovett, "The Shape of Mission in Today's World," 1982 (mimeo).

50. Ibid.

51. F. Claver, FABC Papers 40 (1986) 24.

52. Maureen Walsh, Pacific Mission Institute, Sydney, May 1986 (mimeo).

53. For example, a lay missionary program in which lay people recruit, screen, prepare, and support other lay people in the field, can only have meaning as a temporary step on the way to achieving full partnership and interdependence.

Liturgy and Cultures

11

An African Interpretation of Liturgical Inculturation: The *Rite Zairois*

Chris Nwaka Egbulem, O.P.

THE ISSUE OF INCULTURATION, WITH SPECIAL REFERENCE TO THE LITURGY, has been one of the most central issues for the church on the African continent since the late 1960s. Following inspirations drawn from the Second Vatican Council and statements made about Africa under the pontificate of Pope Paul VI (and later by John Paul II), theologians in Africa have continued to reflect together on how best to help Christian life be incarnated among the people of that huge continent. The task is both urgent and enormous. No one is ready for a repeat experience of the ill luck that was suffered by an earlier Christianity in North Africa, when it was almost completely crushed by the Islamic invasion of the area. A major reason for that demise has been attributed to the fact that the faith professed by the people in North Africa then was never allowed to place its roots deep into the local soil.

The church in Zaire has been a leader in the effort to make the faith feel at home in Africa. Even before the Second Vatican Council, the Bishops' Conference in Zaire had taken up positions that were to encourage the development of Christian

African philosophy and Christian African theology. With the now popular "Faculté de Théologie Catholique de Kinshasa" as its special organ for research and publication, the Zairean Bishops' Conference launched into ecclesiastical projects that have grown to prominence not only locally, but also around the world. One such project is the so-called *Rite Zairois* of the eucharistic celebration.[1] According to the late Cardinal Malula of Kinshasa, Zaire, this celebration is a living sample and result of the liturgical movement and inculturation program in the Zairean Church.[2]

I have been in regular contact with the church in Zaire since 1980 through residence in Kinshasa, return visits, and especially correspondence with confreres, academic colleagues, and friends. At the end of the last decade I completed and defended my research on the Zairean liturgical project, which, I believe, was the first full treatment of the subject in the English language. That effort was undertaken and accomplished under the inspiring direction of David Power (see note no. 5 below). This paper will first give some historical data from the birth through the evolution and approval of the Zairean Mass. A special examination of the notion of inculturation will be made in relation to theological discourse in Africa, with emphasis on what this implies with regard to the liturgy. This will open up to the issue of liturgical sensitivity to traditional African values, which values will be identified in this paper. Then the *Rite Zairois* will be examined as a concrete expression of an African notion of liturgical inculturation.

The Zairean Liturgical Project

The bishops of Zaire gathered in an assembly in 1961 knew that there was a problem with the liturgy celebrated in Zaire. In an emphatic way they wrote:

> The liturgy introduced in Africa is not yet adapted to the proper character of our populations, and therefore has remained foreign to them. The return to the authentic traditions of the liturgy greatly opens the way to a fundamental adaptation of the liturgy to the African environment. Such an adaptation is very necessary for the edification of the traditional (pagan) community on religious grounds, since worship is the most important

element which unites the entire community. Only a living and adapted form of worship can generate the indispensable deepening of the faith which cannot be given through instruction alone . . . An elaborate study and critique of the religious customs as well as a living contact with the people will reveal the fundamental cultural needs, and will furnish the necessary elements for the elaboration of a living African liturgy which is sensitive to the aspirations of the populations.[3]

What is remarkable in the above statement is that the bishops not only saw the problem, but also had a good sense of how best to develop a sound solution to it. The aspects of critical appreciation of the customs of the people and the necessary contact and communication with the people are very vital to the process of developing their projects in the future. Before Vatican II met to discuss and recommend its principles for the "adaptation" of the liturgy to the various cultures of the world, the Zairean Church had already made specific requests to Rome concerning its local liturgical needs. The years of the council and the years immediately following it proved to be somewhat passive by way of local creativity. The outcome of the Second Vatican council did not filter fast enough through Africa. In the meantime, the need for a realistic and honest appraisal of traditional African life by the church had become urgent.

It should be stated that the starting point for the new rite of the eucharist in Zaire is Vatican II's Constitution on the Sacred Liturgy, which was promulgated in 1963. This document dealt specifically with the norms for adapting the liturgy to the various cultures of the world (CSL 37-40). When the new *ordo Missae* was promulgated on 3 April 1969, there was a general feeling in parts of Africa (especially in Zaire) that it did not adequately represent the religious and cultural feelings of African Christians. As a response to this, the Zairean bishops set up a commission to do the work of proposing a eucharistic liturgy that better suited the genius of the Zairean people. They were poised to go beyond the texts prepared in Rome and sent to them. For them, this would mean:

the necessity to open the liturgy to the cultural values of the people of Zaire. On the one part, this means (while respecting the common faith of the Church) the admission of modifications in the forms and expressions of the liturgy in a way that identifies with the genius and character of the life of the Zairean people. On the other part, those cultural elements of the people of Zaire will be subjected to the process of purification and critique in the light of the Christian faith.[4]

It was a publicly professed position of the Zairean bishops at that time that to africanize the liturgy did not just mean adopting some customs usual in the African cultural context, but to create a liturgy which incarnates the mystery celebrated by the Christian community in an expressive and comprehensive manner. When the bishops submitted a schema of the new rite to the Congregation for Divine Worship in December 1969 asking for permission to develop it, the Congregation gave its support for the work necessary for the Zairean bishops to "integrate" the new ordo into Zairean life.[5]

From the beginning of its work, the special liturgical commission in Zaire worked its way through consultations at various levels of church life: parish and diocesan liturgical commissions, committee of bishops, and constant dialogue and correspondence with the Roman congregations. Using the Roman ordo as a starting point, the commission reflected on how the role of a village chief in a traditional assembly could be brought to bear on the Christian celebration of the eucharist. At that time, it was understood that the role of the presider at the eucharist would mirror the role of the chief in the village assembly. As time went on, the emphasis on the role of the presider was modified to include the role of the assembly. In the development of this rite, therefore, three models were somehow merged: the model of the Roman ordo, the model of the chief-presider, and the model of the gathered assembly.

Between 1970 and 1985, the work of refining the proposed text of the rite and the liturgical experimentations were going on simultaneously. There was also a slow catechesis going on both within the Bishops' Conference and among the people. There were issues for which consensus was not possible, especially in what concerned costume and rubrics. The Congregation for Divine Worship together with the Congregation for the Doctrine of the Faith were considering the liturgical and doctrinal positions of the proposed text of the rite. A joint meeting of the representatives of the Roman congregations and the Zairean Bishops' Conference and liturgical commission was held in Kinshasa, Zaire, on 4 November 1986. It was at this meeting that the final ratifications were made in preparation for the eventual approval of the text of the rite. At that meeting, much of the debate and lack of consensus centered around several issues, the most important being the title of the project, and the nature of the explanations given for the invocation of ancestors in the Zairean liturgy.[6] Then on 30 April 1988, following repeated requests to Pope John Paul II by the Zairean bishops for the approval of the text, the Congregation for Divine Worship formally approved the Zairean rite of the eucharist with the official title: *Missel romain pour les diocèses du Zaire.* This title was proposed by Rome. The use of this title made it clear that this rite was intended (by Roman authorities) to maintain Roman identity. As for the invocation of ancestors, although the practice is in the approved text, the questioned explanations were omitted. What survived the purge was an irregular typology made of African ancestors with Old Testament personages like Abel, Abraham, and Melchizedek, as though the dignity of African ancestors depended on these personages. In spite of this, however, the successful emergence of this ritual of invocation of African ancestors in the church's highest form of worship will remain one of the most central identities of this Mass, and of course a major contribution to Christian theology.

The emergence of the Zairean Mass is usually cited as the clearest result of the inculturation movement in Africa. What is this notion of inculturation, and how has it been perceived by the church in Zaire? In the following section these questions will be treated in relation to the liturgy.

Liturgical Inculturation

Our earliest known use of the term "inculturation" occurred during the debates on "mission and non-Christian cultures" at the 29th Missiology Week at Louvain in 1959. Two of the contributions were entitled: "Actualité du problème de l'inculturation" and "Lacunes et problèmes de l'inculturation dans le contexte traditionnel et moderne."[7] The term is, therefore, a neologism, at least in theology. In spite of this, the reality that it represents has been present throughout church history. It is a basic presupposition of this writer that every genuine attempt in church history to have the message and life of the Gospel appropriated into the lived experience of a given culture could be classified as inspired by the spirit of inculturation.

Since the last decade, the term inculturation has been widely used in the areas of theology, missiology, and—in a special way—liturgy. Although the term does not appear in the documents of Vatican II, Anscar Chugungco has suggested that in some instances of the Constitution on the Sacred Liturgy, words like *aptatio* and *accomodatio* could be rendered by the word inculturation.[8] Inculturation is different from adaptation. It goes beyond cosmetic changes. This is what the 1985 Extraordinary Synod in Rome was emphasizing when its participants stated:

> Since the Church is a communion which joins diversity and unity, being present throughout the world, it takes up whatever it finds positive in all cultures. Inculturation, however, is different from a mere external adaptation, as it signifies an interior transformation of authentic cultural values through integration into Christianity and the rooting of Christianity in various human cultures.[9]

Pedro Arrupe's definition of inculturation following the 32nd General Assembly of the Society of Jesus in 1978 stated:

> Inculturation is the incarnation of the Christian life and message in a concrete cultural situation, in such a way that not only is this experience expressed with elements typical of the culture in question (otherwise it would only be superficial adaptation), but also that this same experience transforms itself into a principle of inspiration, being both a norm and a unifying force, transforming and recreating this culture, thus being at the origin of a new "creation."[10]

In this definition neither the Gospel nor the culture is independent of the other. Both interact at a deep level of mutual give and take. In the process a new creation is made.

The project of inculturation proceeds from the incarnational experience of Christ. Pope John Paul II, addressing the Pontifical Biblical Commission in 1979, said that inculturation "expresses one of the elements of the great mystery of the incarnation."[11] Thus liturgical inculturation pertains to the incarnation of Christian liturgical experience in a local worshiping community. Chupungco has described liturgical inculturation as:

> the process whereby the texts and rituals used in worship by the local Church are so inserted in the framework of culture, that they absorb its thought, language, and ritual patterns. Liturgical inculturation operates according to the dynamics of insertion in a given culture and interior assimilation of cultural elements. From a purely anthropological point of view, inculturation means that the people are made to experience in liturgical celebration a "cultural event," whose language and ritual they are able to identify as elements of their culture.[12]

Liturgical inculturation carried to its logical implications opens up to a whole new area of not only making already established liturgical rites meaningful in a given local situation, but also of developing new dimensions in the church's worship patterns, thus bringing some new but yet authentic experiences of worship into the church. This would happen at the level of the sensitive and inspired translation of liturgical texts and the creation of entirely new ones;[13] the transmission of rituals, and the creation of new ones according to local needs.[14] Thus the challenge of liturgical inculturation lies not in explaining away the Roman rite, say, in an African locality, but in celebrating the Christian mystery in question in such a way as to exhibit both the true sense of the mystery and the authentic cultic sense of the given African people.

The Challenge of Liturgical Inculturation in Africa

There is a two-sided problem associated with inculturating the liturgy in Africa.

First, African culture, like all other cultures, is not static but participates in the process of evolution. The search for the genius of African culture runs the risk of invading the church of today with aspects of African life of the past which may today impede progress or which have by their nature become redundant. There has to be a process of discernment: the Gospel can challenge traditional culture.

The nature of Christian worship demands that cultural elements and values to be incarnated into the liturgy undergo critical evaluation. According to the Constitution on the Sacred Liturgy (37), nothing should be admitted which is indissolubly bound up with superstition and error. Instead, they should be in harmony with the true and authentic spirit of the liturgy. For example, that some ancient African tribes sacrificed human beings during religious ceremonies is a fact that neither the Gospel nor today's African life wishes to resurrect. When we therefore talk about African heritage, we must do so in the context of the total growth experienced in its cultural evolution. This is a fundamental concern for inculturation.

The second problem is equally acute. Official church documents tend to give so much prominence to the primacy of the Gospel in such a way that the carrier of that Gospel, the church, is presented as having been fully made already. In that way, it looks like everything seen in the church's way of life is part of the authentic mystery of Christ. The church thus claims to be the judge of culture, the measure being itself (irrespective of its cultural accretions through history). Certain traits of a given culture then become condemned because they do not immediately fit the vision of the church as perceived by the evangelizer.

Authentic inculturation needs to respect the pillars of culture, or as Chupungco puts it, "the dynamics of culture."[15] Inculturation brings the church and the culture into mutual dialogue and sharing, and introduces an experience of bonding. The end result, "a new creation," will bear the mark of authentic Christianity and authentic Africanness. According to Elochukwu Uzukwu:

> If we insist that inculturation involves the meeting between the heart of the Gospel and the heart of African culture so that the Christ becomes the principle of animation to generate a new creation, then we must insist that conversion and on-going renewals are requisites. If a new African reality is presupposed in this experience, its experience in the eucharistic rite would embody commitment to the dead-risen Jesus who animates his African assembly convoked in joy to celebrate his mystery in the meal ritual.[16]

For real liturgical inculturation to happen, the heart of the local situation must encounter the Christ, an encounter which takes ritual embodiment. At the same time, the church's message will have to be "converted" into a mode assimilable to the culture, and expressible in the language patterns of the culture. The term "language" here is not just about words but the entire process of re-presenting the message of the Gospel in a concrete way.

This bifocal nature of authentic inculturation is well expressed by Engelbert Mveng:

> When we speak of inculturation, we mean the evangelization of African culture in such a way as to enable it to be integrated into the eternal Christian heritage and to continue to make this heritage more "catholic." And on the other hand, we mean the africanization of Christianity to the point where it becomes a constituent of the spiritual and cultural heritage of Africa.[17]

Bruno Chenu discerns three stages in the inculturation process: the first is the "violent intrusion" of Christianity which comes to disturb the traditional beliefs of society. The second stage consists of a "trial marriage" between Christianity and the local culture. Here "neither of the partners emerges unscathed from the meeting." Then the final stage is the emergence of "a new creation."[18]

Why do we insist on the double (Gospel-culture) or, shall we say for clarity, the triple (Gospel, culture of the evangelized, culture of the evangelizer) aspect of the challenge of inculturation? We do not possess a pure Christian Gospel devoid of cultural traits. For this reason, inculturation will allow the Gospel as transmitted to be challenged and transformed with the view of liberating it from cultural accretions of other peoples. An African theologian, Justin Ukpong, wrote that inculturation in Africa (and elsewhere for that matter) involves what he called a "confrontation" of faith and culture, in which occurs the interpenetration and interrogation of both in order to yield a reality that is both African and Christian.[19] Liturgical inculturation is not based on what the Gospel does with culture: it is about what the Gospel and culture do with each other in the continuous process of encounter and mutual embrace. Chupungco puts it thus:

There must be reciprocity and mutual respect between liturgy and culture. Culture has also its categories, dynamics and intrinsic laws. Liturgy must not impose on culture a meaning or bearing that is intrinsically alien to its nature. Authentic inculturation respects the process of transculturation whereby both liturgy and culture are able to evolve through mutual insertion and absorption without damage to the identity of each.[20]

There are certain aspects of culture that by their nature witness to the highest realities of the Gospel. Chupungco refers to this concurrence of meaning as "connaturalness."[21] This was how Christian liturgy adopted and maintains the uses of bread and wine, water, oil, incense, candles, genuflections, immersion, laying of hands, anointings, and so on. In all these, the cultural elements retain their traditional expression and vitality.

Three positions will therefore be identified at this time. First, some cultural values by their conditions of connaturalness with the gospel values, can and should have expression in the liturgy. Second, certain cultural characteristics might need to be purged of certain meanings before they can truly bear an evangelical character. The theologian of inculturation, inspired by the Gospel, should liberate such values from images contrary to the truth. Third, what is evidently and wholly contrary to the Gospel must not be admitted into the liturgy.

In the process of liturgical inculturation, what is said of the cultural values here applies to the liturgy itself. This is true when we remember the fact that so much has been accumulated into the Christian liturgy from the various cultures of the world. Whereas certain aspects of the liturgy today may have their references in Scripture, some do not. Even when Scripture and tradition promoted the use of a particular element in the liturgy, it is possible to find a cultural situation where that element bears a most negative meaning. Chupungco raised the question without offering an answer.

Among some peoples, the drinking of wine and the laying on of hands ranks high among the religious and cultural prohibitions. Since the use of wine for the eucharist and the laying of hands for ordination are of biblical origin and are essential to these sacraments, can the dynamics of transculturation in these cases be dispensed with? Can catechesis dissipate the religious and cultural objections against them? Or should the church look into the possibility of adopting some other elements which can equivalently express the meaning of the sacraments?[22]

If the dynamics of culture are to be respected in such cases, it would be inconsistent with the nature of inculturation to attempt to impose those foreign and "ungodly" elements over such people. Evangelical and missionary prudence would require the search and assimilation of other practices and elements which bear the marks of authenticity and gospel spirit. That is liturgical inculturation.

What, then, would be the characteristics of a well-inculturated African celebration (in this case) of the eucharist? Referring to the Zairean Mass, Elochukwu Uzukwu responded:

> The Zairean liturgical experiment would meet our idea of an inculturated African Eucharistic celebration if it projects a Christian celebration which expresses joyously salvation from God in the Christ in a cultic meal-setting, and if it takes seriously assemblies and meal celebrations practiced in the traditional African experience of God, ancestors, spirits, and forces. The celebration would thus express how the African tradition is now under the transforming direction of the Christ whom African Christians confess as savior. Thus in the Zairean rite, one should expect a necessary freedom to express the transforming effect of God's salvific work in Zairean tradition which only Zaireans can truly and deeply experience. In addition, one should anticipate the dialectics of acceptance and rejection as the necessary consequence of the transforming action of God among African peoples to bring about in the Christ a new creation.[23]

Uzukwu, who himself was one of the influential liturgists in and around Zaire during the 1980s, was one of those who kept challenging the Zairean liturgical commission to go much deeper in its efforts to evolve a eucharistic liturgy that is truly African and truly Christian. For me, this would include not only cultic sensitivity, but also the experience of the liberation movement in Africa.

The main issue here is sensitivity to African cultural values. In the course of my research, I set out to make a synthesis of the theological discourse concerning traditional African values during the years following independence across the continent. So much of the literature came out after 1967, the year that Pope Paul VI issued his message *Africae Terrarum* to African churches.[24] By way of reference, I mention the works of Mbiti, Mulago, Thomas, and Luneau, as classic examples of the literature on this subject.[25] In what follows, I will identify what will be proposed here as the juice of traditional African life, without which inculturation in Africa would be utterly fruitless.

The Genius of Traditional African Life

Before looking at the text and content of the approved Zairean Mass, it is important to see what are considered as the pillars of African life which should have some form of expression in liturgical celebration. Apart from the general theological and liturgical enthusiasm in Zaire in the early seventies, there was also a continental movement toward authenticity. Theologians and liturgists were not the only ones eager to get back to their true African roots in order to see how to enrich the church with its blessings: there were also social scientists and ethnologists inquiring into the once forsaken values of traditional African life. The results of their inquiries would motivate the theologians and liturgists in Africa, and the consequent reawakening of these experts to their call of duty helped to instigate a new courage and strength in embracing the authentic values of African life. Any valid appreciation of the Zairean Mass must be done from the point of view of its sensitivity to the core values of African life as they came to be reevaluated. It was already an accepted position in Africa by the early seventies that for any liturgy to be called African in any way, it ought to reflect in a visible way its sensitivity to traditional African values.

I do not intend to do any exhaustive overview here of the debates that accompanied the identification and enumeration of these values. I have already done so in another instance.[26] We will content ourselves here with enumerating and clarifying the values.

Active Presence of the Creator God in the World

First to be considered is the African notion of the active presence of the Creator God in the world. African spirituality gives a most prominent place to the Creator. This God is father and mother. God is present, alive, active, and remains in direct communication and collaboration with creation. Although here with us, God is higher than us. God is the beginning without an end. All that exists has its origin and meaning in God and will terminate in God. In a special way, African spirituality sees the glory of God made manifest in humanity. Across the middle-belt region of Africa, names given at traditional naming ceremonies ordinarily have spiritual references to God, or have religious connotations.

Unified Sense of Reality

Second is the African unified sense of reality. For the African, divinity and humanity are not seen apart. The sacred and the so-called profane interact, and just as body is united to the soul, divinity is indwelling in our world. The visible and invisible worlds interpenetrate. All the beings in the universe and beyond exercise influence one over the other. The world of the spirits participates in the human world. Spiritual needs are as important to the body as bodily needs are for the soul. All are part of human experience, just as life and death are. The human body is like a capsule, an integral whole, incorporating blood, water, fire, air, soil, and all other symbols of life. In short, dualism has little or no place in African thought.

Life as the Ultimate Gift

Third is the African notion of life as the ultimate gift. African spirituality identifies life as the prime act of donation from the Creator to creature. On the human plane, life is the starting point. It is to be received, sustained, enhanced, and safeguarded. Life at all levels is sacred. It is for this reason that marriage and procreation play central roles in the social and religious rites of African peoples. So also are the rituals of initiation.

Between birth and death is the period when the rituals of healing occupy a most important place. This is the effort to regenerate and sustain life when it is threatened by illness or hostile environment. Traditional African healers occupy a most prominent place in the life of the village. Through the power of the spoken word, incantations, divinations, prayers, sacrifices and offerings, the use of roots, herbs, and other natural substances, the healing ministry continues to be promoted in traditional African life. The life and ministry of Archbishop Milingo of Zambia is also a testimony to this aspect of African life.[27]

Family and Community as the Place to be Born, Live, and Die

Fourth is the concept of the family and community as the place to be born, live, and die. African spirituality discerns a vital link between a person and the members of the same family, clan, or community. Being born into a family plunges one into a kind of current, and it is one's ability to be identified within that family and community that will determine one's nature of existence and survival. The life of the individual is therefore lived in participation with others in the community. This is true for the men as it is for the women. (In fact, the position of the woman in traditional African thought is one of honor and respect, although modern trends tend to relegate them to the background. Some of the blame for this has to be taken by the religious and theological positions assigned to women by Christian and Islamic missionaries.) The kinship system which reinforces the traditional notion of the extended family is what has kept the predominant style of the African family alive today. In this sense, it could be said that the African is incomplete when alone. It is no wonder that the unique African style of hospitality has remained a big attraction today, especially to foreigners. This hospitality must be seen from the point of view of its origin in the system of the extended family and community. This too translates into the moral order, in the strict demand for the practice of social justice, and in the promotion of life and the well-being of others.

The Nature and Role of the Ancestors

Fifth is the African conception of the nature and role of the ancestors. The African world actively extends beyond the visible world. The ancestors (sometimes called "the living dead") are those "dead" members of the family or community whose lives left a great heritage and honor to the living, and who continue to influence their families through the legacy they left behind. Not all the dead are ancestors. In fact, I have argued that it is easier to become a Catholic saint than to be an African ancestor (the economic factors excluded). The memories of these ancestors are invoked in various ceremonies and rituals of African peoples. They are invoked as intermediaries between God and the people, in continuation of their earthly function in which they combined headship of their families with ritual leadership.

It is perhaps in this context that we should mention the special respect and place accorded old people in view of their age. The elderly are believed to be in special communion with ancestors both by the fact of their having lived and worked for such a long time under the inspiration of the ancestors, and the fact of their proximity to joining their company. Old age is usually associated with wisdom, dignity, and respect.

Oral Tradition

Sixth is oral tradition in African life. African spirituality accords a great potency to the spoken word. There are three reasons for this. First, the spoken word derives from the divine presence in the world. The sounds of nature (thunder and lightening, for example) are some of the ways God's voice is actualized. Second, the spoken word proceeds immediately from the most privileged of creation, the human person. Words used to bless or curse are believed to possess the power to be effective. Third, the word is not just sound: it names, identifies, and describes a subject. It is what makes history real. The word in African thought encompasses the entire system of communication. This is what is generally referred to as oral tradition in African life, which also includes communication in music, song, dance, poetry, proverbs, storytelling, art, and rituals.

Sanctity of Nature and Environment

Seventh is the African notion of the sanctity of nature and environment. Africans see the presence of the divine in creation. The environment is like the writing board of the Creator. The moon and the stars, rivers and seas, hills and mountains, fish and animals, people . . . all carry the message of God's presence. In other words, created nature and the human environment (visible and invisible) bear the mark of goodness and godliness. This is the first premise in the African notion of the environment. It is for this reason that human activities are generally considered from the religious point of view. All space is sacred. And in spite of the fact that there may be designated locations for worship and sacrifices, the one who is on the way to worship is considered as already in the act of worshipping. The fruits of the earth coming from the labor of men and women are seen as worthy elements for offerings and sacrifices to God.

The seven values described above form the core of the African world-view or, in other words, African spirituality. How these may be expressed in the diverse cultures of the African continent may differ in their details but not in substance. There may be some isolated cases of discrepancy, like the case of the *Nuer* of Sudan who do not have a cult of ancestors. In spite of such exceptions, we still hold to our theory of unity: that there exists enough ground for holding to what has been called "a common Africanness" or "a basic world-view among Africans." This is especially true for the entire sub-Saharan Africa or, more specifically, middle-belt Africa.

Having identified the central values of African life, our next task is to examine in what ways, if any, these have found expression in the approved text and celebration of the Zairean Mass. In this task we must remember that it is not the value as such that has to be clearly expressed: it could sometimes be the symbolic expressions of these values that appear in the celebration. It is important that the text be seen in conjunction with the celebration itself, since it is evident that major differences exist between the two, and that, in fact, the celebration is far ahead of the text by way of sensitivity to local sentiments. We will now consider the approved text of the Zairean Mass. In so doing we will touch on some aspects of the Mass that give it an African identity.

The Approved Text of the Zairean Mass

The approved text of 1988 retains the two main parts of a traditional eucharist: the liturgy of the word and the liturgy of the eucharist, which are preceded by an introductory part and followed by a concluding part. The introductory part includes: entrance of the announcer (welcome of the assembly and invitation to worship); entrance procession of presider and ministers; veneration of the altar; salutation of the people and introduction of the liturgy; invocation of saints and ancestors; song of acclamation (*Gloria*); opening prayer. The liturgy of the word includes: first reading; responsorial psalm; second reading; enthronization and proclamation of the gospel; homily; profession of faith; penitential rite; kiss of peace; prayer of the faithful. The liturgy of the eucharist includes: procession to the altar with gifts; eucharistic prayer; Lord's Prayer; communion and thanksgiving; prayer after communion. The concluding rite includes: blessing and sending forth, exit procession.

A look at a comparative table of the Roman and Zairean Masses reveals that their basic structures are the same. Within the segments of the liturgy however, there are some remarkable differences. The Zairean Mass has a more elaborate opening rite. The role of the announcer in the Zairean Mass is a reflection of native tradition, especially the role of the town-crier in village life. Other differences include the invocation of saints and ancestors in the opening part of the Zairean Mass. Let us also note the position of the penitential rite and the kiss of peace in the Zairean Mass. Whereas the Roman Mass has the penitential rite in its introductory part (before the *Gloria*), the Zairean Mass uses it to conclude the liturgy of the word; and whereas the Roman Mass has the kiss of peace in the liturgy of the eucharist as preparation for communion, the Zairean Mass has it in the liturgy of the word as conclusion of the penitential rite.[28] Within the Zairean Mass, we must recognize an entirely new element, which is the invocation of African ancestors.

Apart from structural differences, there are some ceremonial differences. We already indicated the role of the announcer in the Zairean Mass. He or she fulfills a unique ministry of leading the assembly to a fuller participation in the liturgy. Readers in this Mass ask for and receive a blessing from the presider before proclaiming the word, just as the deacon does before the gospel in the Roman Mass. In a typical African situation, no one in the village assembly would rise to speak without first seeking the presiding chief's permission to do so. The act of "giving the word" to someone is the sole way the power of speech is delegated to individual members of the village assembly.

There is also some difference in the ceremony of the presen-

tation of gifts. The procession in song and dance in the Zairean Mass, and the words used during the presentation itself,
bear marks of originality. Again, the version of the eucharistic
prayer which, although growing out of Eucharistic Prayer II
of the Roman Sacramentary, bears marks of both a native
touch and distinctive theological positions. The Zairean Mass
has officially one eucharistic prayer, whereas the Roman Mass
has nine.

In conclusion, we identify four areas of structural independence: the position of the invocation of the saints, the inclusion of the invocation of ancestors, the position of the penitential rite, and the position of the kiss of peace. Other signs of
independence are: the more powerful role of the presider, the
role of the announcer, the more elaborate processions with
dances (including dances around the altar), and the use of a
distinctive eucharistic prayer. The role of orality and music,
poetry and dance, native costumes and instruments, all contribute to giving the Zairean Mass its native touch.

Further Critique of the Zairean Mass

No one will doubt the highly religious and God-filled nature
of the Zairean celebration. The reason for the gathering, for the
celebrating, for offering, for singing, for dancing, for who we
are, is God. This God is seen to be active in the environment,
and prayers made to God reflect the richness that is found in
the Zairean sky, land, and waters. These prayers are trinitarian, and they bring forth the African sense of the divine presence. However, this liturgy is still dependent on the prayers of
the Roman Sacramentary for the opening prayer, prayer over
the gifts, and prayer after communion. African theologians
and liturgists have frowned on this, noting the dry character of
these Roman formulas. The church in Zaire knows this handi-
cap and hopes to evolve its own prayers. When this happens,
such prayers should reflect the poetic, repetitive, proverbial,
short-phrased, God-centered nature of traditional African
prayers. Above all, there ought to remain room for reflective
spontaneity in the proclamation of liturgical prayers.

In the context of the structural differences already described, we find the Zairean Church reflecting certain ele-

ments of traditional African life. The invocation of saints and ancestors at the beginning of the liturgy helps to establish a creative link between the past, the present, and the future church. Africans have continued to cherish the identity with their ancestors. This invocation is a rite of contact and communion. What is unfortunate here in the liturgy is the complete absence of any names of ancestors. Later, at the end of the preface, the ancestors are again mentioned without names. This is unfortunate because ancestors are not mental concepts but historical people. Among many African tribes (Igbos, Yorubas, etc.), their names are mentioned during rituals. The approved text is still caught up in the debate of who indeed is an ancestor. Besides, one notices a poverty of words in the way the Zairean Mass describes the ancestors. The text should somehow indicate that the ancestors are seen as the source of unity, survival, and life of their offspring: they regulate the moral order and act to render justice in the name of the Creator; they are custodians of law and order in their tribes. Their memorial in the Mass should therefore take a more positive and pronounced style.

Next is the rationale for the position of the penitential rite. In this Mass, the rite is seen as a sign of conversion following the announcement of the word of God.[29] Bishop Anselme Sanon of Bobo-Dioulasso, Burkina-Faso, put it more graphically in comparing African and Roman practices:

> Take the celebration of the eucharist, for example. You people begin it with a penitential liturgy. This is an approach which is altogether contrary to our own mentality. For we have the custom of first of all greeting one another before anything else, and then listening to the message which is brought to us . . . Therefore, according to our own custom, the Word of God and the homily precede the confession of sins, contrary to what is customary.[30]

It is generally accepted across Africa that this placing of the penitential rite better expresses awareness of African religious consciousness. The penitential rite is followed by the kiss of peace, as a conclusion of the rite of reconciliation. It is an outward manifestation of the inward conversion and reconciliation accomplished before the offering, according to the spirit of Matthew 5:25: "Go first and reconcile with your brother, and then come to make your offering." Reconciliation in African tradition is usually followed by mutual embrace or pact of friendship.

Beyond these, we notice the deep expression of family and community spirit in both the text and celebration of the Mass. Participation at the liturgy offers an inclusive feeling of belonging. Women as well as men have creative access to ministry in the liturgy. With the exception of the ministry of the presider (and that of the deacon introduced by Roman pressures), women minister prominently in the sanctuary. The Zairean Church is perhaps the first in Africa to have women "pastors" in some rural parishes. The church is family; the church is community. Hospitality is a central element of this spirit. Visitors to the local church in Zaire will meet the traditional style of hospitality that can sometimes be scandalous, in that people often seek to offer visitors what they themselves do not regularly afford for themselves or their families. But in spite of this, the Mass has no reflection of the tribal conflicts and disunity experienced by many of the participants. Public enemies still share at the eucharist, when African tradition would expect them to reconcile publicly before sharing a meal.

The question of the rite's sensitivity to the issues of liberation, social justice, and peace, is an enduring one. Christians in Zaire are among the poor of that country. Many live under leaking roofs, and so, the three hours or so that the liturgy lasts on Sunday may be their best time in the week. The liturgical project in Zaire has not generated much enthusiasm for the temporal needs of the people, contrary to the traditional demands to look out for the good of the members of the tribe and beyond. There is, however, a new outlook on this issue since the approval of the text in 1988.

The Zairean Mass is celebration. Music, song, dance, are all ways of expressing the life of the people. This reflects the theme of oral tradition in Africa. The whole body is involved in the act of worship. The spoken word offered in proverbial styles, incantations, summons and responses, movements and rhythms, clapping, and shriekings are some of the ways one senses the African character of this Mass.

There is a difference between the text of the rite and the actual celebration. The text is very formal, rigid, non-spontaneous, more Roman than African, very much an academic work. The celebration, on the other hand, is full of life, spontaneous, responding to local sentiments, artistic, and rich with religious symbolisms. A good attempt at recapturing the experience at this celebration has been made by Edward Braxton.[31]

There are two aspects of traditional African life that seem to have very much eluded serious consideration in the evolution of this liturgy. First, the centrality and primacy of life could have been better articulated if there were some ritual of healing in the liturgy. This is a major omission, since healing rituals are among the most central in traditional life on this continent which continues to be menaced by all sorts of disasters to human life and survival. Second, the question of the adoption of local sacramental elements for eucharistic celebration was not really addressed by the commission in Zaire. We have in mind here the sanctity of the environment, and the fact that God has blessed the African soil with nutritional elements holy enough for worship. The importation of wines from Portugal, Spain, and the United States, as well as white wafers, may be some of the aspects of the domination of Roman Christianity that ought to be challenged in the spirit of the inculturation movement.[32]

* * * * * *

What we have presented here could never be exhaustive. Even with the approval of the text of the Zairean rite of the eucharist, the project is still, and ought to continue, in its growth process. We have cited some of its strong points as well as some of its weaknesses. It is yet on its road to being a new creation. And yet it stands out, as others have already attested, as the most inculturated liturgical celebration in Africa today. For this reason it would be presumptuous for any African Church, or any local church community that identifies with African culture and spirituality, to begin a project of liturgical inculturation today without first experiencing in some way the project in Zaire.

So much ground has been covered in Zaire, and this Mass is offering a new vision of what the African Church is offering the world-church. The African Church places a challenge to the church today, in the effort to prepare the ground for the church of the twenty-first century. African-American Christians have already taken this challenge further than many Africans on the African continent, in their search for authentic liturgies that will witness to the African past as well as participate in the culture of North America.

Notes

1. The official title of the approved text is "Missel romain pour les diocèses du Zaire." See *Notitiae* 24 (1988) 455-472. Some earlier versions: "The Zaire Rite for the Mass," *African Ecclesial Review* 17 (1975) 243-248; "Le rite solennel zaïrois de la célébration eucharistique," *Communautés et liturgies* 62 (1980) 57-76.

2. Cardinal Malula's address to Pope John Paul II, Rome, 23 April 1988, in *La Documentation catholique* 85 (1988) 659.

3. Conférence Episcopale du Congo, "Apostolat liturgique - Adaptation du culte," in *Actes de la VIè assemblée plenière de l'episcopat de Congo* (Léopoldville: Secrétariat Général de l'Episcopat, 1961) 362-363.

4. See Jean Evenou, "Le missel romain pour les diocèses du Zaire," *Notitiae* 24 (1988) 454-455.

5. See Chris Nwaka Egbulem, *The "Rite Zairois" in the Context of Liturgical Inculturation in Middle-Belt Africa since the Second Vatican Council* (Washington, D.C.: The Catholic University of America, 1989) 14. Available through microfilm: University Microfilms International, Ann Arbor, Michigan.

6. With regard to the title, the Zairean bishops proposed to us (in order of preference): "Rite zaïrois de la célébration eucharistique," or "Rite de la célébration eucharistique pour l'église du Zaire," or "Rite romano-zairois de la célébration eucharistique." With regard to questions about ancestors, it was asked that four citations be removed from the text. In brief these stated: that the invisible world comprises of God, spirits, ancestors . . .; that God is referred to as ancestor; that we commit sin by abandoning God or the ancestors . . .; and that our sacrificial offerings have reference between us and God or the ancestors. See the full treatment of these issues in Egbulem, *The "Rite Zairois"* 24-29.

7. *Mission et culture non-chrétiennes: Rapports et compte rendu de la 29è semaine de missiologie, Louvain, 1959* (Louvain: Desclée De Brouwer, 1960) esp. 5, 50, 219-223, 235, 311, 315. Aylward Shorter indicated

in his book that the first time it was used "in a theological sense seems to be by Fr. Joseph Masson, S.J., professor at the Gregorian University in Rome, shortly before the opening of the Second Vatican Council in 1962." See Shorter, *Toward a Theology of Inculturation* (Maryknoll: Orbis, 1988) 10. The reference is to Joseph Masson, "L'Eglise ouverte sur le monde," *Nouvelle revue théologique* 84 (1962) 1038. Barthe says that the term first appeared in an official document of the 1977 Synod: "Message to the People of God," as a synonym for the incarnation of catechesis in a culture. He also claims that the word has been known since the thirties; see C. Barthe, "The Theologies of Inculturation," *Catholica* 2 (June 1987) 12.

8. Anscar Chupungco, "A Definition of Liturgical Inculturation," *Ecclesia Orans* 5 (1988) 11, 16. Chupungco went on to say that "SC #65 which allows in mission lands certain initiation elements in use among individual peoples, and SC #77:3 which empowers the Conferences of Bishops to draw up a completely new rite of marriage should in fact be read within the framework of liturgical inculturation."

9. The final document of the Extraordinary Synod, in *The Tablet* (14 December 1985) 1328, no. D.4.

10. Pedro Arrupe, "Lettre sur l'inculturation" of 14 May 1978, as quoted in Bruno Chenu, "Glissements progréssifs d'un agir missionaire," *Lumière et vie* 33 (1984) 75. Translation is mine.

11. Pontificia Commissione Biblica, *Fede e cultura alla luce della Biblia* (Turin, 1981) 5, as quoted by Chupungco, "A Definition of Liturgical Inculturation" 16.

12. Chupungco, "A Definition of Liturgical Inculturation" 17.

13. See the instruction "Comme le prévoit" of 1969, in *Documents on the Liturgy* (Collegeville: The Liturgical Press, 1982) 291.

14. The Constitution on the Sacred Liturgy (77) gave the conferences of bishops the option to draw up a completely new rite of marriage in accord with the usages of peoples and places. See also Chupungco, "A Definition of Liturgical Inculturation" 22.

15. Chupungco, "A Definition of Liturgical Inculturation" 19.

16. Elochukwu Uzukwu, "Inculturation of Eucharistic Celebration in Africa Today," *CHIEA: African Christian Studies* 1 (1985) 17.

17. Engelbert Mveng, "African Liberation Theology," *Concilium* 199 (1988) 18.

18. Bruno Chenu, *Théologies chrétiennes des tiers-mondes* (Paris: Le Centurion, 1987) 144, as referred to by C. Barthe, "The Theologies of Inculturation," *Catholica* 2 (June 1987) 8-14.

19. Justin Ukpong, "The Emergence of African Theologies," *Theological Studies* 45 (1984) 516.

20. Chupungco, "A Definition of Liturgical Inculturation" 19. He then gives examples of how the liturgy "assimilated" cultural aspects from Greek, Roman, and the Franco-German lands, in each case respecting the "dynamics and laws of culture."

21. Ibid. 20.

22. Ibid.

23. Elochukwu Uzukwu, "Inculturation of Eucharistic Celebration" 18.

24. Pope Paul VI, Message "Africae Terrarum," AAS 59 (1967) 1076-1080, 1085-1086; also in *African Ecclesial Review* 1 (1968) 71-84.

25. John Mbiti, *African Religions and Philosophy* (New York: Frederick A. Praeger, 1969); idem, *The Prayers of African Religion* (Maryknoll: Orbis, 1975); idem, *Introduction to African Religion* (London: Heineman, 1975); Vincent Mulago, *La Réligion traditionelle des Bantu et leur vision du monde*, 2d ed., revised and corrected (Kinshasa: Faculté de Théologie Catholique, 1980); Louis-Vincent Thomas and René Luneau, *La Terre africaines et ses réligions: Traditions et changements* (Paris: Librairie Larousse, 1975).

26. See Egbulem, *The "Rite Zairois"* 195-286.

27. E. Milingo, *The World in Between: Christian Healing and the Struggle for Spiritual Survival* (Maryknoll: Orbis, 1984); Aylward Shorter, *Jesus and the Witchdoctor* (Maryknoll: Orbis, 1985).

28. For a comparative table of the Roman and Zairean Masses, see Egbulem, *The "Rite Zairois"* 377.

29. See *Notitiae* 24 (1988) 461.

30. As quoted by B. Jarczyk, "Mgr Sanon, évêque du Burkina-Faso: L'amour avant le pardon," *La Croix* (8-9 December 1985) 16.

31. Edward Braxton, "An African Church for African People," *America* (24 November 1984) 340-343.

32. See Elochukwu Uzukwu, "Food and Drink in Africa and the Christian Eucharist: An Inquiry into the Use of African Symbols in the Eucharistic Celebration," *Bulletin of African Theology* 2 (1980) 171-187.

12

"My Son's Bread": About Culture, Language, and Liturgy

Anthony Kain

I have grown past hate and bitterness
I see the world as one;
Yet, though I can no longer hate,
My son is still my son.
All men at God's round table sit,
And all men must be fed;
But this loaf in my hand,
This loaf is my son's bread.[1]

AUSTRALIA, AND IN PARTICULAR ADELAIDE, SOUTH AUSTRALIA, SEEM TO be geographically at the end of our earth. Go east and you are on your way to the Americas. Go north and you are on your way to Asia. Go west and you are on your way to Africa and Europe. Yet we Australians are a very multicultural people. The first migrations of Aboriginal peoples were forty to fifty thousand years ago. The second migrations, from Europe, were during the late eighteenth, and during the nineteenth and twentieth centuries. A third wave after the Second World War, and a fourth more recent wave of Asian migrations, have brought dramatic changes to the continent.

While studying, first with David Power and others in Washington, D.C., and then in Europe, it was good to live in cultures different from my own Anglo-Celtic heritage and to see at first hand some of the cultures whose peoples had migrated to Australia. The experience further impressed upon me the richness and diversity of our human life and culture in Australia. It also revealed to me how this rich diversity had not been really allowed to flourish in our society. It struck me that there was a language and cultural imperialism at work that prevented this.

This essay is meant to contribute to the exploration of a way to renew a liturgical expression that links the social justice issue of multiculturalism with ritual. It is founded in the experience of the local church of Adelaide, and responds to theological, spiritual, political, and social developments.

Confessing the Sin That Divides

While thinking about the struggle for a unity of liturgical expression that respects the rich diversity of the faith community, I had an experience that, for me, poetically expressed the starting point of the problem. I had my annual leave with a few other priests around the "Top End" of Australia, staying in wonderful places—Kakadu, Litchfield, and Bathurst Island. One evening, while boating on a lagoon, looking at the splendid bird life and the crocodiles, a drama representing a constant struggle was enacted before us.

One of the prize sights of Kakadu is the Jabiru, a huge member of the stork family. We happened upon a pair of them dipping their beaks into the marsh and reeds, looking for file snakes, which are their staple diet. The female found one which immediately wound itself around her beak. Shaking the snake free, she kept its tail in her beak, while it grabbed her foot and hung on for life. The Jabiru's mate was immediately in on the drama, snatching the snake's tail from her beak, seeking to tug it from her leg. There was a nervous humor in us as the stork stood on one leg, the other leg extended ungracefully as her mate tugged on the snake, seeking not so much to help her as to steal her food. The snake's grip was broken, it was pecked to death and eaten by the male, as the female slumped to the ground.

In the great scheme of things this presented itself as a small metaphor, part of a language that was conflictual, emotional, and embryonic. The experience was totally engaging for all of us and asked us questions of life, death, evil, and meaning. In this struggle for nourishment we found a metaphor for that in which people of all races, nations, and ways of life are engaged. It is a struggle which we often enter by stealing from our own kind, or devouring one another.

If we are to start anywhere with the expression of our liturgical unity in a complex society, we need to start with the confession of sin. This is because the history, not only of my land Australia, but of most societies in the world today, is blemished with racism and the stains of colonization. In the case of Australia, the sin begins with the lie of a land that was supposedly uninhabited, and goes on through the decades in all the various kinds of competitiveness and ethnic violence that the human spirit could invent. At more subtle levels it is expressed in a monocultural tendency that Mary Gilmore's poem, quoted at the beginning of this article, names. A different attitude is now happily expressed in a national policy of multiculturalism, but the sin is not yet eradicated.

The multicultural policy and the need to acknowledge sin are affirmed by the Australian Catholic Bishops in a pastoral letter of 1988 on *Racism and the Conversion of the Human Heart*. Such a start reminds me of my first experience of David Power. It was in 1978 in a course in which we investigated with him the "Language of Confession." I remember that the thematic for the course included "affirmation" because the confession of sin needs symbolic expression and because affirmation is a resolution of existential conflict and of a conflict of meanings. This is a rather powerful image in itself, though we never did quite "finish" the investigation that we started. To continually pursue the theme of affirmation seems to me to be central to the ongoing struggle for the renewal of our sacramentality as a church and of our liturgical expression in a pluralistic world.

This associates itself with another memory I have of the courses that I followed. I remember how David Power spoke of sacramentality as having to do with the contrast between life in the flesh and life in the spirit, between death and judgement, and between temporality and eternity. The sacraments and liturgy belong to an understanding of life in which we are caught in a continuing, ongoing, constant struggle between flesh and spirit, between life and death, between darkness and light. To explore the nature of that struggle and relate it to the mystery of God by associating Spirit, Christ, and church in ritual is the never ending task. Without the confession of sin, it cannot advance.

Multiculturalism and Social Justice

At its best, the renewal of the liturgy of the church has been caught up with the exploration of the nature of the struggle for the creation of a harmonious society and church. At its best, the exploration of a multicultural expression in liturgy seeks to take steps toward relating this struggle to the mystery of God. At its worst, liturgy reflects a ritualistic imperialism and remains in a realm that is not engaged with the justice issues of our world. To neglect these seems completely out of touch with the tradition of social teaching in the Catholic Church over the last century, celebrated in the centenary of *Rerum Novarum* in 1991.

There is a timeliness in the encyclical *Solicitudo Rei Socialis* in which Pope John Paul II brings us up to date on social issues. This letter criticizes systems on the basis of the dignity of the human person. In the first chapters we read about the growing sense of the ways in which the unity of the human race is seriously compromised. We read about this as a religious, not just a political, issue, based on the teaching that the church is the sacrament of unity, of unity with God, and of the unity of the human race.

In the fifth part of the letter, entitled "A Theological Reading of Modern Problems," we are asked to reflect on a world divided, a world in which we can speak of the structures of sin. The path toward overcoming such division is the long journey of conversion. Central to this journey is "interdependence" in determining systems of relationship in the economic, cultural, political, and religious elements of our world. The encyclical encourages us to see that when "interdependence" is recognized as a moral category, the appropriate response is one of "solidarity." This opposes the structures of sin and expresses "a firm and persevering determination to commit oneself to the common good; that is to say to the good of all and of each individual, because we are responsible for all."[2] Such solidarity is rooted in the unity of God, the Trinity, and reflects the communion which is the church's vocation as sacrament in and to the world.[3] While there are many other resources that help in this exploration of unity in pluriformity,[4] the analysis in this encyclical gives us a focus that is very helpful.

All this has an obvious association with our exploration of the possibility of a multicultural religious celebration that takes account of the real political and economic world in which we live. It means that the process of liturgical renewal has to be done in dialogue with such analysis and that this has to become more and more the task of local churches. In our local church of Adelaide the relationship between social justice issues and liturgy is growing, fanned by the policies of the Multicultural Office and the Diocesan Social Justice and Peace Commission. A spirituality is growing from this relationship. In its 1989 policy statement on "Multicultural Australia," the Adelaide Diocesan Justice and Peace Commission spoke of the church being called to follow the inclusive path of Jesus and "to find in this practice the already present in-breaking of God's kingdom":

> Christians, then, are called to embody kingdom values in their cultural and political practice. There are two gospel principles at stake here, the principle of inclusive solidarity, and the principle of acceptance and celebration of diversity. Both must be maintained if we are to be true to the kingdom practice of Jesus.

This document then describes ways of operating that have been part of our history, the real situation:

> Inclusion without respect for diversity leads to the dominance of one group, to a cultural imperialism. In Australian history it has led in the direction of assimilation politics.

Further on it says:

> Respect for diversity without an attempt at inclusive solidarity
> leads of isolation, cultural self-satisfaction and self interest. In
> Australia this kind of "ethnicity" is really a mono-culturalism,
> a misunderstanding and deformity of multiculturalism, which
> can lead to a fragmented society.

The experience of our local Adelaide church with our Aboriginal and ethnic groups is, I would think, similar to that of
many areas of the "new world." And as our world responds
more to the refugee situation of our time it is also like many
areas of the "old world" where multicultural and pluralistic
societies are becoming more common. The terms and definitions may differ, but I suspect that the reality is very similar.
Thus in describing our experience I address something which
has a wider application.

The similarity lies in the common experience of sin and
guilt that mark our history and present experience as well as
that of other churches. Here as elsewhere, in face of a multicultural society we are called to see how we can give symbolic expression to the sins of the past and of the present, and to find
the ways to resolve existential conflict and conflicts of meaning. This asks of us that we explore the nature of the struggle
in a very deep way. It urges us as Catholic Christians who see
justice at the heart of the Gospel, to relate this struggle to the
mystery of God by associating Spirit, Christ, and the church.

The Diocesan Experiment

As the ordained member of our local Catholic Adult Education Services during the year 1987-1988, I was asked by the Diocesan Pastoral Team[5] to focus some of the issues of multiculturalism in our church. This was a follow-up to the task with
which I had been engaged during the 1986 papal visit to Australia. The eucharist of the Adelaide leg of that national visit
celebrated "Australia, Land of Many Cultures."[6] In that year I
had established a working relationship with the ethnic groups
of our Roman tradition in South Australia, and this facilitated
the work I was asked to undertake after the visit.

Happily there was some precedent to our undertaking. In

August 1987 the Scalabrinian Fathers[7] celebrated their centenary of foundation with a national convention held in Melbourne on "Pastoral Care in Multicultural Australia." Some twenty-two people from our diocese of Adelaide attended this convention, and on our return I called them together to discuss the possibilities of my task. Two surveys emerged as part of the strategy suggested. The first of these was to be addressed to the ethnic groups, the second to the parishes of the diocese. The questions for both surveys were designed by the group that had gone to the Melbourne conference, and advice was received from the Australian Bureau of Statistics and the Social Administration Department of our local Flinders University.

At the insistence of those who attended the Melbourne conference, the survey started with two questions that asked how the group perceived faith needs and what pastoral approaches best served these needs. It also included this question:

> Multiculturalism accepts people irrespective of their ethnic, cultural or linguistic backgrounds, and promotes their full participation in the Australian community. Each of our cultures and traditions is very rich. Would you like to suggest ways that the wider church of Adelaide could be in touch with your culture/tradition and be enriched by it?

The discussion of these questions drew broad comment and the richest replies, giving many the opportunity to express the real hurts, pain, and struggle that had been their personal and collective reality over the past forty years and longer, indeed much, much longer for Aboriginal Australians. A poignant remark came from one old person: "This is forty years too late."

Much of the experience evoked spoke to me of something critical to the creation of multicultural, multilingual liturgy. Liturgical expression needs to start with the real experience of our culture at this present moment. This means that each cultural group has to understand life, evil, and God in a culturally relevant way. This self-expression of cultural groups does not lead to a fragmented monoculturalism but contributes to the enrichment of the whole. The sins to be overcome, in order to come to the reconciliation that this implies, are those of cultural self-satisfaction, isolation, self-interest.

This critical aspect of culturally relevant liturgical expression was impressed upon me by a young man whom I met at a wedding. I asked him about his involvement with his own ethnic group. In response, he spoke sadly and passionately about the fact that he was not involved any more because he felt that the group did not face the issues that were crucial for him or for itself. His experience, and accusation, was that they were living in a cosmetic world where their idea of culture had to do solely with language classes and folk dancing. The real stuff of their experience and national character was hidden behind this "dreadful facade." He even went so far as to say that the life of the group was almost like the communist plot in his native country, a plot that drowned the reality of identity and struggle by having people dress up in their national costumes, singing their national folk songs (not their revolutionary ones!) and dancing their national folk dances.

Whether or not I agreed with his analysis was unimportant. What he succeeded in doing was to put his finger symbolically on something that had distributed me during the papal visit. While preparing for our eucharist with the pope in Adelaide, I had been inundated with requests for superficial representations of different groups at the Mass. It seemed more important to many that their national costume, their national song or dance or tradition or choir or language be seen "up front," than that the day and its liturgy should look squarely at issues facing us as many peoples seeking to be united in the harmony of Jesus Christ.[8]

Unfortunately, this approach to cultural expression in liturgy goes beyond the one occasion of the papal visit. It is so easy to present a few ethnic choirs singing at different parts of the liturgy. It is so easy to use different languages in liturgy. It is so easy to have people in their national costumes walking in processions and doing liturgical movements. These elements might be necessary, but they become valid only when the real issues are given expression in liturgy, issues that involve transformation of the sinfulness of the social order. During the celebration of the bicentenary of European settlement there were such liturgies, but they were only the beginning of what needs to come.

Theological Perspectives

I would like to offer theological perspectives taken from two theologians, Marcus Borg and Jon Sobrino.

In his book *Jesus: A New Vision*,[9] Marcus Borg has two focal points: Spirit and culture. In the preface he describes Jesus' life as a "vivid testimony to the reality of the Spirit, a reality affirmed and known in virtually every society prior to the modern period."[10] This reality is poorly understood and is even discounted in our world, even by some within the church, Borg suggests. Indeed, many in the church today do not acknowledge the connection between the spiritual reality of Jesus and the culture. There is a tendency to be a "sacristy church," a provider of devotions. Yet Jesus "sought the transformation of his social world."[11] The tendency is to frame a gospel spirituality that leaves social affairs the way they are, avoiding the facts of history. If we do this, we will just be folk dancing and wearing national costumes in liturgical celebrations, while treating Jesus as a devotional remembrance, neither a help to reconcile the hurts and pains of history, nor a truth that enlightens the way to live together as one.

Putting liturgy into a social and historical context is to ask questions about how we understand the human struggle to be one, while often remaining divided. It asks us to face questions that relate this struggle to the mystery of the Holy Spirit associated with Christ and church in ritual.

I remember David Power asking us to explore the sacraments and liturgy as celebrations that mediate the Spirit to us, in such a way that we are one body in and with Christ and pray with him to the Father. In that ongoing struggle between the forces of life and death, flesh and spirit are not external forces acting upon a person or community, but they are forces working within them. The meaning inherent in sacraments and liturgy is not something added to nature or human experience to the real things of our real world. This approach is an abiding memory that stays with me from the time of my studies in Washington and has kept me looking for a spirituality and a liturgy that speak to our historical, social, and multicultural reality.

In an essay on "Presuppositions and Foundations of Spiritu-

ality" in *Liberacion con espiritu*[12] Jon Sobrino gives an insight
that is very helpful in our quest for this spirituality. Sobrino
speaks of prerequisites for every concrete spirituality, suggest-
ing that:

> any genuine spirituality will demand, in the concrete: (1) hon-
> esty about the real, (2) fidelity to the real, and (3) a certain "cor-
> respondence" by which we permit ourselves to be carried along
> by the "more" of the real.[13]

If then we were to look at a spirituality of multiculturalism
as a starting point to create a multicultural liturgy, we would
start with a moment of honesty about our history. To start
with this honesty is, as we have said, to start with the sin in
the reality. Sobrino writes of facing reality with an "unconditional no" and an "unconditional yes."[14] The "unconditional
yes" leads us to love and the demands of Jesus from the Gospel. The "unconditional no" has to be pronounced in face of
the sin in the reality.

Once we have reached this point, however, it is critical that
we be "faithful to the reality, regardless of where it may
lead."[15] Situations will arise that make it hard to follow one's
initial honest response to reality, or where one is tempted to
think of one's response as illusory. We must be ready to follow through with Jesus in obedience to the Father, even to the
silence of the cross and the silence of the Father.

To be caught up in the challenge to be faithful to the real of
our collective, historical attitudes to culture, language, and tradition in Australia is quite painful. For many it has been the silence of the pain of the cross. The temptation is to be untrue to
what we know, to water it down, to be overcome by the power
that seems greater than ourselves. However, this dreadful
power, this dreaded silence, is not the end. We are led beyond
them to hope, "bent on helping reality become what it seeks to
be. This is love . . . Hope and love are the ways we correspond
to the 'more' of reality in its ceaseless quest for plenitude."[16]

Multiculturalism in Australia, as elsewhere around the
world, demands heroism of us as we seek to realize its
"more." The most profound aspects of this reality have to do
with the value of each person, interdependence as a system
which determines relationships, solidarity born of the fact that

we are each responsible for all, in a world where the goods of the earth are meant for all.[17] If we explore the reality honestly, and are faithful to it, and if we are willing to be swept along in the "more" of that reality, then we will eventually be able to pray liturgically in a valid and more authentic way.

The creation of multicultural spirituality is critical. It cannot ultimately be avoided. Yet from all around the world we see the signals that there is much unfinished business in overcoming racial and cultural divisions. Despite the amazing shifts in Eastern Europe in recent years, it has become clear that communism had suppressed not only freedom but also darker attitudes. It is also surprising to note the high number of votes cast for a racist candidate in the 1990 Senate elections in a southern state of the United States of America. In October 1990 the European Parliament found it necessary to endorse a report making 177 recommendations aimed at encouraging racial tolerance. The report also spoke of the fact that right wing parties with pronounced racist views had won seats in parliaments in France, Germany, the Netherlands, and Belgium. Furthermore, it provides the statistic of seventy thousand racist attacks in Britain during a single year. As we face cultural and racial tensions, we are haunted by visions of South Africa, the war in the Persian Gulf, Northern Ireland, and Sri Lanka.

Australia has its own share of tensions. The Australian bicentennial celebrations in 1988 forced us to face our own reality. There had been a silence for too long, a silence similar to the silence of the pain of the cross. As well as the sins against the Aboriginal peoples, in pursuing my task I was confronted at many meetings with the sins against migrants, forced to buy there right to stay in Australia by conforming to what amounted to an oppressive servitude. I had to ask how we could bring this personal and collective experience to ritual, to sacraments and liturgical prayer. I needed to note the difference between separate cultural liturgies and liturgies that brought people together to celebrate solidarity and diversity. When this question is raised, we have to face the tendency for particular cultures to dominate, to include by converting others to their way of language and cultural expression. Realistically, people need to express themselves in liturgy in their own language and culture, but this cannot be done at the expense of a solidarity in diversity that exorcises the sins of isolation, self-interest and cultural self-satisfaction.

Listening to Others: An Example

It seems to me that we have to learn to listen to one another in a way that admits of the authenticity and richness of the other, even if this listening involves us in a radically new experience. I would like to illustrate this by an example from my own experience.

When I was at the "Top End" of Australia, I visited the Tiwi people on Bathurst Island. The Catholic Christian story of this people goes back to the turn of the century when a German missionary, Father Gsell, lived on the shores of the strait between Bathurst and the Melville Island, patiently waiting for his presence and what he stood for to be appreciated. In time, his waiting and patience led to the Tiwi people becoming totally Catholic, in a way which allowed them to integrate their forty thousand year old culture into their belief in Christ and the church in quite an exemplary manner.

With my companions, I flew into Bathurst Island at what was for the people a very special time, when we were able to witness some of their ceremonies. No words can express the total experience, yet I want to speak of it in some detail. The universality of the symbols and the integrity of the ceremonies impressed me in a way which gave me hope for our efforts at liturgical expressions that integrate cultures.

Just after Easter of that year, the Tiwi people at the Nguiu settlement experienced the tragedy of a boat accident in the strait between Bathurst and the Melville Islands. Four of their community were drowned, and on the day that we arrived they had begun two days of memorial ceremonies for a young man who was one of the drowned. As we met the parish priest of the island, we also met the leader of the community and his wife, who invited us to the ceremony. This is one of the things that strikes you about the Aboriginal people; they are always willing to invite you to be part of their life and culture. It is an invitation that we whites are just starting to accept in real openness. It is an invitation that we ourselves need to offer and that needs to be shared among different cultural and ethnic groups.

The ceremony started, in quiet, down by the strait, with four fires lit on the shore. Gathered were the family and the extended family of the deceased, about four to five hundred people. Family relationships and various complex ties between families are important to the Tiwi, as they are to all Aboriginal people. The relationships and the differences are integrated into the ritual through color, dance, gesture, and movement. Bodies were painted with ocher and hair colored with ash. Faces where painted with intricate masks that spoke of ancient fears of being recognized by the evil spirit of death. At the same time the masks seemed to me to be also a way of expressing something of who the person under the mask was. There was real beauty and intricacy and color in the facial designs.

All walked to a sacred place under some ancient mango trees. Ritual dancing and chant began, gradually focusing on an area roofed with palm leaves, in the middle of which stood beautifully carved and painted totems. A procession led by the youth's father, mother, and widow entered the area and surrounded the totems. With chants and dances the life and death of this man, of his community, and of all humanity, was being celebrated. It was truly powerful and sacred.

The immediate family slept under the mango trees all night. At midmorning the ceremony recommenced and continued all through Sunday. It began with a sad chant sung by the father of the deceased. This led to Mass, celebrated simply in front of the totems under the palm-leaf roof. What impressed me especially about the role of the ordained celebrant was his ability to be led into what the people wanted for the Mass. One simple example of this was the way in which he responded to the surprise entrance of the deceased's car towards the conclusion of the Mass. It soon became obvious that the car was there for exorcism, so the priest blessed water and sprinkled the car. The family could then use the car that had stood idle since the young man's death. There was a lovely rapport between the priest and the father of the deceased, which allowed the father to remain the focus of the ceremonies in a kind of concelebration.

After the Mass, the day continued with a mixture of exorcisms performed with holy water and smokey gum leaf. Beautiful lyrical dances by the women and girls contrasted with the powerful, stamping dance of the men and boys, evoking every emotion. The ceremony reached a high point of poignancy when small groups danced, with great display of grief, before one of the totems that took on the persona of the deceased. The wedding photo of the young man had now been placed on the totem, which was embraced and mourned over as though it were the deceased himself. Each person expressed grief there at the totem, offering it to the widow and the family sitting beside it. The ceremony concluded with the washing off of the masks and the ashes from faces and bodies. The widow and her three small children were the last to do this. The totems were then taken to the cemetery and placed around the grave of the deceased. All was now reconciled and the community was now free again, free to walk down the strait, free to use the implements that had belonged to the deceased, free to speak his name again.

I was completely captivated and engaged by this ceremony. I thought of how close to the edge of life these people had lived for forty thousand years and of how the ritual expressed this. The ceremony was an amazing vehicle that led to reflection on life, to judgment about it, and to fresh action. It was also obvious that the Tiwi people took on and reinforced their own reality through the ritual. It situated evil and death in the context of the family, of community, of society, and of eucharist, in that context in which the Tiwi expressed who they were as a people.

Thinking of the great treasure that they still had in this ritual, I also thought sadly of how other Aboriginal communities had lost such rituals. I understood as never before the grief and depression of such tribes in this loss. I thought also of people and tribes around the world who had similarly lost their rituals. I thought of ourselves as Australians struggling to express who we are and what meaning there is to our lives. I thought of how closed we remain to each other. Listening to the rich ritual language of people such as the Tiwi will help multicultural Australia to find expression for its characteristic diversity in unity. Theirs is the Spirit who will lead us to listen to and celebrate our diverse cultural identities, but it calls for a powerful epiclesis if this Spirit is to cover the land and transform it through conversion. Within this epiclesis we can have the anamnesis of who Jesus was and is for our culture.

I think now of how good it was to have been there at Nguiu and of how I was drawn into the people's way of being and of doing. I began as a very interested observer but with the progress of the ritual I became totally engaged. It did not seem to matter that I was not of the Tiwi and that I did not understand their language (though I dared to ask for a good number of translations). It was good to feel at one with this community of people expressing their deepest meaning about life and death in a ceremony thousands of years old woven into the ritual of the eucharist.

The word Tiwi simply means "we people" and you know who they are by taking part in their ceremonies. But who are "we" in Australia? Who are "we" in the world? We are people of "every race, language and way of life."[18] We are incredibly diverse, seemingly inexhaustibly different. We have often seen this as a problem, rather than as something that enriches us all. Some have been shy, embarrassed, about sharing their culture. Some have been oppressive about the superiority of their culture. Often the painful questions of Australian society have to do with separation or assimilation. We try to be monocultural rather than multicultural. Coming here, European immigrants did not seek to learn from the culture of the inhabitants. As a result, our history has not been a happy one and we have not listened either to each new wave of migrants.

* * * * * *

Reflection on this past calls us to lament, to seek forgiveness and reconciliation, to look for a healing of memories, to learn to be honest and faithful about the reality of our lives. Yet as Sobrino says, we are led by this into hope, "bent on helping reality become what it seeks to be."[19]

To create liturgies that draw us together in real ways is to live with acceptance and diversity. The Roman rite cannot exist outside of culture. Listening to each other's cultures, we will be drawn not only into mutual tension but into tension with the Roman rite itself, the sort of tension experienced centuries ago in China by Matteo Ricci. The church learns to speak to cultures, just as it learns to listen to them. Our liturgies must not remain bland attempts at universal rituals but must integrate the rites of peoples. In what we realize through hope and love, attentive to the reality of our multicultural past and present, we find a new twist in the poem with which this article was introduced:

> All at God's round table sit
> And all must be fed
> With this loaf in My hand -
> This loaf is My Son's Bread.

Notes

1. Mary Gilmore, "Nationality," in *The Penguin Book of Australian Verse*, eds., J. Thompson, K. Slessor, and R.G. Howarth (Mitcham, Australia: Penguin Press, 1958) 21.

2. John Paul II, *Sollicitudo Rei Socialis*, On Social Concerns (Homebush, Australia, St. Paul Publications, 1988) no. 38.

3. Ibid. no. 40.

4. Notably the 1989 York Conference of the Societas Liturgica, and such works as: Anscar Chupungco, *Liturgies of the Future: The Process and Methods of Inculturation* (New York: Paulist Press, 1989); Virgil Elizando, *The Future Is Mestizio* (Bloomington, IN: Meyer Stone Books, 1988); Vincent J. Donovan, *Christianity Rediscovered* (Maryknoll: Orbis, 1983).

5. This team consists of the archbishop of Adelaide, a priest who is vicar general, a religious sister, and a laywoman. Collaboratively, they are responsible for the governance of the diocese.

6. It may be useful to note that Adelaide, after Perth, is the most multicultural area of Australia.

7. The Scalabrinians were founded in Italy in 1887 to serve the Italian migration.

8. Many criticisms of the Adelaide papal Mass were based upon such criteria.

9. Marcus Borg, *Jesus: A New Vision* (New York: Harper and Row, 1987).

10. Ibid. preface.

11. Ibid.

12. Jon Sobrino, *Spirituality of Liberation* (Maryknoll: Orbis, 1988).

13. Ibid. 16.

14. Ibid.

15. Ibid. 17.
16. Ibid. 19.
17. See "On Social Concerns" no. 5.
18. Eucharistic Prayer for Masses of Reconciliation II.
19. Sobrino, *Spirituality* 19.

Liturgy and Sacrament
in
Post-Modernity

13

Sacrament:
Event Eventing

David N. Power, O.M.I.

IN COMMENT ON THE SACRAMENTAL THEOLOGIES OF THE FIFTIES AND OF the period after the Second Vatican Council, it has often been said that they rediscovered the historicity of sacramental ritual and its memorial character. This occurred within a broader field of theological interest in God's action in history and of biblical scholarship's revived attention to narrative and narrativity. Such interest coincided with a cultural emphasis on the historicity of human being, where being itself is seen to take form in and through historical events. This is rather different to the mere awareness that human persons live out their lives within history.

In fact, sacramental theology from the time of Irenaeus has reflected whatever is the culturally dominant sense of history, and our time is no exception. The purpose of this article is quite specific. It is to consider what sacramental theology makes of being in time, event, and history. A key problem in considering sacrament as memorial of the pasch of Christ comes from overarching conceptions of history that influence this understanding. The first step will therefore be to consider the approach to history that has largely dominated sacramental theology in times past but which in our age has been unsettled by reason of events and new cultural perspectives. The second step will be to discuss a critique of the Thomistic theology of sacrament that is pertinent to the issues. The third step will be to offer an understanding of sacrament as event, or event eventing, that responds to the problematic and the critique.[1]

The Problematic of Historical Memorial

All the work done in scriptural study and in liturgical theology by way of retrieving a biblical and Judaic sense of memorial leaves the notion of history at work unresolved. There is some fondness, even today, for a Caselian idea of either making present the past event, or being in ritual present to the past event, in which God once acted in history in a definitive way.[2] This seems to give a supratemporal quality to this salvific act, such that it is possible to be part of it at any moment in the course of time.

It would be a great mistake to impose this particular concept of God's relation to history, either on the Hebrew Scriptures or on other Judaic literature of biblical and intertestamental times. It is difficult to recover any one meaning of memorial ritual influencing the rise of Christianity.[3] By and large, one can say that the Israelites saw in the salvific covenant with the people of the Exodus, or with the patriarch Abraham, or with the Davidic dynasty, a promise and assurance that God would ever be present among them and act in their behalf, now as in the past. Biblical studies would also seem to indicate that the original form given to the remembrance of this promise, whether in passing on the faith or in worship, was narrative. Whatever the language of the paschal haggadah (which we do not possess but are obliged to try to reconstruct for the early centuries of the common era) about seeing oneself as though crossing the Red Sea with one's forbears, it is less certain that the people thought that narrative implied a presence to past event in any formal sense. The narrative might simply have offered the redemptive and covenant events as paradigms for the continued divine action to be expected, or even more generically as an assurance that God would act again for the people in some, perhaps unpredictable way. This may have been no more than an abiding conviction that the people's history has been shaped once and for all by these events and continues to be shaped as the history of Yahweh's people by their remembrance, in story, song, and covenant worship.

In other words, appeal to a Hebrew foundation to memorial does not resolve the meaning of liturgical memorial, though it provides symbols that require thought. Rather than looking to a re-presentation of past event, or a present presence to past event, we would do better to consider how representation in story and ritual of a past event, remembered as a divine action, continues to shape history and hope. This is not answered by a simple appeal to the Bible, but necessarily involves some interpretative and philosophical stance on history and time.

History Tamed

Early East Syrian eucharistic prayers[4] blessed God for creation, and for the redemption given in Jesus Christ. They then asked that the church might be truly the gathering of God's people and that the people assembled might be endowed with the forgiveness of sin and immortality. These prayers are quite simple. If they betray any overarching concept of God and God's action, it is that of a wisdom tradition, where knowledge of God in what is revealed in the things of the world and in the endurance of suffering is what matters. It is only with the prayer from the *Apostolic Tradition* attributed to Hippolytus that we find the more lofty ideal of Jesus as the Word of God, creator and redeemer. In its prayer at that point the church goes back as it were into God to find the origins of creation and redemption, and no longer abides with the wisdom drawn from things of the earth and the ways of the just.

This shift in prayer belongs to what in contemporary critique is often called logocentrism. In this context, logos does not mean the spoken word but the word which is claimed to precede speech in the mind and so dictate its contours. Critics of logocentrism are interested in the word spoken and written, for what it says and how it shapes communications and human systems, and how it may be set free of conceptual or ideological impositions. The spoken and written word may either swing clear of any preceding thought that fails to pin itself down in communication, or by virtue of the power of language may say more or other than what the author thought to say.

Given the slippage that occurs between mind and speech, and between speech and the written word, it is not after all so easy to employ the analogy of the passage from the inner word of the human mind to its expression in the theology of God and God's action. Why in one form or another the analogy served a good purpose in presenting and defending the rule of faith in early Christianity may be seen from a reading of the work of Irenaeus of Lyons, which, it is conjectured, influenced the prayer from the *Apostolic Tradition*.

The Christian Gospel proclaimed a direct divine self-gift in Jesus Christ and in the Spirit. It proclaimed Christ the one mediator, not one among mediators. It proclaimed that both creation and redemption were the work of the one God, who loved the world and created and saved it in freedom. Various forms of Greek thought presented a Supreme Being, or a Principle, or a God, who was distant from the world, towards whom or which one had to rise up beyond the things of the world. There was room and need for mediators, above the human order and occupying a sublime position between God and the world, in creating and saving. This philosophy or world view was given vivid, imaginative and mythic, rather than philosophical, form in various kinds of Gnosticism. This representation appealed to some Christians and they tried to harmonize it with the Gospel of Jesus Christ.

While the study of Gnosticism has advanced in recent decades, we are still much dependent for our knowledge of it on Christian writers like Irenaeus, who wrote in enmity against its teachers. In any case, we can see why Irenaeus had to take up the question of creation if he were to proclaim Christ as mediator of redemption. If Christ belonged among the aeons who formed the world in emanating from God, what became of God's gift and presence in him and in the Holy Spirit? If he is to be remembered and revered as the mediator of a salvation which brings divine life to humans, then he must be one with God. It is not enough to see him as the Son of Man who has ascended to God's right hand, or as the Lord who has been given domination through his resurrection over all creatures. Such belief does not necessarily trace the origin of his work back to God. The reality of his redemptive activity can be truly valued only if he has a part in the work of creation, such that the immediacy of God is as true and bounteous in creation as it is in redemption. Affirmed as the Word within God who came out from God to take on flesh, Jesus Christ could be proclaimed as author of creation and of redemption through his communion with the Father in one divinity. At the same time, the reality of his humanity assured the presence of God among humans and the promise of their immortality in God. Thus in explaining the rule of faith embodied in the baptismal rites of the church,[5] Irenaeus proclaimed the free and immediate creation of the world by God the Father in the Word, the redemption of the world through the assumption of human nature by this same Word, ensuing in victorious conflict with sin and death, and the gift of the Spirit for the forgiveness of sins and immortality. By placing all things originally in the mind and free act of God through the inner Word, Irenaeus and other early teachers guaranteed the truth of God's love and of redemption against the view of a world emanating by some necessity through a chain of beings, with consequent disregard for the material world. This formulation of belief in the mediation of the Word in creation and redemption, and in the gift of the Spirit for the forgiveness of sins and immortality, was made part of sacramental prayer in the eucharist of Hippolytus and influenced later blessings.

In such perspective, history itself was originally in the mind of God and revelation is an unfolding of divine intent. While there are many historical events that belong to other peoples, the only history that truly concerned the faithful was the history of salvation according to the order intended and enacted by God. Ironically, by assuring against Gnosticism that God is present in human form and author of acts of historical configuration, Christian writers discounted history and historical contingency.

The notion of history as essentially salvation history, and of a salvation history that enacts a divine order and intention, was given form in various kinds of typological explanation. Fundamentally, this meant reading all Old Testament events in the light of Christ and explaining persons and deeds as types of Christ. On the one hand, their own meaning became clear only after the appearance of Christ. On the other, the meaning of Christ could stand out more fully when they were taken as images and stories in which this is prefigured and so illustrated. Allegorical catechesis is one of the extremes of this perception of God's activity, for it can blithely pass over the inner meaning of any other event or person but Christ. The reading of Scripture as primarily the history of the soul in its communion with the Logos, such as we find in the School of Alexandria, is another extreme, for it tends to discount the deeds of the flesh all together.

Such an approach to the word of the Scriptures found its way into the understanding of sacraments. Insofar as they were a memorial of events, they were considered to be a representation of the deeds of the Word made flesh and so pointed primarily to the supratemporal.[6] Insofar as they were themselves types of Christ, or antitypes of the salvation promised in his death and resurrection they too could be given typological explanation. Celebrated as profound communion in Jesus Christ or in his Body or in his sacrifice, they permitted the actors to pass above the world and history into the things of God and heavenly worship. In accordance with such biblical and sacramental catechesis, the world and its passing events were but the stage on which the followers of Christ worked out their salvation in the hope of that which is above. By reason of the virtue practiced by believers, and through the intercession of the saints, the world might be a better place, less infected by sin, but no historical events counted for much after the death and resurrection of Christ, as indeed none counted for much before it except to the degree that they were a preparation for his coming.

This understanding of Christ's revelation to the world was given theory and consistency in the high middle ages through the established ecclesiastical order and through scholastic theology. Through the retrieval of the works of Aristotle, much more attention was given to things in themselves and to the workings of the universe, but they continued to be given their place within this view of ordered history. Theology and church art included the cycle of daily life and of the seasons in the praise of God's work in the world.[7] The stories of saints filled out the history of salvation in the time after Christ, exemplifying his life and death for their devotees, as well as God's wondrous works done in the power of his name. If kings and rulers figured in this history, it was because they contributed to the godly order in which the justice of God could reign until time's fulfillment in the final judgment, or because they themselves rose above their worldly preoccupations and led lives of prayer and virtue. Order was indeed the prevailing concept that ruled reality. The restoration of justice was given a large place in the theology of Christ's redemptive death as restoration of the divine order.

The integration of the Aristotelian concept of causality into theology served the understanding of creation, redemption, and sacrament in relating them coherently to the theology of God. Since the effect participates in the reality of the cause, the Word of God was seen not only as efficient cause of God's acts *ad extra* but also as exemplar. In the order of redemption, this exemplarity is found in the humanity of the Word made flesh, especially in the sacrifice of his death, which is the chief instrumental and exemplary cause of grace and of sacramental operation. The matter and form which constitute the essential sign of the sacrament signify both the exemplary passion of Christ, the grace conferred according to this exemplar, and the glory anticipated in it. To live in communion with this passion was to live the pasch in passing over from this world to the things of God. To be united in faith with the Word made flesh was to enter already into a contemplative communion with the eternal Word of God.

History Unsettled

Perhaps it is the shock of events which has done most to unseat this ordered view of history and divine providence, which actually carried over into modernity, even in its most atheistic or agnostic forms. The belief in order and in progress was then centered in the human rather than in God, in rationality rather than in providence, but it remained strongly entrenched and exercised influence over the political and economic planning of human affairs. Theology took its own turn to the subject and drew on the human, personal, and collective, for its analogies for God, vested in the persuasion of some ideal human order.

Events however baffle, baffle both belief in a provident and ordering God and in an ordered human freedom, capable of bettering the world. At a recent meeting of theologians, it was suggested that theological reflection needed to speak to the phenomenon of mass death. All had seen images of the corridor of death, leading out of Kuwait to Iraq. All had seen the reports on the death and haphazard burial of children in the refugee camps of Kurdistan. All had seen reports on the floods of Bangladesh which defied the imagination to the extent of stultifying it. All were used to the yearly spectacle of famine in Africa. All were aware that terrorist death in Northern Ireland or Sri Lanka, and gang death in Los Angeles and Washington, or death by AIDS across several continents, are statistics, to which some are compelled to give human faces but populations as a whole commit to surveys.

The northern continents seem to deal with this reality of mass death by distancing it as a spectacle on a screen, just as indeed on a lesser scale individual death has become the stuff of the economy of the viewing parlor. Christians on southern continents are caught in the vain pursuit of appealing for help to the charity of wealthier churches, perhaps trusting that in this way they will find and give a sign of God's providence. Or perhaps they embrace a gospel of liberation, in the hope that dealing with the injustices of global politics and economics, the future may hold less peril. But who can answer where such events belong in the order of providence?

When this assault on faith was brought up, those present at the meeting mentioned responded by a deep intake of breath, a moment's loud silence. They had themselves perhaps tried to answer their children's questions about these matters. If they were ordained ministers, they had maybe tried on some recent Sunday to find space in a homily to speak of God in faith out of the chaos. Or possibly they had heard the realities ridiculously reduced to a petition in the prayer of the faithful, alongside pleas for good weather and strength for neophytes. None professed to have heard an effective cry of faith addressed to the events that belie order and history and the personal dignity of human beings. Looking for such a word only

seems to make us more conscious of the complicity of churches, through long past and recent centuries, in oppressive systems or in the compelled silence of theological over-
explanation in face of chaos and evil. Human suffering has always put a question to faith in redemption, and done so poig-
nantly as in the time of the Black Death. Today, the enormity
of the question means that we are compelled to think again
what it is to remember God's advent in Jesus Christ.

An innate sense of irony makes it possible to mark some
kinds of response with a wake of the reproductive imagination whose demise is to be celebrated as a kind of liberation
from a mean paucity of spirit.[8] Since liturgy is professedly the
locus of historical commemoration that focuses the persuasion
of God's action in history, that may be the place to conduct the
wake. In any case, within sacramental theology it is necessary
to face a double critique of the influence of western metaphysics on notions of history and representation. One is the critique of causality, the other the critique of its effective sup-
pression of language by theories of signifying word.
Awakened from its slumber, the creative imagination may be
freed through this critique to a more powerful if less self-
confident expression of pasch.

Critique of Causality

With Martin Heidegger, the French theologian Louis-Marie
Chauvet believes that western metaphysics, including Thomism, is responsible for the forgetfulness of being in virtue of its
predilection for causality, linked with logocentrism.[9] For him,
metaphysics is instrumentalist thinking. It cannot allow for an
event of being except in terms of its production. That is, everything is thought of in terms of that which gives it being and is
never considered in the pure gratuity of its emergence or of its
being there.

To illustrate his point specifically in regard to grace and sacrament, Chauvet contrasts two relations, that of a boat to the
boat-builder and that of a beloved to a lover. While the boat-
builder actually produces the boat by a kind of activity that can
be watched and measured, the lover does not produce the re-
sponsive love of the beloved. The lover simply stands in a rela-

tion to the beloved which allows the latter to respond, but this response from the self of the beloved is not produced by the lover. This example demonstrates that the things which are truly human, such as love, joy, pleasure, cannot be produced or caused, but can only be symbolically represented in their gratuitous coming to be within a gratuitous relationship. It is this, not production, which has to serve as model for grace and sacrament. If thought of in terms of instrumental causality, grace is devalued to the level of commodity, and even God is fitted into an order of production where univocal conception is hardly overcome by appeals to analogy of being and name by way of the *via eminentiae*. The divine epiphany in the cross defies a causal and providential explanation of event, history, and grace. It is the advent of God in the midst of human suffering as the one who offers love as a gift and seeks a response. The most apt expression of grace is found in the symbol of mutual gift. This is what Chauvet then places at the core of eucharistic memorial and celebration, rather than causality or sacrifice.

The issue is thus aptly stated. Without a doubt, to take some of the examples of Thomas Aquinas too literally, such as that of the saw used in making the piece of furniture,[10] is to give rise to a very materialistic and mechanical conception of sacramental causality. It depersonalizes the order of grace, making it look like a product of some ingenuity. However, there are responses to this critique which highlight other more fundamental elements of Thomistic thought, bringing home the intended limits of the use of the analogy of cause and effect, including the deliberate exclusion of images of production. They do not answer all the problems but by a better appreciation of what Thomas Aquinas did, they offer avenues for the creative retrieval of his thought on sacrament.

Two contemporary French writers, Yves Labbé[11] and Ghislain Lafont,[12] have treated specifically of post-modernity's problem with the metaphysical tradition. The American theologian, William Hill, has in another context responded to the Heideggerian critique of western metaphysics' forgetfulness of being.[13] All three point out that production is not part of Thomas' notion of causality, either in explaining creation or in explaining sacrament. It is the analogy of being, not the image of production, which governs his thought on causality.

Aquinas employed this Aristotelian categorization of causes in order to make the distinction between God as supreme Act and beings by participation in Act, since in a Neo-Platonic conception of participation the participated could too easily be seen as an emanation from the First, or the many as emanations from the One. The difference between God and creatures, between God's action and creaturely action, would thus be glossed.

By using the category of efficient causality to explain the relation of the world to God, Thomas brings out two things about the ontological structure of created being. In the first place, created being exists in dependence on, or beholden to, the one who is totally Act, even while the creator remains intimately present to it by reason of its own very being. The fundamental understanding of divine causality has been negated of all sense of productive activity and expresses the reality of a relationship.

In the second place, Aquinas makes a particular use of the category of cause within his sacramental theology. By using the notion of an ordered instrumental causality involving the person of Christ, his passion, the institution of the church, the significance of the rite, and the response of the recipient in faith to what the rite signifies, Aquinas brought out the interpersonal order of the economy of grace. The gift of grace embodied in the response of faith and love, and formally understood as the communion of the beloved with the lover, comes about within this communion of relationships. The example of the saw sawing is not meant to illustrate the mode of sacramental action, but the fact that the grace bestowed by God's gratuity bears the mark of the relationship with those named as instrumental causes, namely, Christ in his passion, the church, and the minister who brings the former two into the realm of a subject's faith response.

By his strong criticism of productivity, Chauvet may well have brought out the defect of an all too common inclination in sacramental theology, but he may have missed the mark in his explanation of Aquinas. In any case, William Hill would have us be more attentive to the interpersonal of being itself in Thomistic thought, so that the human interpersonal of grace appears as an analogous participation in the relationship which revelation shows us constitutes God's own eternal Act.

In such an analogy, grace would not appear as a value-object or as something produced, but would be seen as response within the beholdedness of being and an invitation to enter into the divine reality of communion.

By attending to the historical circumstances in which he wrote, it is possible to get a better insight into the genius of Thomas Aquinas in using Aristotelian categories in sacramental theology. In the quarrel over the presence of Christ in the eucharist, he had gone beyond the opposition of truth and figure by the analogies of presence *per modum substantiae* and of substantial change, which maintained an interpersonal truth while excluding physicalism. Earlier writers had foreshadowed this distinction, at least in vocabulary, but the issue of how the passion of Christ is present in sacrament or in eucharist had not been addressed. While it was written that Christ himself is present in the eucharist in truth and not in mere figure or sign, using an older language writers continued to affirm the presence of the passion in mystery, or *in mysterio*.[14] Thus presence in mystery seemed to be a middle term between presence in substance and presence in mere sign, but nobody had explained what this meant. In monastic theology, it seemed to have much to do with the spiritual life, or with the share of the faithful in the passover of Christ represented in sacrament and eucharistic memorial.[15] Scholastic theology, however, had not offered any way of paralleling the explanation of presence in mystery with the explanation of substantial presence. This risked leaving the presence of the passion in the order of mere sign, if between "in truth/substance" and "in sign only" there were no *tertium quid*.

The contribution of Aquinas was to follow up on the use of Aristotelian categories to explain the truth of the change of bread and wine into Christ's body and blood, with a parallel use of Aristotelian categories to explain the effective presence of the passion in sacrament. Efficient and exemplary causality furnished the analogy in this case. A past act, such as the passion, cannot be present in the way in which the living Christ who suffered and rose (the *Christus passus*, as Thomas states it) can himself be present. The effective presence, however, which allows the faithful to participate in the passion, may be explained by way of causality, not only efficient but exemplary.

This kind of causality, being that of an intelligent agent which grasps and orders meaning and purpose, allows the beneficiary to be configured to what is exemplified in the instrument. This is the particular and important application of the example of the saw sawing, when it is used outside an order of productivity and thought about in an order of the interpersonal.

Aquinas thus establishes the relation across time between the passion of Christ which is the reality of God's love made incarnate, the institution of the church, and the life of those who partake by faith in sacramental celebration. This is the effective grace of headship, to unite people of all time in one common community of grace and love, as though they were but one person.[16] In reestablishing an order of justice at any given time, Christians model their action on that of Christ in his passion, where the exemplar is not that of a human justice but of a divine justice whose inspiration is the good of friendship and the benignity of mercy, rather than the equalities, redistributions, and retributions of human justice.[17] In highlighting how the passion acts in sacrament as satisfaction and sacrifice, Aquinas focuses on the exemplarity of the chief instrumental cause. It is grace according to this exemplar, where the excess of suffering is surpassed only by the excess of love,[18] that is offered in sacrament.

Thus efficient causality serves to bring out the ontological structure of created being in God's intimacy to it rather than to image a divine activity and a product, and exemplary causality serves to bring out the communion between Christ and Christians in the economy of grace. The inclusion of exemplarity in the notion of efficient cause may, however, cause more problems for sacrament's relation to historical reality than the notion itself of efficient cause. There are in fact two problems. The first is that little room is left for that contingency of historical reality which allows it to be surprising, given that the model and pattern is in the mind of the agent and must but work itself out in time. The second problem is that there is little room for the modulations of the presence of God and Christ to human affairs, and especially to human suffering, that reflect different patterns or modes of compassion. The stress on exemplarity means that history itself is exemplified in the mind of God, according to the divine intellect and will, and human action in history has its own unchanging paradigm in the satisfaction and sacrifice of Christ's passion.

The accentuation of this exemplar of sacrifice and satisfaction in post-medieval theology is ironic. In explaining that Christ's redemption is achieved through sacrifice and satisfaction, Aquinas presented the most efficacious way of remembering the passion for his particular time. It made it possible to integrate its remembrance into a reform of society and church. It was efficacious because of the cultural models at hand to make it intelligible, and because of the wedding of justice and compassion that society then needed. What was then timely later become destructive of time-centredness by being made timeless.

The stress on God's foreknowledge, practical intellect and will, turns out to be an over-explanation of God's action and presence in the world, inevitably giving rise to unsatisfactory distinctions between affirmative and permissive will, or making the most extreme of human pains and natural chaos acts of divine providence. God is imaged too closely on the model of a human planner and the advent or event of God takes on the appearance of an intellectual if benign exercise. The analogies of names, qualities and activities, which go beyond the analogy of being, are reductionist of God's act and presence to a logocentric model. Hence the critique of the place of language within sacramental theology has to become fundamental to the critique of exemplary causality.

Critique of Logocentrism of Language

Language being words, it may seem odd to criticize the word-centredness of theories of language. In such critique, however, logocentrism does not refer to the word spoken or written but to the intellectual word that is deemed to precede all expression. Chauvet suggests that it is this concentration on the thought that precedes expression, or that expresses itself in spoken word, which is at the root of the instrumentalist and productive thinking about grace that belabors sacramental theology. Language is produced by thought and is in turn itself an instrument that can produce thought, and even affection and love, in its hearers. Even the origin of thought follows a productionist schema. According to the scholastic schema, the thing produces the phantasm, and the phantasm the *species impressa*. From the *species impressa*, the intellect produces in itself the *species expressa*, and this can be reproduced in language to pass the thought on to others. Hence the analogy for the use of language as instrumental cause in the use of the matter and form of sacrament.

In his summary of western and scholastic theories, Chauvet does not avoid the risk of caricature. Bernard Lonergan has shown clearly enough that in Aquinas the understanding of the relation between phantasm and understanding, between understanding and concept, or between judgment and love, is that of emanation, not production.[19] Likewise, communication in speech between two persons does not mean that one is putting thoughts into the mind of the other. The teacher teaches and the student is taught, but the students think their own thoughts, not those of the teacher, unless of course they simply memorize, in which case they are without thought. As Thomism would put it, in living things movement is from within, not from without. Again the analogy for understanding the role of sign in sacrament is purified of mechanistic productivity, even while a relationship in being of one to the other is predicated. Faith is from within the soul, even though it is in dependency on the spoken sign of sacrament to which it responds as a word from God.

Despite the restrictions on his interpretation of the scholastic and particularly the Thomistic tradition, Chauvet does point up some problems that make it hard for Thomistic notions of language to serve adequately in sacramental theology. By espousing a conceptually exact signification for sacramental signs, Aquinas was able to restrain some of the allegories of ritual explanation in liturgical treatises. He did not, however, leave room for the creativity of the metaphor, which he took as a persuasive piece of rhetoric rather than as a creative play of meaning.[20] He also espoused an order that quite precisely related the spoken or written word to the thought or inner word that precedes it, and that in turn allowed spoken or written words to convey quite clear ideas to other minds.

This ordered precision left little room for a coming to be in language or through language as language. Language appears rather as the expression of what comes to be otherwise, in what were essentially internal relations of grace, made expressive in sign. Humanity's present dependency on the world of the sensible is simply its present need to have access to the spiritual and intelligible in this manner, and is even linked in some ways with original sin.[21] Confining the role of word to express what can be conceptually conceived within an epistemology of ordered intelligible relations, the exploratory and creative power of word and imagination is doomed to wane.

The contrast that Chauvet makes between metaphysics and thinking from symbols actually shows that theology always appropriates something from other sciences. The novelty in Thomas was to appropriate Aristotle. Chauvet himself does creative work in appropriating from a variety of contemporary sources relative to understanding ritual and symbol. He takes something from the religious sociology of Hubert Mauss, from the psychology of René Girard, and from the language theorems of John Austin. He also takes something from the Neo-Platonist ontology of Stanislas Breton. There is no pure thinking from symbol, but preconceptions and investigatory detours enter into explanation. The advantage of Chauvet's contribution is not the elimination of ontology but the appropriation of work from other fields and the reformulation of the ontological question.

Language within History

In face of post-modernity's accusation that western metaphysics has disembowelled language, Labbé and Lafont[22] see the possibility of allying the analogy of being with narrative, and with an appeal to ethical orientations. It is this alliance which serves to explain the world's relation to God and God's advent in history. The analogy of being is needed to affirm the reality of language's reference outside a closed system of never-ending play with words. It is also needed to affirm God's abiding presence to the world and to human beings, so that creation is not reduced to some past and once-for-all act, and revelation and grace cannot be reduced to an idealist fiction.

Given this ontological basis, narrativity[23] is the way to express being in time and in historical contingency. Narrative expresses the contours of such being. It portrays the necessary immersion in the contingent, and the desire to live meaningfully in terms of some reality not confined within the contingent. By its construal of events, it displays the effort to be in relation to the future and in relation to a measuring of being and act that transcends the present confinement within time, so that all times can be enfolded in that measuring without measure. At the same time, it eschews absolutist thinking that would make of being in time an unfolding of Spirit or the living out on a stage of some predestined plan. Because it shows peoples, poets, and artists endeavoring to construe events into meaning in virtue of desire rather than in virtue of what is already coded, it excludes the possibility that the contingent is only the stage for meaning. Instead it puts the free construal of the contingent, in virtue of value and aspiration and liberative praxis, at the very heart of the event of being. In other words, the narrative account that works a meaningful way through the recollection of facts and happenings is itself taking them into meaning. It shows a way through them into an advent of being that carries past reality with it, rather than leaving it unsalvaged behind. When people suffer, the narrative purpose of remembering these sufferings overcomes the tendency to have them over and done with and forgotten, or to say that the lives of those who suffered were without meaning and purpose. It gathers in the action and aspiration of people in suffering, it shepherds the voices of victims, it goes into the crannies seeking out those unheard, so that being may event out of this reality and not despite it, or even just beyond it.

There is a conflict between a narrative of history that includes everything and orders all events into a meaningful pattern, and the narrative of events that allows for the inexplicability of the whole but aspires beyond this, out of humanity's inevitable particularities and time's unfathomable discontinuities. In the former case, there is a supposed given, and we have but to find it and narrate it. This may simply be the claim to show how and why one thing followed another, so that if one looks hard enough cause and effect emerge. Or it may be the greater, more mythological claim, that finds its way even into history books, namely, that all things happen according to plan and paradigm. The other type of narrative is both more and less ambitious. It lays no claim to ideal patterns, but speaks out of the quest and desire for wholeness in a world that lacks even its clear ideal. It can take up the factuality and contingency of single events or brief periods, and place one narrative after another in the sequence of time in which events occurred, without pretending to show that one of necessity followed the other, nor even by what reasons and motivations it departed from what went before. It accepts the agony of human and historical unconnectedness, but explodes with the desire for connection and the effort to seek it out beyond the contingency of past and present, even while it avoids the vanity of suppressing what does not fit, in order to present an ordered pattern.

Events become integral to human time when they are narrated. In other words, a person's or a people's action or suffering is connected with human life through language. It continues into history through its narration, which is the basic form of its representation, though it may be completed by others, both verbal and iconic. Of any event that takes on a central role in a culture or in forging a people's historical identity, the original narrative continues to be repeated. However, one finds that with the progress of time, or in the face of new events that seem unconnected with this identity, the original event is retold in a new construal. It is by creative representation in fresh narrative that a past event reconfirms its presence in time and history. The promise of the original narration is such that it needs fresh poetic exploration, even while this exploration keeps its connection with the originating event which is looked to as the moment of promise. In other words, a simple recital of an original narrative is not sufficient to keep the living presence of a past event. It needs to be completed by a creative reconstrual which relates its promise to other times.

In Christian revelation, it is the cross of Christ which is proclaimed as the originating event of promise. The gospel accounts are the first written narration of this event and complete the narrative of the passion with the narrative of the resurrection. Hence they continue to be proclaimed as the Good News, affirming the promise of God's advent in the cross. No liturgy is complete without this proclamation, though it takes a year's cycle for it to be complete. There are also liturgical accounts which are much more condensed proclamations, such as the profession of faith in the creed, the narrative moment of the thanksgiving preface and the supper narrative within the prayer. It would be a mistake, however, to think that such proclamations or recitals account adequately for the representation, or living presence, of the event of Christ's cross or of the advent of God in human history. The original narrative must, as it were, go beyond itself in conjunction with the living witness of a community.

Starting with the profession that salvation is given to us in Jesus Christ, the narrative over the course of twenty centuries has taken on an extraordinary variety of configurations. Without being reflected on in that way before these days that impose a seconde naiveté in storytelling, the narrative was reconstrued to take in contingent facts and shapes of given times and practices so that the remembrance of Christ could carry believers through such contingencies. Christ on his cross thus appears as the wisdom of those who find no part in worldly wisdom, as the victor in a struggle with death and sin for those who are the primary victims of earthly powers, as the one whose love is the supreme justice in a society set apart by the rivalry of particular interests, or as the dead Christ of people who find God closer in death than in a life where they themselves are valued less than dead things.

As in the recollection of all events, however, in the church we have also seen the tension between narrative that attempts a totally intelligible history and the narrative that expresses hope beyond the discontinuities that it cannot tame. Alongside the continuing appearance of liturgical, poetic, iconic, and popular narratives that are fitted to the particularities of time and situation, there has been the more erudite effort to find in the pasch the order of things that God wills for the world. This is the issue of logocentrism imported into belief, the persuasion that it is possible to link all times and events and seasons together into one whole narrative that reflects the mind of God. The typological explanation of the Scriptures, the linking of secular events to God's way of preparing people for the Gospel, the making of secular history the stage on which saints live the *exempla* of the virtues of Christ, and the reduction of suffering and catastrophe to events allowed by divine providence for humanity's greater good, are all part of this logocentrism.

The more culturally diverse and less integral way of remembering the passion of Christ makes God's presence more powerful because it is less ambitious and non-logocentric. It says that God advented as love and promise in the suffering and struggle of Jesus Christ, but not in a way that by-passes the discontinuities and contingencies of human history. It is a presence in the midst of that, that gives hope beyond it, but shows not what the origin or eventuality of historical events may be. The very contingency of Jesus' life and mystery and death, the result of a gratuitous evil, humanly speaking leading to nothing for the people whose lives he sought to improve, is the condition of God's event in the world. There is no discernible pattern that makes either it or its outcome predictable. It happens. The Christian community may then link it with a tradition of past and future by a creative use of root metaphors and stories taken from the original covenant, but in showing connectedness in hope across time it need not pretend to productive causality and conceptual exemplarity and an ordered vision of providence.

God events in human history in places and times that are unpredicted and afford no explanation of why it should be this place and this time. Creative narrative can indeed wed the event with advents of other places and times, that also show an unpredictable presence among the disadvantaged of the earth and a hope of carrying suffering itself into the bringing forth of being. It belies itself, however, if it goes beyond that to try to show a planned sequence of some perceived providential disposition. The interlocking of narratives around the paschal narrative reveals a deep structure of being in history that is the event of paschal faith and the event of God's love. This deep structure is however a way to be, that in the midst of the discontinuous, the illogical, the repressive, the claims of other wisdoms, out of that very suffering finds being and communion. The God who thus events, events in contingency, not in the manifestation of providential design, remaining ineffable but close and tangible as Christ's flesh in the covenant security of presence among the suffering.

To retain the word *event* to express the reality of God's revelation is to say that it is not related to the intelligibility of a large picture of history orderly conceived. Instead, it belongs in the midst of events of suffering, hope, and loving triumph that are marked by their contingency, their discontinuity with patterns, their simplicity, their worldly weakness, and that occur when least expected, are in a mere human way without issue, and yet are irrepressible in their vitality for the addressees of the beatitudes. Rather than a providential pattern of meaning, what is affirmed is a divine presence that gives the power of self-affirmation and freedom to the disinherited and the victim.

Sacrament: Event Eventing

The representation of a past event that makes it newly present in human history is achieved through its presence in narrative form and in all the other forms of poetic expression that complete narrative. It is through its narrative remembrance, combining the original proclamation and more culture-centred expressions, that it has a vigor and force that changes and transforms human living and the coming to be of other events. It is in this way that the event of the pasch is represented in sacramental memorial, where the narrative and the praise that responds to it are linked with a ritual that expresses the reality of the gathered community.

This sacramental memorial may be best understood if seen itself as an event. By all means, it has its institutional components and belongs within a tradition of prayer and rite, but it is a creative and eventful moment in that tradition. Through the narrative Christ events again in the community, within the aspirations of its ritual expression, transforming them into new being. The community itself events within its time and society, as a proclamation and witness of this way of God's being among humans and on the earth. The sacramental celebration is not faithful to the event of the pasch which it represents unless it remains faithful to its own eventful character.

This eventful character is kept alive in three ways: narrative, ritual, and witness.

First, it is found in the narrative, which becomes the creative reconstrual of the paschal story as it embodies itself in the midst of the suffering and hope of this populace. The proclamation of the Gospel carries on the tradition, but the selection of pericopes is the first step in an interpretation. Other stories may complete this, as the Acts of the Martyrs once did,[24] or as the stories of the suffering do today in base Christian communities. The homily needs to carry through with the narrative in placing it at the heart of the people as a ferment of hope. The story element of the prayer of thanksgiving weds the gospel proclamation to the chosen images of Christ's paschal presence here and now. It has been seen what some of those were in the past, for example, Christ's victory over death through death, or the restoration through his loving sacrifice of an order of divine justice. For what they are today, one needs to look at the celebrations often referred to as *popular religion*, or at the work of the creative imagination in poetry and drama that captures or anticipates the emerging cultural imagination and sets it on a course of emerging being, refusing to leave it tranquil in its own consumerism.

The second way of expressing the eventful character of sacrament is in the ritual gathering and acting of the people. The traditional forms of rite need to become eventful. The people gather in covenant to each other and to the humanity that surrounds them. Their living sacrifice is their ethical bond to live the times in the name of Jesus Christ. Their ways of inviting, greeting, receiving, nurturing, washing, feeding, communing, activate the tradition as the rites of a community in covenant. The much discussed inculturation of ritual elements is a simple matter of a people's taking the tradition into their own way of being, but as a marginal people, not one that aspires to covenant with the powerful. A people events in a gathering that is their own expression, not one that asks them to suppress the inclinations of their own hearts or to deny their own habitat. A people events in the rites of healing that confront their own sorrows and afflictions, in cleansing water over which the Spirit is invoked in response to their own demons, in a table that is both their own and of the poor of the earth.

Third, Christ events in the sacrament because of the evangelical witness of the community. By action, they take their place in human events. This action is one with their remembrance and their ritual. It shows in deed and hope sustained in the midst of trial and suffering the power of God's Spirit.

Without this witness, the sacraments could not be said to be sacraments of the church, the living Body of Jesus Christ. The proclamation of the cross would be without soil and seed.

To say that it is thus that God is a living presence in human history is a mighty claim. God comes not because all is ordered, but because here there is disorder. Christ and Spirit advent not to make order out of disorder, but to enlighten with promise and faith the deep structures of being in a disordered history where a transcendent hope is forged and a way of being in freedom emerges. We oppose the freedom of God's event if we look for providential dispositions in sin and chaos and suffering, or seek some way of integrating them into a greater concept of world order. In the faith that remembers the sufferings of Jesus Christ, the just and innocent, Christian people but know that God is present in the midst of this suffering. They find the presence of God's Spirit in themselves and in their fellowship with the suffering through their communion in the sufferings of Christ and in the hope of that witness. That is the reason for the hope that is within them. Beyond that, they have no reasons.

Naming the Ineffable

In several places in his book, Chauvet mentions the French philosopher, Stanislas Breton, and his approach to speech about God. In face of the triple religious tradition of analogical discourse, anthropological discourse, and apophatic discourse, Breton prefers the apophatic and the metaphoric in naming God.[25] In what can be said of God, he espouses what he terms *meontology*. There are two notes to this. First, it is a preference for negative language and thought about the divine. In the apophatic language of Neo-Platonism and of some church traditions, God must be separated from the things of this world. Both the way of eminence associated with analogy and the anthropological turn of recent theology say too much of God, whereas we know most of all that nothing of this world can be predicated of the divine. Second, meontology is not a rejection of ontology but sets its limits and marks the point where poetic and metaphoric language take over from ontological. In the view of Breton, for Christians the cross of Christ both sets the limits on ontology and is the ground of apophatic and poetic language. It shows that in revealing self, God withdraws from a world in which religious institutions and philosophical wisdoms make excessive claims. There is a demand placed by this on people and cultures to dispossess the self in face of naming God. Theories about God, or religious institutions that claim authority, are frequently nothing more than a projection of the desires of the human heart for self-possession, or of the claims of the human mind to grasp all reality, on to God. These have to be renounced in order to hear the name given to God in the cross of Jesus Christ. Thus it is this which acts as the symbol and metaphor which beyond the apophatic show the traces of God's presence in the midst of suffering, through an excess of suffering.

In the philosophical works of Breton, there is much insight into the structure of human being. This he takes to be its relation to the other, its *esse ad*, without which it has no *esse in se*. Creative freedom in expression and action is vital to human existence and the relationship to the other, but it is blocked by the logocentrism of western metaphysics. The ultimate referent of the relationship to the other is inconceivable in philosophical thought, and the ineffability of the referent is betrayed by the use of the analogy of names derived from a scheme of causality.

To express the presence of the divine that is given in revelation, Breton prefers a retrieval of Neo-Platonism to Neo-Thomism. In this, more attention is given to God's event-ing than to eminent predication. Taking much from the philosophies of Plotinus and Proclus, he leaves behind the image of emanation of lower being from higher, but conceives the relation of the world to God in terms of the desire of the many to seek reintegration into the One who is the principle of all that is. This is, of course, a distinctive use of the schema of *exitus/reditus* found in Aquinas. Breton does not, however, explain the origin of things in terms of causality which would make room to adopt an analogy of names based on the analogy of being. Even the use of the term *being* to speak of the One can cause confusion. Breton prefers the ineffable of Neo-Platonism, the thought that nothing of anything which proceeds from it can be predicated of the One, and that a person is prepared for enlightenment through a rigorous pursuit of the *via negativa*. In the way of revelation, the cross of Christ invites a stringent walking of the way of negation on the one hand, and on the other, offers the light of the totality of God's love that prevails in the midst of human suffering and abasement. The metaphors which derive from the symbol and narrative of the cross of Christ, or of the pasch, make it possible to name God from within this experience and so to be carried by this naming to a surrender to God and to the imperatives of the Gospel. The importance of this insight for sacramental theology lies in the relationship which it shows between the narrative and the prayer of confession, in its multiple forms, and between the prayer of confession and ethical commitment.

Breton also stresses the point that creatures stand in relation to the One, and the quest for return to the One, as beings who have their principle of operation within themselves. They seek in creativity and freedom to construe and live the relationships which bring them on the road to God, but they cannot do so without the apt use of language and retrieval of images and metaphors from story. The logocentrism of past theologies of creation, grace, and sacrament, inhibit freedom and expression. The accent on the nature of the human as moved mover is too great to do full justice to the free creativity of humans. That on the communication from mind to word in the use of language is an obstacle to the exploration of meaning through imaginative play with images, symbols, and metaphoric predications. The freedom of expression in sacramental celebration, in exploring the potential of both ritual and word, is coherent with the freedom of ethical exploration of the way of the cross in the service of others and in the quest for God.

In what is thus dubbed meontology, there is both an ontological and a linguistic foundation for sacramental theology. The ontological lies in the grasp of humanity's orientation to seek the principle of all things in harmony with the world, and in the rigor of the *via negativa* in naming God that derives from sensitivity to the finiteness of being. Despite the limits on thought about the One, the idea that all things find their being eventually by way of return to the One who is the principle of all that is, includes the notion that the One remains intimately present to things and to humans in the act of their self-creation. This is in fact not incompatible with what is affirmed in the Thomistic analogy of being, when it is separated from conjectures of efficient and exemplary causality but is emphatic of the giftedness and beholdedness of finite being. The affirmation of Pure Act that belongs to this analogy has actually much to do with the way of negation in using words about God, though it is less rigorous in its denial of the possibility of analogous knowledge and the use of analogies in explaining divine mysteries.

The linguistic foundation that comes out of meontology lies in the appreciation of poetic and metaphoric language, which make it possible to reach out beyond the capacities of philosophical language.[26] Here there is some meeting point between the position of Breton and those of Labbé and Lafont, since all three point to the importance of narrative in expressing humanity's being in time and history. All likewise point to the centrality of the symbol of the cross in story and in the use of metaphoric predications. On the one hand, faith in the revelation given in the cross sets the limits on human wisdom and self-realization. On the other, the power of the language in which the memory of the cross is kept fosters the surrender to the God whose trace is found in the love of Christ in the midst of suffering, and who is named from within this story and its appropriation to new situations of suffering. The ultimacy of this surrender is a contemplation that occurs beyond the language and celebration of sacrament. In the practical order, it is compassion and action which emerge out of the faith in God's loving presence in the here and now, without the need for the consolation of the knowledge of a providential order or without the presumption of entering the mind of God as a condition for believing in love. This love events in the community of faith and in the presence of this community in time and place and event, even in the midst of discontinuities and ambiguities to which there is no intelligible pattern.

* * * * * *

As in much else, in this essay the end is in the beginning. Belief in the sacrament as God's event eventing anew situates us in face of the dilemma of mass death and of death reduced to spectacle. It appeals to no theories of providence, no overarching meaning of history, to find in suffering either God's action or the punishment for human sin or the permissive side of God. It expresses a simple and clear faith that God events in the midst of suffering, not because God causes it or allows it, but because it is there and where it is, God is.

Having raised the issue of the notion of history affecting ideas of sacramental memorial, the essay offered some exploration into the sacramental theology of Thomas Aquinas in face of criticism addressed to it. In the course of this, it was possible to retrieve what is basic to the analogy of being that grounds his theory of sacramental causality. It was also possible to see the appropriateness of his introduction of a theory of causality in face of the questions which he needed to address and its contribution to an interpersonal appreciation of the order of grace. Similarly, the address to his own time of the images and theologies of redemption which he adopted was brought out.

Subsequently, the essay pointed to the appeal to exemplarity in the theology of creation, redemption, and sacrament, as that which made the appreciation of history's contingency and of God's relation to history most problematic. There is some fresh ground for sacramental theology when the analogy of being is separated from the factors of causality added to it, and drawn into a creative conjunction with the role of narrative in construing being in time. Further to this, the meontological approach of Stanislas Breton sets the limits of language about God more firmly. Beyond logocentrism, it underlines the exercise of freedom in seeking the path to communion with the One. It leaves room for the retrieval of the story of the cross into sacramental celebration's use of narrative, prayer, and rite. The power of this retrieval carries over into ethical commitment to the way of love in the midst of suffering, however inexplicable or chaotic. It is thus that Christ and the God of Christ are present in the world, it is thus that the power of their Spirit transforms human eventing.

Notes

1. There is no isolation in doing theology. Apart from reading the work of others, a teacher works with students. What is said in this

article comes in part from working with doctoral candidates on three dissertations: with Joseph Fortuna on the theology of Louis-Marie Chauvet; with Sally McReynolds on the philosophy of Paul Ricoeur; and with Jacquelyn Porter on the theological turn of Stanislas Breton. I hope they will not find me guilty of plagiarism, but I doubt that any of them would care to carry responsibility for my own twists of mind.

2. See Cesare Giraudo, *Eucaristia per la Chiesa: Prospettive teologiche sull'eucaristia a partire dalla "lex orandi"* (Rome: Gregorian University Press, 1989) 606-616.

3. For a variety of interpretations of memorial, see Fritz Chenderlin, *"Do This as My Memorial": The Semantic and Conceptual Background and Value of Anamnesis in 1 Cor 11:24-25* (Rome: Biblical Institute Press, 1982) 471-536.

4. In particular, see the prayer from the *Didache* and the prayer of Addai and Mari, English text in *Prayers of the Eucharist: Early and Reformed*, 3d ed., trans. and eds., R.C.D. Jasper and G.J. Cuming, (New York: Pueblo Publishing Co., 1987) 20-24, 39-44.

5. For the exposition on the baptismal rule of faith, see *The Proof of the Apostolic Teaching*, trans. and ed., Joseph P. Smith, Ancient Christian Writers, vol. 16 (Washington, D.C.: The Catholic University of America Press, 1952).

6. For a presentation of the idea of representation in mystagogical catechesis, see Enrico Mazza, *Mystagogy: A Theology of Liturgy in the Patristic Age*, trans., Matthew J. O'Connell (New York: Pueblo Publishing Co., 1989).

7. See Emile Male, *Religious Art in France. The Thirteenth Century: A Study of Medieval Iconography and Its Sources*, trans., Martiel Mathews, ed., Harry Bober, Bollingen Series, vol. XC-2 (Princeton: Princeton University Press, 1984).

8. See Richard Kearney, *The Wake of the Imagination: Toward a Post-Modern Culture* (Minneapolis: University of Minnesota Press, 1988).

9. Louis-Marie Chauvet, *Symbole et sacrement: Une relecture sacramentelle de l'existence chrétienne* (Paris: Cerf, 1987).

10. *Summa Theologica* III, q. 62, art. 1, ad 2m.

11. See Yves Labbé, *Humanisme et théologie: Pour un préambule de la foi* (Paris: Cerf, 1975); *Essai sur le monothéisme trinitaire* (Paris: Cerf, 1987), and his review article, "Réceptions théologiques de la 'Postmodernité': A propos de deux livres récents de G. Lafont et L.-M. Chauvet," *Revue des sciences philosophiques et théologiques* 72 (1988) 397-426.

12. Ghislain Lafont, *Dieu, le temps et l'être* (Paris: Cerf, 1986).

13. William Hill, "Rescuing Theism: A Bridge between Aquinas and Heidegger," *The Heythrop Journal* 27 (1987) 377-393.

14. For example, see Lanfranc, *Liber de Corpore et Sanguine Domini* (PL 150:425).

15. See Alf Härdelin, "Pâques et rédemption: Etude de théologie monastique du XIIe siècle," *Collectania Cisterciana* 43 (1981) 3-19.

16. *Summa Theologica* III, q. 49, art. 1, c.

17. *Summa Theologica* III, q. 48, art. 2.

18. Ibid.

19. Bernard Lonergan, *Verbum: Word and Idea in Aquinas* (Notre Dame: University of Notre Dame Press, 1967).

20. *Summa Theologica* I, q. 1, art. 9.

21. *Summa Theologica* III, q. 61, on the necessity of sacraments.

22. See the works cited in notes 11 and 12.

23. It goes without saying that some of the most timely work on imagination is found in Paul Ricoeur, *Time and Narrative*; see also Hayden White, *The Content of the Form: Narrative Discourse and Historical Representation* (Baltimore and London: The Johns Hopkins Press, 1987).

24. See B. de Gaiffier, "Le lecture des Actes des Martyres dans la prière liturgique en occident," *Analecta Bollandiana* 72 (1954) 134-166.

25. On faith and reason, see Stanislas Breton, *Foi et raison logique* (Paris: Seuil, 1971); see also *Le Verbe et la croix* (Paris: Desclée, 1981).

26. For a brief presentation of Breton's thought on metaphor, see "Faut-il parler des anges?", *Revue des sciences philosophiques et théologiques* 64 (1980) 225-240.

Appendix

Something to Celebrate

Ciaran Earley, O.M.I.

DAVID POWER HAS BEEN FOR ME AN INSPIRATION, A FRIEND, AND A LIFE-giving force, pushing me to find new ways to evangelize and be evangelized at every stumbling block of my formation and ministry as an Oblate, in Ireland, in Brazil, in Rome, and now again in Ireland. To talk of him is to tell my story.

In the mid-sixties David became superior of the Oblate seminary in Piltown. For many of us, our time there under his leadership was one of the most significant periods of our lives: the values he promoted have deeply influenced our ministry. Option for the poor, now widely accepted as a hermeneutic principle of Catholic theology, was part of his everyday consciousness and permeated his theological teaching and pastoral leadership. We, his pupils, instinctively find ourselves drawn to the side of the excluded, the wounded, the oppressed; and to working as best we can for change from their perspective.

He also insisted that any ecclesial undertaking has to be based on the concrete experience of those involved, and on critical reflection on that experience. That is how I and my Oblate companions found ourselves working in a steel factory in the North of England for six weeks one summer, each night sitting down with Anglican industrial chaplains to make sense of what had happened during the day. "Good News" is only credible when related to human experience.

In the seminary he showed his commitment to equality by encouraging the development of structures of participation, so that everyone could have a voice in shaping the life of the college. He also helped us form "primary groups" in which students and staff came together to talk about our lives, to reflect, to pray, and to support one another.

He cherished the Scriptures as a source of illumination of life, and nurtured within us a great respect for their use in all ministry.

True to his own convictions, one summer in the early seventies he and four seminarians went to live in a tenement flat in a disadvantaged area of Dublin. The students worked in different projects among the people, and David's role was to accompany them and help them in their pastoral reflection. He was far ahead of his time—a veritable "frontier apostle": three days after the project began, word came from the archbishop of Dublin that the experiment be abandoned.

It is not surprising that on arrival in Brazil, I was easily attuned to the pastoral priorities of the Brazilian Church, especially the promotion of basic ecclesial communities which embody the values that had been so carefully cultivated in the seminary. In my own parish our main efforts were directed toward the formation of a network of small evangelization groups. Insofar as possible, we offered education and training to be leaders in the use of the Scriptures, in the running of groups, and in the service of the community. The more we became involved in the process of formation in action, the more insistently did the fundamental question trouble me: what is the message we are to be announcing?

It was in 1973 that David, after many ecclesiastical adventures, arrived in Brazil to give a series of lectures to Irish and American Oblates. I decided to approach him with a question. The previous year Juan Luis Segundo had been helping us assess our missionary work, and had spoken of the importance of being able to say what you believe in, briefly and personally. In other words, he had proposed the challenge of formulating our own version of the Kerygma. I duly approached David and asked if he would put down on a sheet of paper what he considered to be the essential Good News we are meant to announce in "word and deed." Two hours later—after his siesta—David emerged with the Kerygma scrawled in four sentences on the torn page of a copy book:

1. The Kingdom of God is within and among you.
2. The sinful environment impedes the living of the Kingdom values.
3. The way of salvation/liberation is the way of the cross.
4. Community/fellowship with people is communion/ fellowship with God.

Later, three of us sat down with him around a tape recorder and discussed those four sentences for close to five hours, extracting as much meaning as we could. To all our queries and challenges, David was able to respond clearly, cogently, and credibly. It made so much sense that a few of us went off to an isolated place to translate these concepts into an eighteen-hour experiential course which we could run with our people.

Thirty young adults took part in the first Kerygma course, held in a center called the Oasis in Uberlandia. For three full days they wholeheartedly took part in the activities and exercises which embodied the vision and values of the Kerygma. They found their lives affirmed and challenged by the great symbols of the Kingdom—sin, cross, and resurrection—in a new way that seemed so real and empowering. Soon afterwards, we brought the course back to our own diocese. Many people who participated in it were afterwards to become quietly militant leaders in the communities. Vilmar de Castro was just such a person. At the age of twelve he came in from the country to make his first communion. Later he begged us to set up a late-night youth community for young people who worked in a bakery. It was called "Five Loaves." He became the coordinator. Soon he became a catechist. When he took part in the Kerygma, it was chilling to see how seriously he took everything, particularly the section on the cross. "To suffer to do away with suffering" was the famous definition of the cross given by Leonardo Boff which we used in the course. Vilmar became leader of a basic ecclesial community.

Ministry of the Land was the name given in the seventies to the church's involvement in agrarian reform and the movement for rural workers' rights. Vilmar became prominent in this dangerous ministry. On 26 October 1987 he was assassinated as he made his way in the early morning to the little rural school where he was the teacher. And the word became flesh.

In 1976 I experienced a tremendous bleakness which today we call burn-out. David advised me to do the tertianship course run by the Divine Word Missionaries in Nemi outside Rome. There were sixty missionaries in the course from seventeen different countries. It was in Rome that I experienced David Power, the intellectual healer. He was teaching at the Gregorian University at the time and had many other responsibilities. With patient kindness he met me each Thursday. We would visit some part of Rome and talk, and then return and work together on a series of seven short courses for use with the people in the communities. It is only in hindsight that I see the extent of the compassion of a great scholar choosing the right remedy for a wounded brother.

In Ireland years later, in a workshop called "Partners in Mission," I met a parish priest from the inner city: he invited me to come into his parish in the dockland of Dublin to set up and run the Kerygma course. He arranged accommodation for me, yes, in the same flat occupied by David and company ten years earlier.

Systematic neglect by modern governments and the decline in port traffic has left this part of the city in a state of decay, and deprivation has taken its toll on the quality of life of the people over the years. Long term deprivation, low income, and high unemployment have led to increasing ill-health, low level of education, and social disorder. Physical and social stress are higher there than in most places in the city. This was the setting in which we were to try to announce the Kerygma, devised by David in the dry heat of central Brazil. What would be "Good News" in Sherrif Street and Seville Place, Dublin? Johnny and I agreed we would have a go at enabling a core group of people to reinterpret their experience in the light of the message and life of Jesus. We hoped this would start a new process of development of ecclesial community. Johnny furnished me with a list of names of people who:

* in the past had shown interest;
* were representative of different areas, groups, ages, and sexes;
* had tried to do something and had suffered for what they believed in.

In three months of foot-slogging and persuasion, I knocked on doors, tried to explain what I was about, and tentatively invited people to take part in a "faith and life" project called the Kerygma Course. Eventually thirty people—fourteen men, eleven women, two priests, and three sisters—took part. The course, consisting of six three-hour sessions, was held over six successive nights. During those nights we compared the values and pattern of Jesus' life in Palestine with our own life in Dublin's North Wall, comparing and contrasting his vision and struggle with our own.

How do people in Dublin's inner city describe the Kingdom of God? Here are some examples of what people said:

> * The Kingdom of God is not within me when I am full of fear; it is within me when I am at peace with myself. It is not within me when my confidence is destroyed; it is when I know I'm precious in God's eyes.

> * The Kingdom of God is not among us when we want control over others; it is among us when we treat everyone as brother and sister. It is not when we are filled with thoughts of revenge; it is when we are able to forgive.

> * The Kingdom of God is not around us when we are blind to the problems of our area; it is around us when we face up to the situation we live in. It is not when we don't want to know; it is when we get involved. It is not when we discourage others; it is when we invite others to join us in building things up.

When the people discussed the cross, they said things like:

> * It means swallowing your hurt pride to resolve a problem constructively at a meeting.

> * It means making the effort to listen and understand why your marriage partner is speaking or acting in a certain way.

> * It means burying the law of the least effort to go out on the streets and get involved.

Everyone turned up every night. On the last night we celebrated the eucharist in the day-care center where the course had been held. People, now really aware of their own collaboration with the coming of the Kingdom, had so much to celebrate. There is a song which reflects their lives and their struggle to change things. We sang it that night. It has this verse:

Freedom doesn't come like a bird on the wing,
   It doesn't come down like the summer's rain.
Freedom, freedom is a hard won thing.
   You have to work for it, fight for it,
Day and night for it. And
   Every generation has to do it again.

During that eucharist people had these kinds of things to say about the course:

* It brought hope and light and life to the group.

* It has changed my attitude to life and people completely.

* The Kingdom of God on earth is linked with the Kingdom of Heaven through the goodness of God in our own deeds.

* It brought out that Jesus and myself are so much alike in the way we live our everyday lives.

* Environment can get us down but we can stand up to it.

* A great feeling of togetherness and fraternal generosity.

* It has shown me I'm not alone in my suffering, that by team-work within our community we can achieve most of our objectives with patience, with love and honesty and Christ's help.

In later years I didn't see so much of David, but his fundamental inspiration has still remained in my ministry. Perhaps the way David's life interwove with mine offers a model for the ministry of the theologian: helping people make sense of our faith praxis, clarifying, encouraging, giving us vision and hope, empowering us. The theologian is to bridge the gap between the living theological tradition and the experience of those who struggle to be God's people and to fulfill God's dream for all.

David Noel Power, O.M.I.: Biographical Note

Kenneth Hannon, O.M.I.

DAVID NOEL POWER WAS BORN IN DUBLIN, IRELAND, ON 14 DECEMBER 1932. He had his early education at the Christian Brothers School, Dun Laoghaire, which he completed in 1949. He made his novitiate, and then professed vows as an Oblate of Mary Immaculate on 29 September 1950.

Upon completion of the novitiate, he was sent to Rome for his studies and took the licentiate in philosophy in 1953 and in theology in 1957 at the Gregorian University. He was ordained priest at the Basilica of St. John Lateran in Rome on 22 December 1956.

His first assignment upon completion of his studies was to the Oblate Scholasticate at Piltown in Ireland. His responsibility was to teach dogmatic theology, which he did for seven years, covering the whole cycle of all the treatises in that discipline. In addition to his teaching in dogmatics, he was told to "do the rubrics" as well. This offhanded assignment of the newest faculty member, typical of the time, began the distinguished career of scholarship and teaching which we celebrate in this volume.

In 1964 Father Power returned to Rome, to the Pontifical Institute San Anselmo, to begin the doctorate in sacred theology with a specialization in liturgy. Beginning his doctoral studies at this time afforded the opportunity to be in Rome as the Second Vatican Council was ending, and to become acquainted with some of the important figures at first hand. His residence through this period in the Oblate International Residence for priest students placed him in contact with Oblates from some twenty-five countries around the world, studying for advanced degrees in different disciplines. Power was appointed superior of this residence during his last two years of study, 1966-1968. He defended his dissertation and received the S.T.D. in 1968; the dissertation was published the following year as *Ministers of Christ and His Church*. The dissertation already evidences the distinctive quality of his work in the field. By training and inclination, David Power is first of all a systematic theologian who takes the liturgy, traditions and texts, as the particular field of his inquiry.

Through Herman Schmidt, who directed his dissertation, Power became involved in the work of the international theological review *Concilium*, and began to co-edit the volumes of the liturgy section with Schmidt in 1969. He has continued this participation, eventually with Luis Maldonado and then Mary Collins to the present. The early days of the review gathered many of the great theologians of the council, among them Rahner, Schillebeeckx, Congar, and Küng, and placed Power in serious dialogue with them as the editorial board met to define the review's topics and work. He undertook this task while serving as superior and director of formation at the Oblate House in Piltown from 1968-1971. During this time he also taught systematic theology at the Milltown Institute of Philosophy and Theology in Dublin. In the autumn of 1969 he was guest lecturer at Maynooth's St. Patrick's College, lecturing on the theology of the priesthood.

When his term at Piltown ended in 1971, Power returned to Rome where he served first as director of studies (1971-1972) and then as superior and director of formation at the Oblate International Scholasticate (1972-1977). During this period he lectured in sacramental theology at the Gregorian University and St. Thomas Aquinas University (Angelicum) and in systematics (Christology) at Regina Mundi. His two-part article in *The Way* (1975) on "Symbolism in Worship" introduced him to a broader readership at this time. He was eventually appointed assistant professor in sacramental theology at the Gregorian, a position he held from 1974 until his departure from

Rome in 1977. During this period he also began to teach and lecture more broadly: in Texas in 1972, in Southern Africa in 1971 and again in 1976, in Brazil in 1973, and in Sri Lanka in 1977. These international and missionary involvements along with his continued participation on *Concilium*'s editorial board have had a continued influence in his research, writing, and teaching.

Even before he finished his assignment in Rome, interest was expressed in Power's joining the faculty of theology at The Catholic University of America in Washington, D.C. He accepted appointment as associate professor in systematic theology and liturgy there in 1977. In 1983 he was promoted to the rank of ordinary professor and continues in that position to the present. In this phase of his career he has continued to lecture widely—in the Philippines in 1979 and 1983, in Pakistan and in Australia, also in 1983 and in 1991. From 1986 until 1989 he served as chair of the Department of Theology at Catholic University. His membership in academic societies in the United States includes the Catholic Theological Society of America, the American Theological Society, the American Academy of Religion, and the North American Academy of Liturgy. He served the Academy of Liturgy as president in 1987-1988. That society honored him with its *Berakah* award in 1991 in recognition of his outstanding contribution to the study of liturgy and the advancement of the renewal of liturgy in North America.

Ever the critical and patient researcher, Power has consistently offered insight and stimulus in his writing and lecturing. As teacher, he has made those skills available and accessible to class after class of scholars, ministers, and pastors, from different parts of the world. As pastor and missionary, he has readily and eloquently given his attention to the needs of the church. As a Christian, he has sought to contribute to the efforts which must continue to be made in inter-faith and ecumenical dialogue. All of this he has done with the peculiarly dry Irish wit which can sometimes make sweet wine even from unripe grapes.

A Bibliography of David Power's Work

Prepared by Kenneth Hannon, O.M.I.

Works are grouped under several general headings. Thus there are duplicate entries in some cases. Works are listed chronologically (books and articles are mixed) within groupings to allow one to follow development within an area. Unless noted otherwise, all articles in *Concilium* can be found in English, Dutch, French, German, Italian, Portuguese, and Spanish. A list of *Concilium* volumes edited by David Power is provided separately.

Theology of Sacrament, Symbol and Sacramental Worship

"Symbolism in Worship." Parts 1, 2, 3. *The Way* 13 (1973) 310-324; 14 (1974) 57-66; 15 (1975) 55-64, 137-146.

"The Odyssey of Man in Christ." *Concilium* 92 (1974) 85-106; revised and reprinted as "Human Odyssey in Christ" in David N. Power, *Worship: Culture and Theology*. Washington, D.C.: The Pastoral Press, 1990. Pp. 85-101.

"A Theology of Community." *Way* Supplement 34 (1978) 95-106.

"Doxology: The Praise of God in Worship, Doctrine and Life." *Worship* 55 (1981) 61-69.

"Sacraments: Symbolizing God's Power in the Church." *Proceedings of the Annual Convention of the CTSA* 37 (1982) 50-66.

"Contemporary Developments in Sacramental Theology." *Catholic Theological Review* 5 (1983) 7-13.

Unsearchable Riches: The Symbolic Nature of Liturgy. New York: Pueblo Publishing Co., 1984.

The Sacrifice We Offer: The Tridentine Dogma and Its Reinterpretation Edinburgh: T. & T. Clark Limited, 1987.

"The Sacraments in the Catechism." In *The Universal Catechism Reader: Reflections and Responses*, edited by Thomas J. Reese. San Francisco: Harper Collins Publishers, 1990. Pp. 109-125.

Specific Rites - Theology

INITIATION

"The Odyssey of Man in Christ." *Concilium* 92 (1974) 85-106; revised and reprinted as "Human Odyssey in Christ" in David N. Power, *Worship: Culture and Theology*. Washington, D.C.: The Pastoral Press, 1990. Pp. 85-101.

"Blessing of the Baptismal Water." In *Commentaries on the Rite of Christian Initiation of Adults*, edited by James A. Wilde. Chicago: Liturgy Training Publications, 1988. Pp. 91-98.

"La mise en oeuvre du rituel de l'initiation chrétienne des adultes aux Etats-Unis d'Amerique." *La Maison-Dieu* 185 (1991) 104-115.

EUCHARIST

"How Can We Speak of Sacrifice and Mean It?" In *Baptême - eucharistie - ministère: Réflexions de théologiens catholiques sur le document oecuménique 'La Réconciliation des églises,'* edited by Gerard Békés. Rome: Editrice Anselmiana, 1976.

"Words That Crack: The Uses of 'Sacrifice' in Eucharistic Discourse." *Worship* 53 (1979) 386-404; reprinted in *Living Bread, Saving Cup: Readings on the Eucharist*, edited by Kevin Seasoltz. Collegeville: The Liturgical Press, 1982. Pp. 157-175.

"Editorial Conclusions: Receiving What Has Been Handed On." *Concilium* 152 (1982) 87-91.

"Mass." *Encyclopedia Americana* 18 (1982) 433-436.

"The Sacrifice of the Mass: A Question of Reception and Rereception." *Ecclesia Orans* 2 (1985) 67-94.

The Sacrifice We Offer: The Tridentine Dogma and Its Reinterpretation. Edinburgh: T. & T. Clark Limited, 1987.

"The Anamnesis: Remembering, We Offer." In *New Eucharistic Prayers: An Ecumenical Study of their Development and Structure*, edited by Frank C. Senn. New York: Paulist Press, 1987. Pp. 146-168.

"The Eucharistic Prayer: Another Look." Ibid. Pp. 239-257.

"Eucharist." In *Systematic Theology: Roman Catholic Perspectives*, vol. 2, edited by John Galvin and Francis Schüssler Fiorenza. Minneapolis: Augsburg Fortress, 1991. Pp. 261-288.

"The Priestly Prayer: Tridentine Theologians and the Roman Canon." In *Fountain of Life,* edited by Gerard Austin. Washington, D.C.: The Pastoral Press, 1991. Pp. 131-164.

Eucharistic Ministry: Revitalizing the Tradition. New York: Crossroad, 1992.

"Eucharistic Celebration: Action, Word, Sight." *liturgical ministry,* vol. 1 (Summer 1992). Pp. 78-84.

PENANCE

The three articles under this heading have been revised and combined in "The Sacramentalization of Penance" in David N. Power, *Worship: Culture and Theology.* Washington, D.C.: The Pastoral Press, 1990. Pp. 213-241.

"The Sacramentalization of Penance." *The Heythrop Journal* 16 (1977) 5-22. Translation: "La sacramentalización de la penitencia." *Sellecciones de Teologia* 18 (1979) 49-56.

"Confession as Ongoing Conversion." *The Heythrop Journal* 16 (1977) 180-190.

"Editorial Conclusions: The Fate of Confession." *Concilium* 190 (1987) 127-131.

PRESBYTERATE

Ministers of Christ and His Church: Theology of the Priesthood. London: Geoffrey Chapman Publishing Co., 1969.

Christian Priest: Elder and Prophet. London: Sheed & Ward, 1973.

"Appropriate Ordination Rites: A Historical Perspective." In *Leadership Ministry in Community,* vol. 6 of *Alternative Futures for Worship,* edited by Michael Cowan. Collegeville: The Liturgical Press, 1987. Pp. 131-137.

"Guidelines for the Development of Rites." Ibid. Pp. 139-150.

"Evolution of the Priesthood: Adapting to Pastoral Needs." *Church* 4 (1988) 16-21.

ANOINTING

"Let the Sick Man Call." *The Heythrop Journal* 18 (1978) 256-270; revised and reprinted as "Let the Sick Call" in David N. Power, *Worship: Culture and Theology.* Washington, D.C.: The Pastoral Press, 1990. Pp. 243-259.

"The Sacrament of Anointing: Open Questions." *Concilium* 214 (1991) 95-107.

FUNERAL

"The Funeral Rites for a Suicide and Liturgical Developments." *Concilium* 179 (1985) 75-81; reprinted in David N. Power, *Worship:*

Culture and Theology. Washington, D.C.: The Pastoral Press, 1990. Pp. 261-269.

ACOLYTE, LECTOR

Gifts That Differ: Lay Ministries Established and Unestablished. New York: Pueblo Publishing Co., 1980. Second edition, 1985.

DIVINE OFFICE

"Home or Group Prayer and the Divine Office." *Concilium* 52 (1971) 92-103.

TRIDUUM

"The Easter Triduum: Crucified, Buried and Risen." *Pastoral Music* 14 (1990) 23-26; reprinted in *Initiation and Its Seasons*, edited by Virgil C. Funk. Washington, D.C.: The Pastoral Press, 1990. Pp. 67-72.

BLESSING

"On Blessing Things." *Concilium* 178 (1985) 24-39; reprinted in David N. Power, *Worship: Culture and Theology*. Washington, D.C.: The Pastoral Press, 1990. Pp. 191-210.

"Editorial Conclusions: Receiving the Tradition." *Concilium* 178 (1985) 121-126.

Worship: Theology, History, Interpretation

"Sacramental Celebration and Liturgical Ministry." *Concilium* 62 (1972) 26-42.

"Two Expressions of Faith: Worship and Theology." *Concilium* 82 (1973) 91-105.

"The Song of the Lord in an Alien Land." *Concilium* 92 (1974) 85-106.

"Cultural Encounter and Religious Expression." *Concilium* 102 (1975) 102-112; reprinted in David N. Power, *Worship: Culture and Theology*. Washington, D.C.: The Pastoral Press, 1990. Pp. 39-52.

"Uso e Senso della Scrittura nelle Celebrazioni Liturgiche." *Concilium* 11 (1975/2) 167-178. Also in Dutch, French, German, Portuguese, and Spanish. The volume did not appear in English.

"A Theology of Community." *The Way* Supplement 34 (1978) 100-111.

"Unripe Grapes: The Critical Function of Liturgical Theology." *Worship* 52 (1978) 386-399.

"Words That Crack: The Uses of 'Sacrifice' in Eucharistic Discourse." *Worship* 53 (1979) 386-404; reprinted in *Living Bread, Saving Cup: Readings on the Eucharist*, edited by Kevin Seasoltz. Collegeville: The Liturgical Press, 1982. Pp. 157-175.

"Cult to Culture: The Liturgical Foundation of Theology." *Worship*

54 (1980) 482-495; revised and reprinted in David N. Power, *Worship: Culture and Theology*. Washington, D.C.: The Pastoral Press, 1990. Pp. 3-24.

"Doxology: The Praise of God in Worship, Doctrine and Life." *Worship* 55 (1981) 61-69.

"All Things Made New." *Liturgy* 2 (1982) 7-11.

"Liturgy, Memory and the Absence of God: Response to Geoffrey Wainwright." *Worship* 67 (1983) 326-329.

Unsearchable Riches: The Symbolic Nature of Liturgy. New York: Pueblo Publishing Co., 1984.

"The Sacrifice of the Mass: A Question of Reception and Rereception." *Ecclesia Orans* 2 (1985) 67-94.

"Liturgical Praxis: A New Consciousness at the Eye of Worship." *Worship* 61 (1987) 290-305; reprinted in David N. Power, *Worship: Culture and Theology*. Washington, D.C.: The Pastoral Press, 1990. Pp. 127-142.

The Sacrifice We Offer: The Tridentine Dogma and Its Reinterpretation. Edinburgh: T. & T. Clark Limited, 1987.

"Evolution of the Priesthood: Adapting to Pastoral Needs." *Church* 4 (1988) 16-21.

"The Holy Spirit: History, Scripture and Interpretation." In *Keeping the Faith: Essays to Mark the Centenary of Lux Mundi*, edited by Geoffrey Wainwright. Philadelphia: Fortress Press, 1988. Pp. 152-178.

"Communication in a Communion of Faith." *Doctrine and Life* 38 (1988) 136-143.

"Editorial Conclusions: Music and the Experience of God." *Concilium* 202 (1989) 148-151.

"Room for All: Chosen, Committed." *Church* 5 (1989) 19-22.

"History and the Sunday Assembly." *Chicago Studies* 29 (1990) 289-306.

"Power and Authority in Early Christian Centuries." In *That They Might Live: Power, Empowerment, and Leadership in the Church*, edited by Michael Downey. New York: Crossroad, 1991. Pp. 25-38.

"Twenty-Five Years On—Seen from the Roots: The Migration of Powers." In *Sung Liturgy: Toward 2000 A.D.*, edited by Virgil C. Funk. Washington, D.C.: The Pastoral Press, 1991. Pp. 43-63.

"When Words Fail: The Function of Systematic Theology in Liturgical Studies." In *Proceedings of the North American Academy of Liturgy*, 1991. Pp. 18-26.

Eucharistic Mystery: Revitalizing the Tradition. New York: Crossroad, 1992.

Worship and Culture

"A Theological Perspective on the Persistence of Religion." *Concilium* 81 (1973) 91-105; reprinted as "Christianity as Religion" in David

N. Power, *Worship: Culture and Theology*. Washington, D.C.: The Pastoral Press, 1990. Pp. 25-38.

"Cultural Encounter and Religious Experience." *Concilium* 102 (1975) 102-112; reprinted in David N. Power, *Worship: Culture and Theology*. Washington, D.C.: The Pastoral Press, 1990. Pp. 39-52.

"The Sacramentalization of Penance." *The Heythrop Journal* 16 (1977) 5-22. Translation: "La sacramentalización de la penitencia." *Sellecciones de Teologia* 18 (1979) 49-56; reprinted in David N. Power, *Worship: Culture and Theology*. Washington, D.C.: The Pastoral Press, 1990. Pp. 213-241.

"Let the Sick Man Call." *The Heythrop Journal* 18 (1978) 256-270; revised and reprinted as "Let the Sick Call" in David N. Power, *Worship: Culture and Theology*. Washington, D.C.: The Pastoral Press, 1990. Pp. 243-259.

"The Odyssey of Man in Christ." *Concilium* 92 (1974) 85-106; reprinted as "Human Odyssey in Christ" in David N. Power, *Worship: Culture and Theology*. Washington, D.C.: The Pastoral Press, 1990. Pp. 85-101.

"Liturgy in Search of Religion." *Philippine Studies* 28 (1980) 344-353; reprinted in David N. Power, *Worship: Culture and Theology*. Washington, D.C.: The Pastoral Press, 1990. Pp. 55-65.

"Cult to Culture: The Liturgical Foundation of Theology." *Worship* 54 (1980) 482-495; revised and reprinted in David N. Power, *Worship: Culture and Theology*. Washington, D.C.: The Pastoral Press, 1990. Pp. 3-24.

"Households of Faith in the Coming Church." *Worship* 57 (1983) 237-254; reprinted in David N. Power, *Worship: Culture and Theology*. Washington, D.C.: The Pastoral Press, 1990. Pp. 105-125.

"People at Liturgy." *Concilium* 170 (1983) 8-14; reprinted in David N. Power, *Worship: Culture and Theology*. Washington, D.C.: The Pastoral Press, 1990. Pp. 273-283.

"Liturgy and Culture." *East Asian Pastoral Review* (1984/4) 348-360; reprinted in David N. Power, *Worship: Culture and Theology*. Washington, D.C.: The Pastoral Press, 1990. Pp. 67-84.

"On Blessing Things." *Concilium* 178 (1985) 24-39; reprinted in David N. Power, *Worship: Culture and Theology*. Washington, D.C.: The Pastoral Press, 1990. Pp. 191-210.

"The Funeral Rites for a Suicide and Liturgical Developments." *Concilium* 179 (1985) 75-81; reprinted in David N. Power, *Worship: Culture and Theology*. Washington, D.C.: The Pastoral Press, 1990. Pp. 261-269.

"Worship after the Holocaust." *Worship* 59 (1985) 44-53.

"Hope Is the Joy of Saying Yes." *Pastoral Music* 11 (1986) 20-26; reprinted in David N. Power, *Worship: Culture and Theology*. Washington, D.C.: The Pastoral Press, 1990. Pp. 175-190.

"Liturgical Praxis: A New Consciousness at the Eye of Worship." *Worship* 61 (1987) 290-305; reprinted in David N. Power, *Worship: Culture and Theology*. Washington, D.C.: The Pastoral Press, 1990. Pp. 127-142.

"Liturgy and Empowerment." In *Leadership Ministry in Community*, vol. 6 of *Alternative Futures for Worship*, edited by Michael Cowan. Collegeville: The Liturgical Press, 1987. Pp. 81-104.

"Le calendrier de l'église: Les saints sont-ils négligés ou mal représentés?" *La Vie spirituelle* 69 (1989) 691-699; translation in David N. Power, *Worship: Culture and Theology*. Washington, D.C.: The Pastoral Press, 1990. Pp. 143-152.

"When to Worship Is to Lament." *Worship: Culture and Theology*. Washington, D.C.: The Pastoral Press, 1990. Pp. 155-173.

"Twenty-Five Years On—Seen from the Roots: The Migration of Powers." In *Sung Liturgy: Toward 2000 A.D*, edited by Virgil C. Funk. Washington, D.C.: The Pastoral Press, 1991. Pp. 43-63.

Worship: Culture and Theology. Washington, D.C.: The Pastoral Press, 1990. This collection contains most of the articles in this section.

"Worship and a New World: Some Theological Considerations." In *The Changing Face of Jewish and Christian Worship in North America*, edited by Paul F. Bradshaw and Lawrence A. Hoffman. Notre Dame and London: University of Notre Dame Press, 1991. Pp. 161-183.

Ministry, Pastoral Office

Ministers of Christ and His Church: Theology of the Priesthood. London: Geoffrey Chapman Publishing Co., 1969.

"Sacramental Celebration and Liturgical Ministry." *Concilium* 62 (1972) 26-42.

Christian Priest: Elder and Prophet. London: Sheed and Ward, 1973.

"Liturgical Ministry: The Christian People's Poiesis of Time and Place. *Worship* 52 (1978) 211-222.

"Hierarchy." *New Catholic Encyclopedia* 17 (1979) 249-250.

"Ministry (Ecclesiology)." Ibid. 412-414.

Gifts That Differ: Lay Ministries Established and Unestablished. New York: Pueblo Publishing Co., 1980. Second edition, 1985.

"The Basis for Official Ministry in the Church." *Jurist* 41 (1981) 314-342.

"Ministries of Word and Eucharist." *The Way* 25 (1985) 44-53.

"Liturgy and Empowerment." In *Leadership Ministry in Community*, vol. 6 of *Alternative Futures for Worship*, edited by Michael Cowan. Collegeville: The Liturgical Press, 1987. Pp. 81-104.

"Appropriate Ordination Rites: A Historical Perspective." Ibid. Pp. 131-137.

"Guidelines for the Development of Rites." Ibid. Pp. 139-150.

"Church Order." In *The New Dictionary of Sacramental Worship*, edited by Peter Fink. Collegeville: The Liturgical Press, 1990. Pp. 212-233.

"Power and Authority in Early Christian Centuries." In *That They Might Live: Power, Empowerment, and Leadership in the Church*, edited by Michael Downey. New York: Crossroad, 1991. Pp. 25-38.

"Order." In *Systematic Theology: Roman Catholic Perspectives*, vol. 2, edited by John Galvin and Francis Schüssler Fiorenza. Minneapolis: Augsburg Fortress, 1991. Pp. 291-304.

"A Theological Assessment of Ministries Today." In *Trends in Mission. Toward the Third Millennium. Essays in Celebration of Twenty-Five Years of SEDOS*, edited by William Jenkinson and Helene O'Sullivan. Maryknoll, New York: Orbis Books, 1991. Pp. 185-201.

"Episcopacy." In *Dictionary of the Ecumenical Movement*, edited by Nicholas Lossky, José Miguez-Bonino, John Pobee, Thomas Stransky, Geoffrey Wainwright, and Pauline Webb. Geneva: World Council of Churches, 1991, and Grand Rapids: Wm. Eerdmans. Pp. 359-361.

"Ordination." Ibid. Pp. 750-752.

"Presbyterate." Ibid. Pp. 819-820.

"Priesthood." Ibid. Pp. 821-822.

Volumes of *Concilium* Edited by David Power

With Herman Schmidt:

Vol. 52	*Prayer and Community*
Vol. 62	*Worship of Christian Man Today*
Vol. 72	*Liturgy and Ministry*
Vol. 82	*Liturgical Experience of Faith*
Vol. 92	*Politics and Liturgy*
Vol. 102	*Liturgy and Cultural Religious Traditions*
	The Use of Non-Biblical Texts in the Liturgy (This volume did not appear in English.)

With Luis Maldonado:

Vol. 112	*Liturgy and Human Passage*
Vol. 122	*Structures of Initiation in Crisis*
Vol. 132	*Symbol and Art in Worship*

With Mary Collins:

Vol. 142	*The Times of Celebration*

Vol. 152   *Can We Always Celebrate the Eucharist?*
Vol. 162   *Liturgy: A Creative Tradition*
Vol. 178   *Blessing and Power*
Vol. 190   *The Fate of Confession*
Vol. 202   *Music and the Experience of God*
Vol. 214   *The Pastoral Care of the Sick*

Contributors

Michael Downey is theologian in residence at Lexington Theological Seminary, where he teaches courses in Christian spirituality and worship. He is spiritual director for Protestant and Catholic students at the seminary. His publications include *Clothed in Christ: The Sacraments and Christian Living* (1987) and *That They Might Live: Power, Empowerment, and Leadership in the Church* (1991).

Regis A. Duffy, O.F.M. is associate professor of theology at the University of Notre Dame. He is the author of *Real Presence* (1982), *A Roman Catholic Theology of Pastoral Care* (1983), and *On Becoming Catholic* (1984).

Ciaran Earley, O.M.I., a former missionary in Brazil, now works in the Pastoral Department of the Dublin Institute of Adult Education. He is co-author with Gemma McKenna of *Actions Speak Louder* (1987) and *Partners in Faith* (1991).

Chris Nwaka Egbulem, O.P. is lecturer in systematic theology and liturgical studies at the Washington Theological Consortium, and speaks across the U.S.A. on inculturation and evangelization, especially in African American communities.

Joseph J. Fortuna is assistant professor of liturgy and sacramental theology at St. Mary Seminary (Center for Pastoral Leadership) in Cleveland, Ohio.

Richard N. Fragomeni is a presbyter of the diocese of Albany, New York, and assistant professor of word and worship at Catholic Theological Union in Chicago. He is a founding member of the North American Forum on the Catechumenate and has been most active in the implementation of the RCIA in the United States and Canada.

Kenneth Hannon, O.M.I. is professor of pastoral and liturgical theology at Oblate School of Theology in San Antonio, Texas. He has served on the Boards of the Federation of Diocesan Liturgical Commissions and the Southwest Liturgical Conference.

Stephen Happel is associate professor in the Department of Religion and Religious Education at The Catholic University of America, Washington, D.C. His most recent book is *Conversion and Discipleship* (1986) written with James J. Walter.

Mary Catherine Hilkert, O.P., a member of the Sisters of St. Dominic of Akron, Ohio, is associate professor of systematic theology at Aquinas Institute of Theology in St. Louis. A contributor to many periodicals, she is co-editor with Robert Schreiter of *The Praxis of Christian Experience: An Introduction to the Theology of Edward Schillebeeckx* (1989).

Kevin W. Irwin is associate professor of liturgy and sacramental theology at The Catholic University of America, Washington, D.C. Among his publications are *Liturgical Theology: A Primer* (1990), *Liturgy, Prayer and Spirituality* (1984), and the three volume commentaries on the liturgical year: *Advent-Christmas* (1986), *Lent* (1985), and *Easter: A Guide to Eucharist and Hours* (1991).

Anthony Kain is pastor of the multicultural suburban parish of Woodville-Findon, Adelaide, South Australia. He is the co-founder of the Australian Academy of Liturgy and is involved with various national and diocesan bodies in teaching, writing, and liturgical consultation.

Warren Kinne, S.S.C. is the central coordinator of the Lay Missionary Program for the Society of St. Columban in Navan, Ireland. His most recent publication is *The Splintered Staff* (1990).

Sally Ann McReynolds, N.D. is assistant professor of theology at St. Mary College, Leavenworth, Kansas.

David Noel Power, O.M.I., to whom this book is dedicated, is an internationally known theologian, author, and lecturer. He teaches in the Department of Theology at the Catholic University of America, Washington, D.C. Among his numerous books is *Worship: Culture and Theology* (1991).

Geoffrey Wainwright, an ordained minister of the British Methodist Church, is Robert E. Cushman professor of Christian theology at Duke University, Durham, North Carolina. A member of the World Council of Churches' Faith and Order Commission, he chaired the final production of *Baptism, Eucharist and Ministry* at Lima, Peru, in 1982.